KU-568-410

ASPECTS OF EDUCATIONAL
TECHNOLOGY

Aspects
of Educational Technology
Volume XVI

Improving Efficiency
in Education
and Training

*Edited for the Association for Educational
and Training Technology by*
Andrew Trott, Harry Strongman and Les Giddins

General Editor
A J Trott *Bulmershe College*

**Kogan Page, London/Nichols Publishing
Company, New York**

First published 1983
by Kogan Page Limited
120 Pentonville Road, London N1 9JN

Copyright © The Association for Educational
and Training Technology, 1982
All Rights Reserved

British Library Cataloguing in Publication Data
Aspects of Educational Technology
Volume XVI: Improving efficiency in education and
training – ISSN 0141-5956; 16
1. Education – Aims and objectives – Congresses
I. Trott, Andrew II. Strongman, Harry
III. Giddins, Les IV. Series
370'.0941. LB41

ISBN 0-85038-566-0 (UK)
ISBN 0-89397-148-0 (USA)
ISSN 0141-5956; 16

Printed in Great Britain by
The Anchor Press Ltd and bound by
Wm Brendon & Son Ltd,
both of Tiptree, Essex

Published in the USA by Nichols Publishing Company,
PO Box 96, New York, NY 10024

371.39
ASP

Contents

Author Index

Editorial

The major theme of the Educational Technology International Conference in 1982 was that of the effectiveness and efficiency obtainable in education and training. This issue was felt to be appropriate at a time when most governments of the world were making demands upon educational institutions of all kinds to reduce numbers of students, and to reduce expenditure whilst still maintaining quality. The selected papers reflected these pressures in various ways. A number examined the effectiveness and efficiency obtainable through changes in methodology, others concentrated upon improving processes in a systematic way, while others detailed advances in technology. The workshops provided practical exemplars of these changes, enabling delegates to experience and question a range of innovatory techniques and products.

Two main sub-themes ran through the conference proceedings: the first was concerned with microteaching — the skills approach in various applications — and the second explored links between education and industry. The skills approach reflects a particular interest of the host institution, Bulmershe College, and the number of papers and workshops which addressed this sub-theme emphasized the involvement and international interest in this field. The other sub-theme of education/industry links concentrated upon a particular concern of the local education authority in which the college is situated. The importance of this issue was indicated by the diversity of papers and workshops which related to it and by the wide range of people who attended.

One of the interesting aspects of the conference was the emphasis placed by the opening and closing speakers upon educational research. George Leith drew together strands which had been interwoven into conferences since 1968, giving them purpose and a new incisive edge; whilst Ken Austwick compared his present thoughts with those he had expressed 10 years ago, and asked thought provoking questions concerning the present and future role of educational technology. These two papers, taken together, comment upon the changing nature of educational research, the controversies surrounding acceptable methodologies, and the need for more research into the measurement of effectiveness and efficiency.

Current economic conditions have brought about a decline in the number of people attending educational conferences, and this trend was a noticeable feature of ETIC 82. However, for those who came to Bulmershe, the reductions brought two benefits, one regarding the organization of the conference and the other related to its general ambience. Because fewer people attended, fewer papers were presented, and so the number of parallel papers was reduced. Thus the feelings of frustration felt by delegates in the past, because there were many simultaneous papers, were lessened. The other benefit was that delegates were able to meet and talk with nearly everyone attending. ETIC 82 will be highly regarded by the many people who see the prime purpose of conferences as an informal meeting place to discuss relevant issues with other practitioners in the field.

   The theme of effectiveness and efficiency was put into practice in the
organization of the conference timetable. The papers were scheduled
conventionally, but some of the other presentations were given different
treatments. Workshops were preceded by introductory papers, and some were
repeated so as to give a greater opportunity for people to attend. One important
experiential session was allocated a whole day.

   A noticeable factor was the improvement in the use of media to present papers.
For many years ETIC organizers have commented upon the use of educational
technology by educational technologists. It is to be hoped that this improvement
continues at ETIC 83.

   Our special thanks are recorded to Loulou Brown, who worked so hard on the
production of this edition, and who, even when two of the editors were on
assignments abroad, worked with admirable determination and enthusiasm.

Andrew Trott
Harry Strongman
Les Giddins
Bulmershe College, Reading, November 1982

Keynote Address

Whatever Happened to Programmed Instruction, Mastery Learning, and Microteaching...? Some Reflections on a Neglected Area of Educational Technology

G O M Leith
University of Cape Breton, Canada

'There are fashions in science, and some scientists climb on the bandwagon almost as readily as do some painters and musicians. But although fashions and bandwagons may attract the weak, they should be resisted rather than encouraged.'   *Karl Popper*

Vanity Fair

Educational research and development have been perceived as giving poor returns for investment over a wide range of endeavours. Thus we find that reviews of research, in which an experimentally introduced method is compared with others, generally conclude that the balance of evidence does not favour one method over another. Group methods versus class teaching, discovery versus direct instruction, linear versus branching programmed learning, microteaching with or without models, TV instruction versus conventional teaching — the no-difference result occurs again and again, or, if some significant result turns up, just as many go in the opposite direction.

Teachers have become disillusioned with the pronouncements of research and development teams and individuals, many of whom are considered to be remote from the classroom, unacquainted with what goes on in schools and lacking concern for the real-life problems of teachers in interaction with children. When doubts about curriculum changes, such as those in modern mathematics, which were unwelcome to many at their inception, are voiced by the subject matter experts themselves; when the results of classroom grouping methods, such as mixed ability classes and open schools, which were often accepted unwillingly, are called in to question; and when the validity of previously relied-upon products of research, such as mental tests, is acknowledged by many to be suspect, teachers become sceptical.

It is, in fact, fashionable nowadays to denigrate claims that educational research and development have a scientific basis, and to uphold ideas which deny the possibility of objective inquiry into human behaviour and conduct. Indeed, the present vogue is to identify educational research with the creative arts rather than with empirical investigation. Thus Adelman and Walker (1975) see as: 'the aim of such research . . . to construct reports which provide *vicarious experience* for their audience'.

Tony Becher (1980) goes further and proposes:

'an alternative methodology . . . which models itself on the approaches of the historian, the anthropologist and the interpretative artist . . . the generalizations for which it seeks are of the kind expressed in novels, plays or works of art, not of the kind expressed in scientific texts'.

This orientation was in evidence already in 1958, when Becker, an important pioneer of the alternative methodology, explained that: 'the technique of participant observation consists of something more than merely immersing oneself in data and "having insights" '. He hoped that: 'qualitative research may become more a "scientific" and less an "artistic" kind of endeavour'.

One of the reasons for taking up the approach is 'to reject the paternalism of traditional research within education' (Nixon, 1981) and, though Swift (1965) denies left-wing bias, Nixon goes on to explain that: 'what is needed is nothing short of a radical democratization of the research community'. Indeed, the 'humanist tendency' promotes an anti-elitist position and, with a great deal of proselytizing zeal and arcane terminology, Nixon suggests that everyone should become his own researcher.

The movement is dialectically the antithesis of programmed instruction, mastery learning and microteaching, and also of systems analysis and experimental research and development in education. These latter are rejected because there is a philosophical antipathy to objectivity, measurement, hypothesis-testing, causal inference, experimental design and statistics. On the other hand, the approaches variously called (among other names) symbolic interactionism and ethnomethodology, hold to a subjectivist account of knowledge, believe in relativism, and take the interpretation of intentions and meanings within a nexus of social rules as the basis for explaining social interaction. Consequently, research involves the investigator in long-term immersion in the social context (in education — the classroom) in order to discover, in the same way as an ethnographer or social anthropologist, the rules of interaction which disclose the symbols, meanings and values of the actors in the social drama. The researcher finds a complex network of relationships and meanings which may well be unique to that situation. But the aim is to give sensitivity and understanding to the researcher (teacher) about his or her own classroom interaction situation rather than to concentrate on experimental (scientific) research (the finding of regularities and laws and the making of predictions), which is rejected. Causal explanations are legitimate for human beings when regarded as physical objects, eg when they fall or give the knee-jerk reflex, but irrelevant when social rules and individual intentions are involved. It is interesting that much of the sociological action-research which antedated the attention paid to the school 'milieu' focused on drug addicts, mental hospital patients, attempted suicides and a variety of 'rejected' and minority groups.

Thus, systematic approaches to research are rejected on philosophical or ideological grounds. They are also put aside because the results obtained in experiments are held to be of little or no practical value to teachers, or because the application of the principles is too complex to be carried out in practice, or because research suffers from a fundamental defect in that subjects never react as passive objects but interpret or construe the situation in their own ways. The radical sociologists who inspire the classroom research movement seem to view the whole of experimental research in education as based on naive ideas formulated independently of acquaintance with learners and teaching. They regard attempts to avoid the confusion of variables, and to introduce a range of values of a treatment to seek evidence of dependence or independence, as invalid because experimental controls and conditions are never representative of the classroom situation. Similarly, the samples employed are only representative of a hypothetical population.

Indeed, the existential phenomenological action research movement regards reports of experimental and quantitative research in education and in sociology as communication between experimenters rather than as diffusion of information for practical use. The lack of involvement of teachers with research and innovation in their own work is seen as one of the strongest reasons for substituting participant observation and action research for the present structures of research activity.

The Demise of Innovations

Yet programmed instruction, the Keller Plan and microteaching have faded and have been weakened not so much by the practical fruitfulness of the results of action research as by weaknesses which seem to afflict many innovations, even after they have been installed. The fault appears to arise from the fact that accepting and implementing a novel innovation, one which cuts across conventional or accepted principles and practices, demands an extreme commitment of missionary zeal. The enthusiasm of the promoters heightens expectations and leads to inflated claims. At the same time, the innovation, which may represent a high degree of novelty of approach and creativeness, undergoes sharpening and levelling processes of stereotyping and fixation. If conflicting stereotypes arise (and it may be useful here to consider linear and branching methods of programming) they attract rival supporting factions. Complexities and uncertainties in the original schemes become ironed out.

Thus programmed learning too readily regressed to a text-book-with-holes format, and mastery learning which was usually better than conventional teaching in comparative studies (McKeachie, 1974) has been widely simplified and adapted to fit a timetabled lecturing system based on textbook chapters with a schedule of repeated tests. Microteaching also seems to have become stereotyped in the form of minicourse models of teaching skills, albeit with replications in different languages. In much the same fashion, perhaps, the 'ethnographic' alternative methodology is, itself, already becoming a caricature of the exemplary approach whose paradigm is Whyte's 'Street Corner Society'. Just as Rogerian non-directive therapy generated volumes of dialogue transcriptions between the therapist (T) and the patient (P), there are already collections of case studies containing selections from verbatim transcripts of classroom interactions between teacher (T) and pupils (P_1, P_2). In explaining how to conduct educational case studies Walker (1980) tells us that: 'the emphasis is towards "*collecting* definitions of situations" (multiple representations), and the presentation of material in forms where it is open to multiple interpretations'. He goes on: 'The case study worker constantly attempts to capture and portray the world as it appears to the people in it. In a sense, for the case study worker what *seems* true is more important than what *is* true'. Lyman and Scott (1970), introducing the case study approach, tell us that:

'A new wave of thought is beginning to sweep over sociology. Aspects of the wave have been given an assortment of names — "labelling theory", "ethnomethodology", and "neo-symbolic inter-actionism" — but these do not cover its entire range of critique and perspective. A new name must be found to cover a concept which presents not only a unique perspective on conventional sociology, but is also a radical departure from the conventional. We feel an appropriate name is the "sociology of the absurd".'

A Neglected Distinction

A distinction made by Trager and Hall (1953) between *line integrators* and *point integrators* helps to explain why innovations are promoted with evangelistic fervour and later become unadventurous routines. It illuminates fundamental differences between individuals who operate in contrasting learning strategies, with differences in social interaction patterns and also helps to explain why some sociological theorists and activists are unable to tolerate systems, definition, measurement and analysis, and call instead for inductive, intuitive, spontaneous, flexible, open approaches to education and 'research'.

The *line integrator* is characterized as one who works within a given system. His function is to make his system work. He learns quickly and well, if what is given is integrated into some kind of system. To him, memory work is not arduous. He tends to ignore contradictions between the internal logic of his own system and events outside them. Some of the best scientific work is done by line integrators who, given a system, will work to build its solid foundation.

The *point integrator*, however, is likely to question the principles involved in any scheme. He has to make each point his own; is disturbed by contradictions within a frame of reference or between it and the outside. His function is to create new systems as conditions change, but he gets restless in a static situation. Having discovered and integrated his points, he tends to lose interest and move on, leaving the 'line integrator' to fill in the picture. In science, he is accused of being unscientific and of neglecting to prove his points. Examples of point and line integrators at the highest level are Einstein, a point integrator, and Napier, a line integrator who was the inventor of logarithms and whose single-handed labour and industry were responsible for the calculation of the first tables.

It is undoubtedly for the sake of follow-up research activity that Kuhn (1963) gives his approval to the type of science education which stresses text-book knowledge and which leads to science students being better able to solve problems which have a single correct answer than to think of multiple answers to open-ended questions (Hudson, 1966; Leith, 1972a). And it seems to be the line integrator whose characteristics have provided the aims and models of educational methods.

When teachers are asked to describe or choose the type of student they prefer, there is a manifest preference for rigid, conforming and orderly pupils. The active, independent, assertive student is least preferred. (Feshbach, 1969; Beigel and Feshbach, 1970; Good and Grouws, 1972.)

Again, when teachers are asked to describe the characteristics of their 'best' students a profile is consistently drawn of a conscientious, persistent, methodical, patient individual, who conforms to rules and completes tasks in good time. (Lavin, 1965; Entwistle and Entwistle, 1970.) Indeed, it was found that conforming, compulsive, rigid, insecure learners were given higher marks during the term than students with different propensities who were academically more able and performed better in examinations (Kelly, 1958).

The educational system is designed to fit line integrators who maintain and support it, and ignore contradictions between the system and what lies outside it. (Leith, 1982b.) Point integrators want to challenge the system, but are not given to consolidating and underpinning novel alternatives. As Trager and Hall (1953) point out, they sometimes have difficulties with line integrators who do not understand their points. An example is the plight of a highly intelligent, mature student who was able to select the expected answers to multiple-choice tests, but found the questions to be based upon assumptions in which she did not believe. The teacher could not understand why the student was unwilling to give the required answers, even though she knew which alternatives were expected.

'Education Should Be Everywhere the Same'

Flanders' interaction analysis was developed to assess the value of 'indirect teaching' involving pupils in a greater degree of oral participation. Nevertheless, it represents many features of educational inquiry which are eschewed by action researchers. First, in their view it employs prepared category systems for classifying interactions. In their view, this necessarily prejudges what may be found, and prevents the opportunity for the emergence of genuine understanding. Second, it assumes that the classroom will represent a narrow range of teacher-pupil relationships, in all of which there will be 'direct-frontal' teaching, according to Arye Perlberg. Consequently, there is no opportunity for learning where there are many different activities when the teacher is not the central focus, such as in the open classroom, or in small group project work, etc. However, there have been attempts to make video-recordings which can be viewed and reviewed for purposes of revising ideas of what certain events mean before the analysis is finally made. A study by Adams and Biddle (1970) exemplifies these techniques. They employed two concealed cameras to video-tape the events of 32 social studies and mathematics lessons given in 16 different classrooms in Grades I, VI and XI in the USA. Their teachers were a carefully balanced set of older and younger men and women, none of whom had less than two years' teaching experience. After making detailed analyses (the average number of activities noted per lesson was 371) they reached the conclusion that individuality in classrooms is discouraged. The kinds of behaviour displayed are remarkably limited.

'Task behaviours predominate, defined exactly and prescribed exactly (after the fashion of programmed learning), individuality can only be manifested to the extent that pupil A gets further in the program than does pupil B.'

'On the other hand, if what individuality really means is that pupils learn differently — it is the *process* that calls for the recognition of individuality, not the end product . . . we should expect to see evidence of this within the classroom situation. On the evidence of our study this is not the case.'

During the period when behaviourism was the predominant approach in psychology, it was assumed that there are universal laws of learning which apply to all humans and other animals. Skinner extended the principles of reinforcement, shaping, chaining, generalizing and discriminating, from pigeons and rats to humans. Teaching machines were Skinner Boxes, with the experimental subject on the outside. Underwood (1964) acknowledged that there are large individual differences in the rate of learning which 'produce pesky statistical problems resulting from the wide range of scores', but pointed out that, given the same level of learning (whether achieved rapidly or slowly), the rate of forgetting is the same.

This difference in the rate of learning became for Carroll (1970) and Bloom (1974) the basis of mastery learning. Microteaching, which began by applying some of Skinner's techniques to 'teaching skills' (small steps, immediate feedback and shaping by cues and prompts), came to adopt an 'imitation' view of learning, proposed by, for example, Bandura (1963). This is appropriately one of the strands of theory in behaviour modification, in which the process of shaping is short-circuited by presenting a model to be copied (Leith, 1978, 1979).

Not all behaviourists, however, take the view that learning must be of one kind. Broadbent (1973) regrets the thinking, among most researchers, which looks for a constant rule of behaviour, applying to all persons, and the same person on all occasions. He makes it clear that different strategies of performance can be adopted by different people, or at different times by the same person. We should, therefore, be concerned to devise, elaborate and compare many different ways in which the mind can be organized.

From the perspective of an examination of the educational uses of anthropology (not ethnomethodology) Singleton (1973) refers to differences in cognitive styles associated with linguistic and cultural differences. He urges that schools should abandon the assumption that there is a single method for knowing, and that they should develop multiple-method learning environments.

A defender of the liberal-arts education system, R M Hutchins, wrote nearly 50 years ago:

'Education implies teaching. Teaching implies knowledge. Knowledge is truth. The truth is everywhere the same. Hence education should be everywhere the same.'

Nevertheless, in a later context and writing about general education, he added that:

'the variations which should be encouraged fall not in the realm of content, but in that of method. Allowances for individual differences should be provided for by abolishing all requirements except the examinations and permitting the student to take them whenever in his opinion he is ready to do so.' (Hutchins, 1936)

Neglected Differences

Educational establishments have been slow to accept the notion that learners may need to receive different treatments in order to achieve the same goals. One reason seems to have been an inability to conceive that factors other than abilities, aptitudes, age and sex are involved. While these factors certainly occur, there is little consistency in the evidence. Bracht's survey of 103 studies found five which showed aptitude/treatment interactions. It is not surprising, therefore, that many of the differences have been missed. One example which we devised in Birmingham was a comparison of inductively and deductively arranged programmes which were each accompanied either by realia to exemplify the rules or by outline diagrams. The learners were categorized by intelligence and sex. No differences between the main factors of method, mode, or sex emerged, though those above average in intelligence learned more and took less time. However, in the above-average IQ group one method was successful with a particular mode, and unsuccessful with the other, while the opposite combination had the contrary effect. Learners of below-average IQ showed a similar criss-cross pattern except that the results were completely reversed (Harvey, 1968). Similar findings were revealed in additional studies, which have not been published.

Our most consistent and fruitful basis of research into differences in learning has involved a series of studies in which we successfully focused on the definition of conditions, which optimize success in learning for some and inhibit it for others, and different conditions which have the reverse effect (Leith, 1974c).

Several of these studies were summarized in a paper given at the 1968 APLET Conference (Leith, 1969a). Typical of the research is an experiment carried out in co-operation with David Shadbolt. We compared the success of college students' learning from two types of learning materials, which had been validated previously, to ensure an overall no-difference result. The first was highly structured, had a step-by-step progression, and gave frequent feedback for the students' (usually) successful responses. There was an easy-to-difficult and simple-to-complex unfolding pattern. The second reversed the order, beginning with the most complex situation and requiring students to propose explanations of phenomena. The explanations were invariably incomplete or in error, the feedback pointing to aspects not covered by the explanation. Thus, the contrast was between a form of direct instruction and a form of discovery learning, requiring a succession of tests of hypotheses which were validated or invalidated. The final tests for both methods included a preponderance of transfer items, including questions on related topics not taught. The overall result, which was the same as that of thousands of educational comparisons, was, of course, expected. The hypotheses being tested were that some students — those who were tolerant of ambiguity and uncertainty, who were willing to take intellectual risks and were not dismayed by making errors and correcting them — would be successful with the discovery learning treatment. This approach would not, it was proposed, be helpful to students who were unable to entertain uncertainty. On the other hand, the consistent, steady, progressive build-up of systematically organized step-by-step activities would be inhibiting to the students who preferred personal exploration without constant guidance, but encouraging to the more particularly persistent students.

In order to divide the sample into men and women who scored high and low on the scale, a measure of the following qualities was administered: a tendency to become restive if there is insufficient variety, a search for stimulation, a tolerance of ambiguity and a dislike of the imposition of clear-cut rules, in addition to a test of general anxiety. It was, in fact, a test of extraversion/introversion which seems to have much in common with point and line integration. It was called the HB Personality Inventory (Hallworth, 1962).

Extraverts were significantly better in the final test of learning and transfer if they had been given the discovery learning treatment, whereas introverts were significantly better if they had received the direct instruction method. Essentially, the same result was obtained in a comparison between a randomly-arranged set of problem-solving tasks, and a similar format with problems arranged in sequence, with full prompting (Leith and Wisdom, 1970).

The research project was continued by varying the age level and subject matter, and refining the treatments to be compared until elements were found which could be varied precisely, rather than the relatively global and qualitative differences which were first introduced. The treatments which provoked disordinal interactions were position of rules or summaries (Leith, 1970; Leith and Trown, 1970). For example, large-step versus small-step programmed instruction (Leith, 1970) in a situation where rules were to be derived and formulated following problem-solving experience with knowledge of results, giving or not giving 'official' versions of the rules (Leith and Trown, 1970) and, in microteaching, giving microteaching experience with feedback, as opposed to receiving microteaching and evaluating it (Leith and Britton, 1979; Leith, 1982a).

It would be possible to follow the inductive path for a prolonged period, checking off yet other situations in which one extreme of a dimension of treatment favours extraverts and the other favours introverts. The sequence of experiments involving extraversion was one of several lines of inquiry, some of which turned out to be fruitful. Aptitudes, especially in conjunction with sex, gave some good results, one of which is referred to above. Achievement motivation, rigidity, and level of aspirations were also tried out. There was one non-significant experiment in which more-or-less tedious versions of a linear, small-step programme were compared with each other to find if different amounts of reactive inhibition could be generated. However, all versions obtained identical results with extraverts and introverts, whether anxious or non-anxious.

The point is that early in the series a more general explanation was looked for than that of fitting the lists of descriptive attributes of introverts and extraverts alongside dimensions of educational method.

From clues gained from experience of work with learners, in experimental and teaching situations, several pointers were identified. For example, nervous and introverted students would get 'overheated' when using some of the problem-solving materials developed for research, and would protest that the tasks were impossibly confusing.

Outgoing students took the randomly-arranged problems in their stride, but rapidly became bored and restive when given the same problems arranged in progressive order with statements of principles and many hints and prompts (including the correct answer). This latter approach gave maximum learning and transfer to introverts, however.

Again, it was frequently observed that some students were unsatisfied with the technique, solution, or answer given by the teacher, and would try out other ways or ask 'awkward' questions. They would become frustrated if the order of procedure could not be varied. Meanwhile, some pupils would become distressed if definitive answers were not supplied or could not be found, while others were quite happy for something to remain uncertain or ambiguous.

Studies of the effects of co-operative learning also led to well-defined results involving extraversion and anxiety. The first experiments in which the effects of social interaction were assessed showed that mixed-ability pairs worked better than homogeneous pairs, and individuals. More specifically, lower-ability members of mixed-ability pairs tended to gain as much learning and transfer as the brighter members, who, in turn, were somewhat better than their peers in the control group (Amaria, Biran and Leith, 1969; Amaria and Leith, 1969). Following this pilot study, several further experiments were run permitting a complete, systematic analysis of all combinations of extravert and introvert with anxious and non-anxious, above- and below-average ability to be set up. The verbal interactions of a representative sample of the entire set of combinations were recorded on sound-tape, and transcribed and submitted to an interaction analysis (Bales, 1950).

The findings were very precise. The greatest learning and transfer came about when two sets of conditions were simultaneously fulfilled. The first was that both members of a pair must be the same in extraversion/introversion level (ie both extraverts or both introverts). The second was that they should have different levels of anxiety (one anxious, the other not anxious). The analysis of the verbal interaction transcripts supported this finding. At the same time, it showed what kinds of interaction were related to success.

In fact, four of the interaction categories showed strong correlations — two positively and two negatively. Pairs of learners with opposite levels of anxiety obtained twice as much on the transfer test as pairs having the same level. Part of the explanation seems to be that the former spent about 125 per cent more time in asking for orientation, information and confirmation than the latter pairs. They also spent up to 50 per cent less time showing antagonism, deflating each other and asserting themselves; up to 60 per cent more in showing solidarity, raising each other's status, giving help and rewarding each other. They also disagreed less, and were less passively rejecting and withholding help. It should be noted that these findings applied to mixed- and to similar-ability groups, personality factors having a greater effect than intelligence. It is also worth noting that children with identical anxiety profiles were able to increase learning and transfer in themselves and in a compatible partner by interacting in a supportive, positively reinforcing manner; or lower the amount of learning and transfer in themselves and an incompatible partner. In the latter case, the same type of individual would be criticizing, uttering scathing remarks and being generally unco-operative (Leith, 1974a). The results are supported by the finding that positively-worded social reinforcement systematically improves learning, while negatively-worded reinforcement reduces it systematically, if consistently given (Leith and Davis, 1969).

A more powerful explanation of the findings was sought in Eysenck's (1972) account of arousal, which he links to extraversion and introversion. Introverts are claimed to be chronically aroused and need to inhibit this tendency. Strong stimulation, however, may arouse introverts beyond an optimal level of arousal for some tasks — when they will become confused and disorganized. Extraverts, on the other hand, are under-aroused and, to maintain an optimal level, need to have strong stimulation. Hence, extraverts are constantly seeking variety and change. Without it they become bored and restless. Anxiety or emotionality is indirectly linked to the arousal system, so that high anxiety and introversion linked together tend to go beyond the optimal level of arousal, but, without anxiety, the level of introversion may be about right. Being extraverted and emotional may give an individual the required amount of motivation to do something. Extraversion without anxiety, however, may not give sufficient drive.

One test of this is performance on creativity tests, where different amounts of stress can be introduced to add to the excitation raised by the anxiety level. Stressed extraverts achieve creativity test scores which are as high as those of non-stressed introverts. Similarly, the effect of stress on introverts is to reduce the number of alternatives and novel responses generated by them. Non-stressed extraverts, too, are not very productive (Leith, 1981). Anxiety added to stress reduces creativity scores. Anxious individuals responding without external stress, however, will obtain good scores.

A further experiment was carried out to test the arousal hypothesis on co-operative learning (Leith, 1974b). This time, the learners were university students taking a course based on the use of a textbook. A set of questions designed to help students to think about their reading was prepared. Some students used the question-raising material individually, while others learned in pairs. Some pairs had the same personality, others were different. The predictions were that introverts working alone would be better than extraverts working alone, while extraverts together would be as good as introverts alone. It was also put forward that, in a mixed personality pair, the extravert would learn better than the introvert. These predictions were found to be correct. The reasons follow directly from the arousal explanation. Extraverts need extra arousal which does not come from the boring task of textbook reading. However, two extraverts together stimulate each other. Extraverts can get some stimulation from interaction with introverts, but introverts are stimulated to an excessive extent by interaction with extraverts and, in such situations, learn less. Two introverts, working together, hardly influence each other at all, and consequently they retain an optimal level of arousal.

There are many facets of the research which have yet to be clarified. For example, the way in which the results of experiments on discovery methods versus direct instruction (ie methods which stimulate arousal versus methods which are less activating and excitatory) occur with young children. The factor in our experimental work which distinguishes the discovery method from the direct instruction teaching of younger children is anxiety rather than extraversion. It has shown up in experiments by Leith (1969a), Trown and Leith (1975), and is present in an unpublished analysis of creativity and stress with nine-year-olds, that the influence of anxiety on achievements in learning changes over with increasing age. Thus, anxiety in youngsters encourages learning, and anxiety in older students decreases learning (Leith and Davis, 1972).

Reflections

In my earlier writings (Leith, 1969b; Leith 1974a), features of educational technology which might have a continuing place in education were examined. For example, it was predicted that, paradoxically, if the ideas of programmed learning were accepted more readily, it would stop being considered a distinctive technique or a medium of instruction. The principles, that is, of formulating objectives, carrying out task analyses, preparing and trying out learning situations, methods and materials and revising and improving them in the light of feedback from learners, would become absorbed into the generally accepted procedures of instructional preparation.

The attempts to provide alternative modalities in Mastery Learning, such as those of text, audio-visual, or personal tutorial (Sullivan, 1969) helped to change attitudes towards different modes of presentation, though there is no longer the incentive of overwhelming numbers to maintain the Keller Plan, or to make further innovations along these lines necessary. In fact, five years seems to be a good life for such a sweeping change in educational organization and teaching methods. This is just enough time for the pioneers (the point integrators) to put the innovation into viable form, train some line integrators and move on to new positions and try out other novel approaches.

Changes in the general structure of innovation have often paralleled, or have followed, the sequence of changes in industry. Thus there have been periods when interest has been concentrated upon human relations in the school and classroom. There was a movement towards an improvement in efficiency, and there was also a production-line automation period and later a vertical grouping devolution, similar to the Volvo work-group organization. We have also had flexible, individual scheduling, which was perhaps a response to the loss of punctuality and the phenomenon of a fall-off in attendance at lectures, as much as a staggering of clock-on times to match individual needs in industry.

Rose (1978) has given an illuminating account of industrial sociology, beginning with the implications of Taylor's scientific management approach to work. The early pioneer of educational technology, Rice, who wrote the *Futility of the Spelling Grind* in 1897 was obviously applying Taylorian scientific management to teaching and learning. He found that half the time spent on such lessons as spelling drill would produce an equally good result. In other words, we should take the whole perspective of social change and development into account in looking for ways to make educational technology effective. Thus it is likely that at last the promised revolution in computer-assisted learning (which was confidently predicted to take place in the 1960s) may be at hand. The dramatic lowering of costs and smaller size of computers puts them well within the reach of school classrooms and families. So it may be considered feasible to develop the variety of teaching-learning strategies required to cater for the full range of individual differences in learning. The research described in the previous section on co-operative learning in pairs is put forward as a starting point for preparing different interactive programs. Learners might test themselves in advance on an orientation program, or simply try various tracks until a compatible computer 'instructor' style has been located. In principle, many programs could be designed to increase or diminish stress, eg rate of presentation and difficulty level, and to unfold a linear or hierarchical structure or else a spiral or network structure, as well as to present the teaching material in inductive discovery forms, in addition to didactic forms of discovery. Trown and Leith (1975) have shown that precise allocation to teaching methods is possible by reading off values from the intersection of regression lines. Indeed, it seems entirely feasible that computers themselves after initial 'experience' with new programs would work this out.

Perhaps the moment has come to revive all the skills of learning systems design, which were shelved, in order to produce trained instructional computer programmers and explore new techniques of improving learning. It should be recognized that this area is a field in which innovations continue to occur, but only when there are challenging projects to carry out. Van Dee, Postma and Leith (1973) designed a set of self-instructional modules providing hands-on experience in learning to operate and prepare programs for a small computer which required only hours to complete, with feedback and self-evaluation, instead of the week-long course offered by the manufacturer. Mathias and Leith (1971) prepared a unit of learning activities to teach chemistry students to interpret infra red spectra print-outs, which gave complete mastery of complex perceptual and cognitive schemata for visual interpretation and heuristic decision-making — again in a few hours instead of many lecture and laboratory sessions. Providing knowledge and know-how of these same learning-system design principles to student-teachers at all school levels, from infant to further education, enabled them to obtain much higher classroom teaching marks in their teaching practice than fellow students in a randomly selected control group in a college of education second-year cohort, who were taking alternative modular courses (Leith and Britton, 1979). In addition, the re-design of a microteaching programme so that it involved a comparison with group-determined criteria of teaching success in a smaller number of more complex skills than usual, and without filmed models of performance, has been shown to give lasting advantages to teachers who undergo this brief training in which they and their peers act as both teacher and class (Britton and Leith, 1982).

Conclusions

It may be pointed out that, in common with the research and development practices of a very large number of educational technologists, the experimental and development work described here has included a spectrum of research methods which range from participant observation (eg Postma and Leith, 1973; Visser, Postma and Leith, 1974), pilot runs, try-out samples and individual trials (eg Leith, Amaria and Williams, 1969) all the way to laboratory experiments carried out to elucidate precise points of learner processing and cognitive strategies (eg Leith, 1967). Those of us who practise educational technology do not denounce particular methodologies as such, only the claims made to exclusive probity and the rejection of rival methods and research orientations. It is clear that some individuals find the lack of precision in some methodologies unsupportable, whilst others are horrified and outraged to suppose that the bloom of ambiguity and the indeterminateness of multiple interpretations of certain concepts might be ruthlessly expunged. These temperamental differences between individuals are the psychological analogue of the sociology of knowledge syndrome. They give no weight to judgements of the validity of ideas, principles and methods — which have to be assessed by entirely different criteria.

References

Adams, R S and Biddle, B J (1970) *Realities of Teaching: Explorations with Videotape.* Holt, Rinehart and Winston, New York.

Adelman, Clem and Walker, Rob (1975) Developing pictures for other frames: action research and case study. In Chanan, G and Delamont, Sara *Frontiers of Classroom Research.* NFER, Slough.

Amaria, R P, Biran, L A and Leith, G O M (1969) Individual versus co-operative learning 1: influence of intelligence and sex. *Educational Research,* 11, pp 93-103.

Amaria, R P and Leith, G O M (1969) Individual versus co-operative learning 2: influence of personality. *Educational Research,* 11, pp 193-199.

Bales, R F (1950) *Interaction Process Analysis: A Method for the Study of Small Groups.* Addison Wesley, Cambridge, Mass.

Bandura, A (1963) *Social Learning and Personality.* Holt, Rinehart and Winston, New York.

Becher, A (1980) Research into practice. In Dockrell, W B and Hamilton, D (eds) *Rethinking Educational Research.* Hodder and Stoughton, London.

Becker, H S (1958) Inference and proof in participant observation. *American Sociological Review,* 23, pp 652-660.

Beigel, A and Feshbach, N (1970) A comparative study of student teacher, teacher corps and undergraduate preferences for elementary school pupils. Paper presented at the annual meeting of the California Educational Research Association.

Bloom, B S (1974) Time and learning. *American Psychologist,* 29, pp 682-688.

Britton, R J and Leith, G O M (1982) The effects of microteaching on teaching performance: a two year follow up. *BACIE Journal,* 27, 1, pp 27-30.

Broadbent, Donald E (1973) *In Defence of Empirical Psychology.* Methuen, London.

Carroll, John B (1970) Problems of measurement related to the concept of learning for mastery. *Educational Horizons,* 48, 3, pp 71-80.

Entwistle, N J and Entwistle, D (1970) The relationship between personality, study methods and academic performance. *British Journal of Educational Psychology,* 40, pp 132-143.

Eysenck, H J (1972) Personality and learning. In Wall, W D and Varna, V P (eds) *Advances in Educational Psychology,* University of London Press, London.

Feshback, N (1969) Student preferences for elementary school pupils varying in personality characteristics. *Journal of Educational Psychology,* 60, pp 126-132.

Good, T and Grouws, D (1972) Reaction of male and female teacher trainees to descriptions of elementary school pupils. Technical Report No 62, Centre for Research in Social Behavior, University of Missouri at Columbia.

Hallworth, H J (1969) *The H B Personality Inventory.* University of Birmingham, Birmingham.

Harvey, L (1968) Unpublished MEd Thesis, Faculty of Education, University of Birmingham.

Hudson, L (1966) *Contrary Imaginations.* Methuen, London.

Hutchins, R M (1936) *The Higher Learning in America.* Yale University Press, Newhaven, Conn.

Kelly, E (1958) A study of consistent discrepancies between instructor grades and term and examination grades. *Journal of Educational Psychology,* 49, pp 328-334.

Kuhn, Thomas S (1963) The essential tension: tradition and innovation in scientific research. In Taylor, C W and Barron, F (eds) *Scientific Creativity: Its Reorganisation and Development.* John Wiley, New York.

Lavin, David E (1965) *The Prediction of Academic Performance.* The Russell Sage Foundation, John Wiley, New York.

Leith, G O M (1967) An investigation of the role of stimulus and response meaningfulness in verbal learning. *Programmed Learning,* 4, pp 284-289.

Leith, G O M (1969a) Personality and learning. In Dunn, W R and Holroyd, C (eds) *Aspects of Educational Technology* **II**. Methuen, London.

Leith, G O M (1969b) *Second Thoughts on Programmed Learning.* National Council for Educational Technology, Occasional Publication 1, London.

Leith, G O M (1970) The acquisition of knowledge and mental development of students. *British Journal of Educational Technology,* 1, pp 116-128.

Leith, G O M (1972a) *Personality, Intellectual Style and Study Background.* Research Report No 14, Department of Research in Education, the University of Utrecht.

Leith, G O M (1972b) The relationships between intelligence, personality and creativity under two conditions of stress. *British Journal of Educational Psychology,* 42, pp 240-247.

Leith, G O M (1973) The effects of extraversion and methods of programmed instruction on achievement. *Educational Research,* 15, pp 150-153.

Leith, G O M (1974a) Programmed learning in science education. In UNESCO, *New Trends in the Utilization of Educational Technology for Science Education.* The UNESCO Press, Paris.

Leith, G O M (1974b) Individuals or dyads? A comparison of two methods of instruction in social psychology. *Empirische Studies Oder Onderwijs,* pp 143-146. H D Tjeenk Willink, Groningen.

Leith, G O M (1974c) Individual differences in learning: interactions of personality and teaching methods. *Personality and Academic Progress,* Association of Educational Psychologists, London.

Leith, G O M (1978) The psychology of learning. In Unwin, D (ed) *Encyclopaedia of Educational Media, Communications and Technology.* Macmillan, London.

Leith, G O M (1979) Implications of cognitive psychology for the improvement of teaching and learning in universities. *Educational Review,* 31, pp 149-159.

Leith, G O M (1981) Personality and intellectual style. Seventh International Conference on Improving University Teaching. University of Taukuba.

Leith, G O M (1982a) The influence of personality on learning to teach: effects and delayed effects of microteaching. *Educational Review,* to appear.

Leith, G O M (1982b) In quest of the Mugwump: an analysis of interactions between teaching and learning styles. (to appear)

Leith, G O M, Amaria, R P and Williams, H (1969) Applications of the principles of programmed learning to the preparation of television lessons in elementary science and mathematics. *Programmed Learning,* 6, pp 209-230.

Leith, G O M and Britton, R J (1973) The influence of learning techniques of programmed instruction on teaching performance in school. *Educational Research,* 15, pp 227-231.

Leith, G O M and Britton, R J (1979) The effects of microteaching and personality on teaching performance. Fifth International Conference on Improving University Teaching. London.

Leith, G O M and Davis, T N (1969) The influence of social reinforcement on achievement. *Educational Research,* 11, pp 132-137.

Leith, G O M and Davis, T N (1972) Age changes in the relationship between neuroticism and achievement. *Research in Education,* 8, pp 61-70.

Leith, G O M and Trown, E A (1970) The influence of personality and task conditions on learning and transfer. *Programmed Learning,* 7, pp 181-188.

Leith, G O M and Wisdom, B (1970) An investigation of the effects of error making and personality on learning. *Programmed Learning,* 7, pp 120-126.

Lyman, S M and Scott, M B (1970) *A Sociology of the Absurd.* Appleton, Century, Crofts, New York.

McKeachie, W J (1974) Instructional psychology. In Rosenzweig, M R and Porter, L W *Annual Review of Psychology,* 25.

Mathias, H and Leith, G O M (1971) *The Interpretation of Infra-Red Spectra.* University of Sussex, School of Molecular Sciences and R M Phillips Research Unit, Falmer, Sussex.

Nixon, Jon (ed) (1981) *A Teacher's Guide to Action Research.* Grant McIntyre, Ltd, London.

Postma, Otto and Leith, George (1973) *The Objectives of the Mass Spectrometry Course.* Department for Research and Development in Education, the University of Utrecht.

Rice, J M (1913) *Scientific Management in Education.* Hinds, Noble and Eldridge, New York.

Rose, M (1978) *Industrial Behaviour.* Penguin Books, Harmondsworth.

Singleton, John (1973) The educational uses of anthropology. In Weaver, Thomas (ed) *To See Ourselves: Anthropology and Modern Social Issues.* Scott, Foresman, Glenview, Illinois.

Sullivan, A M (1969) A structured individualized approach to the teaching of introduction psychology. In Dunn, W R and Holroyd, C (eds) *Aspects of Educational Technology* **II**. Methuen, London.

Swift, D F (1965) Educational psychology, sociology and the environment: a controversy at cross-purposes. *British Journal of Sociology*, 16, pp 336-347.

Trager, George L and Hall, Edward T (1953) *The Analysis of Culture*. Washington, DC.

Trown, E A and Leith, G O M (1975) Decision rules for teaching strategies in primary schools: personality treatment interactions. *British Journal of Educational Psychology*, 45, pp 130-140.

Underwood, B J (1964) Laboratory studies of verbal learning. In Hilgard, E R (ed) *Theories of Learning and Instruction*. University Chicago Press, Chicago.

Van Dee, Andrea, Leith, George and Postma, Otto (1973) The programming of the Olivetti 101 computer. Department for Research and Development in Education, the University of Utrecht.

Visser, Sophie, Postma, Otto and Leith, George (1974) The reorganisation of the gas chromatography course. Department for Research and Development in Education, the University of Utrecht.

Walker, Robert (1980) The conduct of educational case studies. In Dockerell, W B and Hamilton, D F (eds) *Rethinking Educational Research*. Hodder and Stoughton, London.

Section 1:
Effectiveness and Efficiency in Education and Training

1.1 Using Mass Media to Teach Adaptive Skills

R G Dawson and R I. Miller
Human Resources Research Organization

Abstract: This paper presents a description and demonstration of audio-print training materials developed to facilitate the adaptation of US military personnel to life in a foreign country.

It was determined that materials implemented through traditional systems could not be delivered in a cost-effective manner to large numbers of military personnel located in various locations throughout Europe. A review and critique of possible media and delivery systems resulted in the choice of a mass media approach using the Armed Forces radio network and the *Stars and Stripes* newspaper. This choice of delivery systems was based on the knowledge that most military personnel in Europe have access to, and make use of, the Armed Forces radio and *Stars and Stripes* newspaper.

It was also determined that traditional training materials would not meet the specific needs of the trainee population. Characteristics of the military personnel which were relevant to the choice of training methods include:

1. Soldiers often do not seek out services, but try to learn things on their own.
2. Many soldiers lack the time, and duty assignments preclude their enrolment in classes.
3. Soldiers tend to use services which are accessible to them in terms of location and time.
4. Many soldiers are most receptive to training which is based on real-world needs and which has a 'hands-on' orientation.

Based on trainee characteristics and desired characteristics of the training method, competency-based training approaches were thought to be the most effective. The characteristics of competency-based instruction incorporated in the materials will be described in detail.

As a result of the analysis of possible delivery systems, trainee characteristics and desired instructional methods, this series of training modules on adaptation of US military personnel to services in Europe has been developed and pilot-tested. The pilot test was conducted to determine the effectiveness of the materials in providing cost-effective instruction over a wide-spread area to trainees who may lack motivation and the basic skills necessary to benefit from traditional instructional methods and media.

Introduction

'Doing it in Deutschland' is not a phrase for a bumper sticker in Germany. It is the title of a training programme for American soldiers in Germany which is unique in its purpose, its design and delivery system.

From the time first-term enlisted soldiers step off the plane in Frankfurt, until they end their tour overseas, they are confronted with a multitude of demands, many of which are new and difficult. How well these soldiers are able to cope with the diverse aspects of military life in Europe, both on and off duty, has profound implications for the Army. The research strongly suggests that soldiers' ability to cope effectively with everyday life affects their adaptation to their new environment, their job performance, and their retention, decisions, and, consequently, their level of mission readiness.

Demands on New Arrivals

When first-term enlistees arrive in Europe, they are bombarded with new multiple demands, some of which are directly job-related, such as:

- ☐ becoming more familiar with military life after only a brief period of basic training and advanced individual training in the United States;
- ☐ integrating oneself into the new unit both on and off duty;
- ☐ acquiring job-related skills not learned in previous training which will be required within the new unit.

Other demands relate to their precipitous entry into a foreign country, such as:

- ☐ orienting oneself to living in Germany, which involves learning about that country's culture, language, customs, services, life-styles and currencies;
- ☐ learning about, and making use of, agencies and organizations within the Army which will assist in the areas of housing, medical and dental care, financial matters, family and child care services, recreational pursuits, education, legal assistance and various other situations faced by soldiers;
- ☐ handling the emotions, particularly the stress, which accompany abrupt changes in one's life (eg, movement to a new geographic location, separation from family and friends and entering a new work environment).

Throughout the first term in Germany, new demands are made of the soldier both on and off duty. These demands are not independent of each other. How well a soldier is able to cope with off-duty situations impinges upon how well that soldier is able to meet on-the-job requirements and vice-versa.

The Demands of Overseas Tours

The demands outlined above which initially confront the soldiers will continue throughout their tour of duty. Others that occur during an overseas tour might include:

- ☐ forming and maintaining friendships and working relationships;
- ☐ acquiring skills needed to pass Skill Qualification Tests and advance to higher skill levels;
- ☐ accomplishing tasks required for promotion;
- ☐ deciding whether or not to re-enlist;
- ☐ engaging in community activities — both American and German;
- ☐ conducting one's life within the institutional requirements of the military and German law;
- ☐ meeting the usual needs related to citizenship, family, health, finances, consumerism, etc which may be modified by the uniqueness of the new environment;
- ☐ beginning the adjustment process related to leaving Europe.

It can be seen from even a cursory look at the context of a first-term enlistee's life in Germany that many demands confront the soldier throughout the tour overseas. The ability to meet these demands is dependent upon the individual's repertoire of knowledge, skills and affective attributes (values, interests, dispositions, etc) and the degree to which the person can select, integrate, and apply those personal resources consistent with the requirements of those demands.

A soldier who has a limited range of skills and affective attributes from which to draw is less likely to adapt successfully to the environment from which those demands are emanating. The soldier must be assisted in the acquisition of the vital life-coping skills which, in turn, might facilitate successful adaptation to the new environment.

The Identification of Topics

The Human Resources Research Organization (HumRRO) collected information from interviews, questionnaires and tests with first-term enlistees, as well as meetings with, and surveys of, non-commissioned officers and representatives of agencies which provide services to soldiers. Among the findings of this research was the identification of a set of demands which meet the following criteria:

1. Perceived to be important by all three groups (first-term enlistees, NCOs and agency representatives).
2. Faced by 50 per cent or more first-term enlistees, by their own self-report and the observations of NCOs and agency representatives.
3. Faced frequently by first-termers.
4. Problematic for first-termers to meet adequately.
5. USAREUR-specific and/or host-nation related in the requirements needed to meet the demand.

The set of eight demands listed in Figure 1, out of the original pool of 127 believed to be commonly faced by soldiers in Europe, provides the objectives and content for the 'Doing It In Deutschland' series.

Soldier Characteristics

The data from the HumRRO study and other related research allow for some generalizations about first-term enlistees which have implications for the design of a programme intended to teach them the adaptive skills needed to cope with life in USAREUR (US Army in Europe). Many soldiers have limited reading ability, dislike reading, and/or do not learn well from print-only instruction. Soldiers tend to be most receptive to training which is based on real-world needs and which has a 'hands-on' orientation. The use of more than one medium helps to maintain their attention and enhances learning, as does the inclusion of humour.

The above characteristics of soldiers as learners have been integrated with the principles of performance-oriented training in the design of 'Doing It In Deutschland'. First, a multi-media format is used. An audio-tape and print component complement one another. Neither is meant to stand alone. The print portion is written at a readability level appropriate to the audience and contains many visuals. Pictures, cartoons, representations of signs, symbols, maps, schedules, menus, forms or other items related to each programme's topic are interspersed among the instructional information, practice activities and assessment exercises.

Second, the programmes are designed to be entertaining as well as instructive. The audio component is a humorous episode for each topic. The episodes involve the main cast of secret agent-type characters in adventures which require them to perform the skills being taught. Thus, in THE MUNICH CONNECTION, their mission involves using public transportation and reading maps, schedules and signs, purchasing tickets, and behaving appropriately on buses, streetcars and trains. Figure 2 contains an excerpt from the script for THE MUNICH CONNECTION.

Third, the programmes incorporate the characteristics of performance-oriented training. The objectives are specified in terms of relevant life-role demands. Time is flexible in terms of how long a soldier takes to achieve competence. Correct performance is demonstrated on the tape and explained in print. Opportunities are provided for practice. Activities include those which require the soldier to get out into the community. Assessment is an integral part of each programme.

The Implementation of the Programmes

It was evident from the HumRRO study that training materials alone will not remedy the problem regardless of how effective they might be. The materials must be delivered in a cost-effective manner to large numbers of those soldiers in need of the training. It was learned, for example, that soldiers often do not seek out services, but rather tend to try to learn things on their own or informally through

1. *Public Transportation*

   Use public transportation systems effectively.

2. *Community Resources*

   Know of, and be able to use, the services offered by agencies which assist soldiers to cope with life in USAREUR.

3. *Legal Aspects of Living in Germany*

   Observe host nation laws, including traffic rules, and obey German police.

4. *Interactions with Host-Nation Citizens*

   Observe acceptable/preferred behaviours within the host nation; such as quiet hours, 'unwritten rules' of behaviour, and social behaviours. Develop tolerance/respect for the language, values and behaviours of host-nation citizens.

5. *Shopping on the Economy*

   Communicate effectively with store personnel when shopping.

6. *Eating Out on the Economy*

   Know how to order and pay for food and behave appropriately in restaurants.

7. *Banking and Personal Finance*

   Use banking facilities during overseas tour; manage personal finances.

8 *Education/Training*

   Use opportunities for education and training consistent with personal and job goals and needs.

Figure 1. *Topics for 'Doing It In Deutschland'*
(High priority, USAREUR-specific/host nation-related demands)

Strac Willie:	Dr Zap, Dr Zap, Dr Zap!
Dr Zap: (groggy)	Huh, wha . . ., what's up?
Strac Willie:	I need a light.
Dr Zap: (more awake)	What?!
Strac Willie:	I need a light. I'm sure you got matches in that satchel of yours.
	One of these days all those papers are going to go up in smoke.
	Just move over a taste. The bag's wedged between you and the seat. Just let me get the bag — I'll find the matches.
	(sounds of rustling papers)
Strac Willie:	I ought to take out fire insurance on Dr Zap. He's a walking hazard with this bag.
Chester:	Say, Strac, what are you doing? You can't smoke in here.
Strac Willie:	Sure I can.
Chester:	But I thought you couldn't smoke on German transportation.
Strac Willie:	No, that's only true for *Strassenbahns* and buses.
	On trains you can smoke on any cars where it says *raucher*. It's usually written below a symbol of a cigarette burning.
	If you see *Nichtraucher*, that means no smoking. The symbol for that is the same cigarette burning, only on a white background with a slash mark through it.
	That sign on the door means I can smoke. So if you will excuse me . . .
Chester: (crackling paper)	Sure. And I think I'll have a Hershey bar.
Strac Willie:	Now, that's a flash of brilliance, Boondoggle. I think I'll have one too. But, first, put your trash where it belongs. There's a fine for littering.

Figure 2. *Excerpt from the script for THE MUNICH CONNECTION*

Figure 3. *The 'Coping Contest' from THE MUNICH CONNECTION*

their peers, NCOs, family or friends. Additionally, many soldiers either lack the time, or conflicts with duty preclude their enrolment in classes and/or their use of many agency services. Furthermore, soldiers tend to use those services which are most accessible to them in terms of location and time.

Therefore, in order to reach the largest number of soldiers, a mass media approach is being tried. Most soldiers both have access to, and in fact make use of, American Forces Network (AFN) radio which is broadcast throughout Germany, and the *Stars and Stripes* newspaper which has a daily distribution of 93,000 in Germany.

The initial delivery of the series of eight programmes is scheduled for Autumn 1982. For several weeks before the series begins, 'spots' will be aired on AFN-radio, and television will inform listeners of the coming programmes. During this time, articles and advertisements will also appear in the *Stars and Stripes*. On each of eight Sundays, the *Stars and Stripes* will include a supplement which will provide the printed materials for the programme.

The eight-page newspaper insert will contain information to be read before the broadcast; visuals to be looked at during the broadcast; reference materials for use in practice activities and real life; multiple and diverse opportunities to apply and practice the skills; and a self-assessment. For gaining and maintaining interest, there are cartoons, letters to the 'Coping Corner', puzzles and games and the 'Coping Contest'. (The 'Coping Contest' for THE MUNICH CONNECTION is shown in Figure 3.) Finally, an evaluation form on which readers/listeners can provide their reactions to the programme is included as part of the contest tear-off/mail-in section.

During each of the eight weeks a different episode of the series will be broadcast over AFN-radio throughout Germany. It is anticipated that each show will be aired at a number of times on different days based upon an analysis of listenership and availability of air time. During the week in which a programme is being aired, it will be distributed to Learning Resource Centres in each military community for use by them and by other programmes (eg, educational programmes, Army Community Service or the United Service Organization). In this way, the programmes will be available to people who did not hear it on AFN or people who want to hear it again.

'Doing It In Deutschland' is a pilot programme which is based upon extensive research and which incorporates proven principles of instructional design. Yet, it is an experiment. A comprehensive evaluation will be conducted to assess the benefits which result. The basic question will be: 'Does "Doing It In Deutschland" help soldiers to cope with life in the Army in Germany?'

1.2 Populations and Formats in Prospect and Retrospect

B S Alloway
Huddersfield Polytechnic

Abstract: At a time of increasing acceleration in the development of technologies, concern with the worldwide economic situation and the re-appraisal of human achievement and values, our learning in the future needs to reconsider the past.

In education and training the introduction of 'technology', however defined, seems to continue to cause either academic coolness or wild enthusiasm. Both reactions call upon the educational and training technologist to provide information, interpretation and experiential proof that technology has a sound, theoretically based, yet practically demonstrable outcome.

However, we are now faced with an extremely wide-ranging technology and, at the same time, a learning population actively seeking knowledge from pre-school to retirement, from all parts of the world and with very different individual requirements. Can the educational and training technology specialist hope to service such a vast array of demands?

This paper will attempt to show that, by the adoption of a variable format approach, it is possible to make a well defined programme of sub-technologies serve many different situations, both at home and abroad. Examples from such a range of situations will be demonstrated.

Populations

In educational terms, a population may be considered as (i) an individual (tutorial), (ii) a series of individuals (open learning systems), or (iii) a group of people (children or adults) who tacitly, or by some form of obligatory or legal requirement, undertake a learning experience.

According to the type, purpose and environment of such learning experience, this population may be categorized as pupils, scholars, students or trainees, each name implying a different relationship to the total learning hierarchy. Yet traditionally, in each group a common curriculum would be employed, a well established set of teaching techniques would be used, and a fixed strategy for the academic or training year would be commonplace.

Apart from a wide range of specialisms, experiences and qualifications being brought together in the later learning years (as experienced in the latter section of this paper) there are considerable individual differences within a population. For instance, the majority of teachers and instructors make some form of adjustment in their instructional tactics to take account of differences in attitudes, interests, motivation, aptitudes, achievements, satisfaction and accomplishment, etc. Adjustments also have to be made for the constraints and stimuli of each population's special 'interaction ambience' between peer group members and academic or training staff. This reaction can make the experiences of nominally parallel learning activity quite different, and enable groups to reach entirely different learning levels. Within each group a 'supplementary curriculum', unique to each class configuration, may add also to the population's prospective learning.

Formats

A majority of pedagogic formats rely heavily upon teacher/instructor dispensation of information, followed by an activity to encourage learner retention and, eventually, a re-exposition by the learner, which provides the evaluation data (often by examination). The possibility of other formats has engaged the minds of many practitioners during the past 25 years, and some excellent results have been reported at previous ETIC conferences. Two of these alternatives have been the subject of experimental work by the author who, during the development of a series of educational technology modules, attempted to design a system of learning-evaluation that would enable both new knowledge of subjects and skills to be tested, together with the unique creative contribution that each individual should be able to bring to a learning experience.

The two types are (i) an implementation report based upon the total course input and the opportunity to use such knowledge and skills within the course members' homes, or overseas institutions, and (ii) a 'case study' dissertation, whereby at each stage of the course students are asked to apply each module to their own teaching or training situation, to monitor results and then present an evaluation within the dissertation.

The vehicle by which such experience of format has been obtained during the 10-year development is a set of educational technology modules that can be used selectively in a wide range of part-time and full-time courses. There are now 21 of these modules, seven in each of the following groups.

(a) Communication media
(b) Design and production techniques
(c) Applications of systems analysis.

Courses based upon selected groupings of the modules (according to learner need) allow the bringing together of each individual's existing knowledge, with the new information and participative skills programmed into the specific course. The set gives the opportunity to include from traditional areas, ie audio-visual media, cinephotography, educational broadcasting, etc, through educational technology theory (objectives, design, modes, media, participation, testing and evaluation) and on to more recent sub-technologies such as colour video production, micro-teaching ergonomics, microcomputer applications and information technology.

However, the evidence of study varies with each different type of course, and the application of assessment techniques is matched to the population needs and demands. The following examples of attempts at a more flexible evaluation style are shown below.

A one-year modular evening course for professionals in libraries, training establishments, information services, National Health Service, and primary, secondary, further and higher education. Observations have shown that study implementation seems most successful when members have to apply a regular amount of the course work to their weekly employment tasks, but a long-term project design enables considerable opportunity for individual ideas to be developed in parallel with the course.

A 12-week full-time course for overseas senior staff, using the modules to explore the organization and management of educational technology. In this case the evaluation format was based on three tasks:

1. Specification of the home territory responsibility, authority, sphere of influence, opportunity, and estimated probability of being able to make an implementation change upon return to their own countries.
2. Selection of any seven from the 21 modules, for an in-depth study of areas that stand a more-than-average chance of being accepted by educational and training authorities.
3. The preparation of a phased programme of implementation, including the control of finances, budgeting, purchasing, storage, library/media centre, course design involving educational technology, and management techniques.

Student No /Medium	Talk	Chalk	Chart	Mag Bd	OHP	CCTV	Realia	Slides	Handout	Other
1	100	10	20	20	30	0	20	0	0	?
2	100	80	20	0	0	0	0	0	0	?
3	100	30	30	0	10	10	0	10	10	?
4	100	40	100	0	60	0	0	0	0	?
5	100	50	70	0	60	0	0	0	0	?
6	100	60	40	0	0	0	0	0	40	?
7	100	40	40	30	20	0	0	0	0	?
8	100	100	50	10	20	0	0	0	40	?
9	100	60	50	10	0	0	0	0	0	?
10	100	80	10	0	0	0	0	0	80	?
(Figures above represent percentage of teaching time in which media were used)										
Aggregate %	100	56	43	7	20	1	2	1	17	?

Figure 1. Information gathered from a newly-qualified overseas graduate teaching group. Choice based on one year's postgraduate teaching experience 'Use of Educational Technology Media'

Dissertations for higher qualifications within a Polytechnic setting. As a major part of advanced and post-graduate diplomas in education it has been possible to offer the module set as a basis for dissertation study. Combinations of the modules from each of the three sub-sets enable a considerable economy of effort in routine structures, and therefore a concentration upon investigative and creative scholarship. Some examples of 40,000-word dissertations were shown at this conference.

Modular courses taken to overseas countries (up to one-month periods). These applications of the modular set create an opportunity to assess the possibilities for specific development according to the existing facilities and the developmental policy of the educational and training authorities. It is advisable to take out all of the materials, software, books, equipment and written course material, because if you are several thousand miles away from the UK, many difficulties can arise from the lack of basic commodities. Apart from shortened forms of the above evaluation techniques, it is possible to add a realistic human performance element in the setting in which members of a group will normally have to operate. One such survey, taken prior to the start of a two-week implementation course, is shown in Figure 1. Needless to say, such usage was conditioned by possession and availability of materials.

Where might the new learning potentials be established in the formats of the future and how can experiences from the past be combined to show innovative change? Some of the experiments that the author is currently involved with include the following:

1. A combination of structured learning, with various forms of creative expression, some of which are detailed above. The importance of this combination might be further explored in the context of many training activities, in that the common structured sequence 'imitation, accuracy, pace and stamina' is so often followed by considerable creative adaptability in the working environment. This is due to the constant need to improve on performance, update products and reduce fatigue.
2. Current rethinking of training, especially where related to rapidly changing production demands, is tending to emphasize the value of short spells of specific training. Economies in learning times by accelerated training formats directed to today's production or service needs open up many possibilities for the pre-structuring of training courses and materials.
3. The well tried 'old methods' and 'traditional media' may have much left in them which could be mined, using new applications and possibilities by employing different techniques. Much new technological hardware in reprographics, computing, video and photo-processing enables faster, more accurate and more responsive results for both instruction and learning.
4. The universal development of computer, microprocessor and microcomputer applications in industry, commerce, the market place, the home, and especially the primary school, leaves no doubt that at least the microcomputer should be used wherever possible in education and training.
5. Previous long-term academic syllabuses and training programmes will perhaps have to change more easily and rapidly. These factors require continuous research, development and new designs. A modular approach to production has been found to give greater efficiency and economy in the world of industrial production. How valid is the greatly increased adoption of such formats in our education and training, which provide the human populations for both production and consumption?

1.3 Pictures as Retentional Aids to Prose Learning: An Examination of Reiterative Strategies and Contextual Image

R Bernard
Concordia University, Canada
and
C Petersen
American Institute for Research, Lincoln, Nebraska, USA

Abstract: Pictures have been issued as adjuncts to prose for centuries (Orbis Pictus, 1658), but have only recently begun to attract research attention. It is thought that pictures increase learner interest, and add attractiveness to the printed page. The attentional role is primarily for motivational purposes and, as such, the picture is intended to add interest and appeal to otherwise barren textual formats. Illustrations fulfilling the explicative role directly portray aspects of the content which are not clearly defined or explained by words alone. Finally, retentional pictures function much like other adjunct aids (eg advance organizers, or overviews) to increase the retentional value of the prose.

Through an examination of the prose literature, it was determined that two types of organizing structures exist, each of which has, at least conceptually, a retentional image counterpart. Further, it was thought that application of these structures to the design of picture/prose interactions might result in a consistent strategy for the design of alternative adjuncts. Reiterative images might provide the same benefits in terms of organizing function. Likewise, contextual organizers provide a mediational bridge between the learner's past experience and knowledge and the passage content. Images designed to provide such a link between the learner and the content have been found to be effective (Bernard, Peterson and Ally, 1981) especially when the context of the passage is not clearly understood in advance by the learner. Further research, however, is needed with images used in this fashion to establish their usefulness.

In the past year, four studies have been conducted to determine the conditions under which these strategies are effective in promoting the retention of prose content. Three have taken a reiterative approach to image design, and one has looked at the contextual function of images. The purpose of the paper proposed here is threefold: (i) to report briefly and in non-technical language the outcome of these experiments, (ii) to discuss these outcomes in the light of the theory from which they are derived and the practical benefits which they suggest, and (iii) to present and discuss issues of methodological concern, both to the practitioner interested in using these strategies, and the researcher interested in pursuing this work further.

Sections from the textual materials are presented, along with the images used in each experiment as a means of illustrating the design strategies that were used in each case. Finally, the generalizability of this research will be considered, with particular attention paid to the design of the images themselves.

Introduction

If asked why pictures and illustrations are so regularly included in instructional textbooks and other printed educational materials, many people would cite reasons such as: 'They make the printed page more appealing'; 'They motivate the learner to read the prose'; or 'They represent information which is not easily describable in words'. Unquestionably, these are worthwhile design objectives. However, Duchastel (1978, 1981a, 1981b) and Levin (1979) have argued that pictures can perform an additional function when used interactively with prose, that is, pictures may increase the retentional value of the written content. Following on from their notion, we have conducted a series of six studies in the past year in an attempt to determine:

(a) if pictures and illustrations in text can improve learning and retention of the prose;

(b) if there are certain learner, pictorial or prose conditions which promote increased retention immediately after reading and over time.

This paper is a broad summary of three of these studies.

The Research

We began our research with a general paradigm drawn from the literature of prose processing. An illustration designed to promote prose retention could either have a contextual relationship to the prose or a reiterative relationship. We saw a contextual picture functioning in much the same way as an advance organizer (Ausubel, 1968) or an overview, providing additional clarifying information or, in some way, representing the structure of the entire passage or a large section within it. On the other hand, reiterative illustrations were conceived as more narrowly circumscribed within the limits of specific information in the text. A reiterative illustration would be designed to duplicate paragraph-level content in pictorial form, and would provide memory support, because the information is represented in dual coding (Paivio, 1971). Like inserted questions, reiterative pictures would probably have a more localized effect than a contextual picture, aiding memory for specific pictured information, but having no overall facilitative effect.

Contextual and reiterative retentional functions were conceived from the rather extensive literature of prose processing and the more limited literature dealing with picture and prose interaction. However, space limitations preclude a detailed explication of this literature. (For more information see Bernard, Peterson and Ally, 1981; Duchastel, 1981a, 1981b; Brody, 1981; Levin, 1979; Levin and Lesgold, 1978.) It is quite likely that other conceptualizations exist. Contextual and reiterative functions, however, provide a convenient starting point for the exploration of pictures used as retentional aids to prose learning.

The remainder of this paper is divided into three major sections:

(a) A presentation of the general method employed in these studies.

(b) A brief treatment of the specific results of each study.

(c) A general discussion of the results of all of the studies.

General Method

Materials

In every case except one (Study One) the prose passages used were especially constructed and validated for the purposes of the experiment. At least two content specialists were used in each case, as well as reference materials and existing texts on the subjects. Similarly, the illustrations were conceived and designed with the aid of this same content expertise. In general, all of the illustrations were constructed after the passages were written from the highest level concepts in the section being represented. Labels or other words embedded in the illustrations were used where appropriate to make the illustration more meaningful and to tie them to the prose content. A graphic artist produced the final black and white line version of the illustrations. Table 1 provides the topic of each passage as well as the number of illustrations included in each passage.

Dependent Measures

In all of the studies learning was assessed by means of a multiple-choice test (20-30 items) covering the contents of the prose. Reliabilities for these tests ranged from .69 to .81 (Cronbach's α). In all of the studies but one (Study One) an additional

Study	Prose topic	Number of illustrations	Subjects	Independent[1] variable	Dependent[2] variable	Control variable	Design
One	human brain; aphasias and resulting symptoms are detailed	2	introductory education students n = 104	CI vs CP vs control vs placebo control	immediate and delayed MC	cognitive style (measured but not used)	4 x 2 with repeated measures
Two	theories of learning; behaviourism, cognitivism, humanism	3	introductory educational psychology students n = 78	CI vs control vs image with covert and overt response	immediate and delayed MC and FR	reading ability (used as covariate)	4 x 3 with repeated measures
Three	the human circulatory system; the functioning system	5	introductory biology students n = 53	RI vs control print vs audio presentation	immediate and delayed MC and FR; pictured and non-pictured items	reading ability (used as covariate)	2 x 2 x 2 with repeated measures

1 CI: contextual image; CP: contextual prose; RI: reiterative images
2 MC: multiple-choice; FR: free recall

Table 1. *Summary of the major parameters of the three studies*

free-recall test was given. Subjects were asked to recall as much as they could from the passage contents and write it in the form of complete statements. The free-recall test was always administered prior to the multiple-choice test, so that the cued test would not act as a recall device. In addition, both of these measures (in different random orders in the case of the multiple-choice test) were administered at a delayed point in time (from one to six weeks later). Prior to any testing, all subjects (except in Study One) were administered a test of reading ability (Nelson-Denny, 1973).

Procedure

Materials were randomly assigned to subjects (as an alternative to random assignment of subjects to materials) in numbered packages. The subjects then proceeded through the package materials in order from beginning to end. Where feasible, no time limit was placed on answering the multiple-choice test. The time limit for reading the passage was based on baseline administration times obtained from the pilot testing of the materials.

Additional Information

For additional information concerning the design, number and type of subjects and variables for each study, refer to the listings in Table 1.

Results

Study One

The first study was designed to assess whether a contextual illustration appearing in a pre-passage location would provide low prior knowledge learners with the additional conceptual support, so as to make the passage contents more meaningful and therefore more memorable. The illustration and an equivalent prose treatment (similar to an advance organizer) were designed to provide additional context for the more specific information contained in the passage. Two control conditions were used; one which received the passage alone and one which read a placebo of equivalent length. All groups (four in all) were administered an immediate and delayed post test. Thus, the study employed a 4 x 2 repeated measures design.

The results of the analysis of variance indicated a significant ($p < .001$) interaction of time and treatments. *Post hoc* comparisons revealed that the interaction was caused by the decline over time of the passage-only control group. This group scored about the same level as the placebo control condition on the delayed test, while the group which received the contextual illustration and prose equivalent remained relatively high (ie about 30 per cent higher than the control groups at the delayed testing time).

Study Two

The results of Study One suggested that a contextual illustration designed to provide necessary conceptual structure (*cf* Bransford and Johnson, 1972; Royer and Cable, 1975) to the passage contents could improve retention of the prose content. Additionally, the results of Study One were generally supportive of Duchastel's (1981b) prediction that the benefits of retentional illustrations are not likely to appear immediately but will show after longer testing intervals.

Study Two was an extention of Study One. Here, we wanted to find out whether contextual illustrations preceding the major organizational units in a passage could improve overall retention of the passage. Study Two was similar to Study One, except that we tested a more commonly-employed illustrative strategy; that of interspersing the illustrations with the text. A special three-section passage was written for Study Two. The passage dealt with three learning theories: behaviourism, cognitivism and humanism. After a number of attempts at designing illustrations for this rather abstract content, we decided on a form of illustration based on Knowlton's (1966) analogical picture type. The major conceptual feature of each learning theory was portrayed as a concrete analogy (eg a man climbing to the top of the self-actualization mountain). Into this was inserted a mnemonic, and five major concepts from the passage contents.

One of our major purposes in Study Two was to determine the effects of encouraging the learner to use the illustration as a retentional aid. There were two elaboration conditions in this study (Reder, 1980). One of these, the covert elaboration condition group, received the illustration in its normal position, plus instructions to mentally answer a question which appeared under it — a question which encouraged the reader to think about the contents of the picture. The other elaboration condition, the overt group, received instructions to write a few sentences about the relationship of the picture and passage in the space provided. We expected that this condition would produce the best results, as it is common for adults to treat pictures in a cursory manner (Brody, 1981) and this condition required the subjects to provide evidence that they had looked at and tried to understand the illustration.

The results were surprising, however. We found that the means of the overt condition were considerably below all other means and significantly below ($p < .05$) the passage-only and the passage plus picture conditions on the multiple-choice test. The passage plus picture condition produced the highest means, although they were not significantly higher than the passage-only condition. Several interpretations of this result are possible. One is that time spent on picture interpretation reduces learning from the prose. Another is that encouraging learners to elaborate upon an illustration verbally, and especially in writing, caused them to recode the picture verbally. This has been found to reduce memory for the picture (Levie and Levie, 1975) and any verbal information which might be associated with it. According to this view, the positive effects of cue summation (Severin, 1967), and combined verbal and imaginal coding would not be present.

Study Three

Study Three was an attempt to explore the potential of reiterative illustrations with prose presented in two different modes: visually (print) and orally (spoken). Previous research with children (Levin and Lesgold, 1978) has indicated consistent findings in favour of picture conditions when the prose is presented orally, but mixed findings when students read the prose. We were interested in finding out if these results hold for adults as well. In addition, we were interested in determining how the insertion of reiterative illustrations in a passage affects memory for the non-illustrated information around the picture. To test this, we structured the passage to include five illustrations which related specifically to five of the 12 prose paragraphs. The illustrated paragraphs were alternated with the non-illustrated paragraphs. By examining test items related to these different sections across the four treatments, audio and print presentation with and without pictures, we could judge how people responded to pictorially and non-pictorially supported information.

The results indicated no overall main effects or interactions on the combined multiple-choice test (ie picture items plus non-picture items). However, there was a strong main effect ($p < .05$) in favour of the illustration conditions when items taken from the illustrated prose were considered alone. This result is not surprising. Illustrations support the information they are designed to support. Do they, in addition, support the other non-illustrated information in the passage? The answer, according to the results obtained here, is no. We found a three-way interaction of presentation mode (print vs audio), illustrative condition (illustrated vs non-illustrated) and time of testing on the non-illustrated test items (see Figure 1). Only the print-alone condition remained high over the delayed testing interval, falling 5.5 per cent over time. Audio-alone and print plus illustration, while initially as high as the print-alone condition, fell 21 per cent and 24 per cent respectively over the delayed period. The audio with illustrations was initially low (ie 30 per cent below the print without illustrations group) and remained low on the delayed test (ie 32 per cent below the print illustration group). These results point to the possibility that reiterative illustrations, like the ones used in this experiment, may have a very local effect. They encourage memory for the specific information they are designed to reinforce, but reduce memory for the non-illustrated text, especially over longer testing intervals. The expected aiding effects of pictures (Levin and Lesgold, 1978) on orally presented text were not found in this study.

Discussion and Conclusions

The studies presented here were conceived as exploratory in nature. Replication and additional exploration is required before final statements can emerge. Therefore, the following discussion and tentative conclusions are offered.

In general, the studies reported in this paper suggest that, under certain conditions, illustrations can provide facilitative memory support for instructional prose. It seems reasonably clear that, in order to be effective, an illustration must be used by the student as a memory aid. This means that the student must be aware of the purpose of the illustration as well as how the illustration fits into the overall scheme of the passage. Clarity on these two points appears to be an essential ingredient to obtaining effective results. However, the findings in Study Two suggest that attempts to encourage the learner to process the picture more deeply through verbal elaboration may not produce the intended beneficial results. Further experimentation, however, is necessary before the validity of this finding is assumed.

Related to this, of course, is the question of what exactly a picture or illustration provides the learner, assuming that the purpose of the illustration is clearly specified. If the picture provides something which students are not likely to be able to provide for themselves, the chances of effectiveness are increased (Salomon, 1978). Study One demonstrated that the contextual information supplied by the picture aids recall enormously. However, Study Two did not support this conclusion nearly as emphatically. While the picture-only condition in Study Two produced higher means than the no-picture condition, the difference was not significant. The pictures obviously did not provide enough support to warrant their inclusion in the passage.

Study Three provided evidence that pictures used to reiterate the passage contents can improve retention, but only for the verbal content which is addressed by the illustration. In fact, non-illustrated verbal information may actually be less well remembered as a result of the illustration. If illustrations and pictures, like inserted questions and underlining, provide cues as to the relative importance of particular content in the text, the mere absence or presence of pictures may turn out to be as important as the content portrayed. A study of the relative effects of various cueing aids might provide additional insight into the question of textual design. If illustrations do provide a cueing function, then the selection of content to be illustrated should be carefully made. In fact, an analysis of the prose text in which the conceptual structure of the passage is outlined (eg Schallert, 1980) should precede the selection and design of illustrations.

In summary, the studies reported here provide only tentative evidence that images can offer retentional support for textual prose. However, the results are encouraging and the authors believe that further refinements in instrumentation,

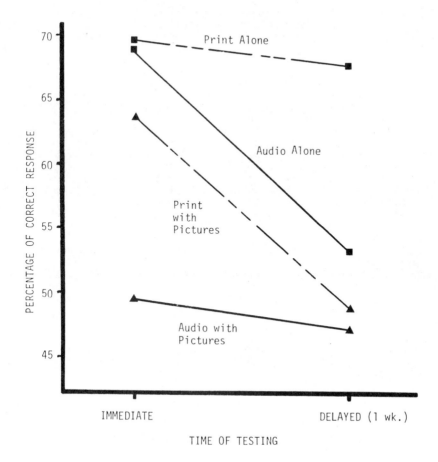

Figure 1. *Three-way interaction of testing time, presentation mode and picture condition for non-pictured items*

administrative procedures and sample selection will eventually produce more definitive guidelines for practice. Work on the underlying theory is also important if we are eventually going to understand how the manipulation of design variables influences learning and remembering from text.

References

Ausubel, D P (1968) *Educational Psychology: A Cognitive View.* Holt, Rinehart and Winston, New York.

Bernard, R M, Petersen, C and Ally, M (1981) Can images provide contextual support for prose? *Educational Communication and Technology Journal,* 29, pp 101-108.

Bransford, J S and Johnson, M K (1972) Contextual prerequisites for understanding: some investigations of comprehension and recall. *Journal of Verbal Learning and Verbal Behaviour,* 11, pp 717-726.

Brody, P J (1981) Research on pictures in instructional texts: the need for a broadened perspective. *Educational Communication and Technology Journal,* 29, pp 93-100.

Duchastel, P C (1978) Illustrating instructional texts. *Educational Technology,* November, pp 36-39.

Duchastel, P C (1981a) Research on illustrations in text: issues and perspectives. *Educational Communication and Technology Journal,* 28, pp 283-287.

Duchastel, P C (1981b) Illustrations in text: a retentional role. *Programmed Learning and Educational Technology,* 18, pp 9-15.

Knowlton, J Q (1966) On the definition of picture. *Audiovisual Communication Review,* 14, pp 157-183.

Levie, W H and Levie, D (1975) Pictorial memory processes. *Audiovisual Communication Review,* 23, pp 81-97.

Levin, J R (1979) *On functions of pictures in prose.* Theoretical Paper 80. Wisconsin Research and Development Center for Individualized Schooling.

Levin, J R and Lesgold, A M (1978) On pictures in prose. *Educational Communication and Technology Journal,* 26, pp 233-243.

Nelson, M S and Denny, E C (1973) *The Nelson-Denny Reading Test.* Houghton Mifflin, Boston.

Paivio, A (1971) *Imagery and Verbal Processes.* Holt, Rinehart & Winston, New York.

Reder, L M (1980) The role of elaboration in the comprehension and retention of prose: a critical review. *Review of Educational Research,* 50, pp 5-53.

Royer, J M and Cable, G W (1976) Illustrations, analogies and facilitative transfer of prose learning. *Journal of Educational Psychology,* 68, pp 205-209.

Salomon, G (1978) *Interaction of Media, Cognition and Learning.* Jossey-Bass, San Fransisco.

Schallert, D L (1980) *Relational Mapping as a Discourse Analysis Method.* University of Texas at Austin.

Severin, W (1967) Another look at cue summation. *Audiovisual Communication Review,* 15, pp 233-245.

Section 2:
The Development
of Packages
and Programmes

2.1 The Council for Educational Technology Training Programme: An Exploratory Excursion in South West England

D Harris *University of Bath*
R Tarrant *Council for Educational Technology*
R Winders *Plymouth Polytechnic*

Abstract: The paper gives details of the current stage in the South West region of this programme funded by the Council for Educational Technology (CET). Two regions are functioning in the pilot project: an urban area and a rural area. The SW region is the rural area.

The project is attempting to identify possibilities for transfer of ideas between education and training and vice versa. In a rural area the distances to be travelled are a key aspect.

The strategy used by the SW region in initiating the project is outlined. The role of changes in information technology as a potential means of alleviating problems and needs identified is also described and there are case studies of existing practice and changed practice.

The whole project is in the context of the Council for Educational Technology's five technologies: resource assisted teaching, resource based learning, remote interactive learning, mediated learning, and management of teaching and learning resources. A brief explanation of these technologies is included.

Introduction

The Council for Educational Technology Training Programme is aimed at supporting the trainers of practitioners (teachers or trainers) in education, industry, commerce, public administration and the armed services. It is not only for giving guidance and information on the new approaches in training, but also for the exchange of ideas within and between education and training.

The SW region covers from Lands End (or, more precisely, the Isles of Scilly) to the North of Gloucestershire, and from Cornwall to the eastern edges of Dorset and Wiltshire. The main centres of population are Plymouth, Exeter, Bristol, the Bournemouth-Poole area, Swindon and the Cheltenham-Gloucester area. There are also other large towns or cities (Bath, Paignton, Salisbury, Taunton, Torquay and Weston-super-Mare). The remainder of the area comprises small towns and villages, and is largely rural. In the context of the UK, distances are quite large (Gloucester to Penzance is 225 miles, Penzance to Bournemouth 190 miles). In some areas there are no motorways or railways to speed travel. Some areas are relatively untouched by new technologies. For example PRESTEL only came to the northern part of the region in 1981 and has not yet arrived on a local basis in Exeter, Plymouth and the southern part of the region. It is clear that outside the larger urban areas the training of practitioners involves problems of distance.

The Framework

A framework of five approaches to learning was identified by CET. The definition and relationships between the five approaches were refined during the project to:

Inside organizations
1. Resource assisted teaching (RAT)
2. Resource based learning (RBL)

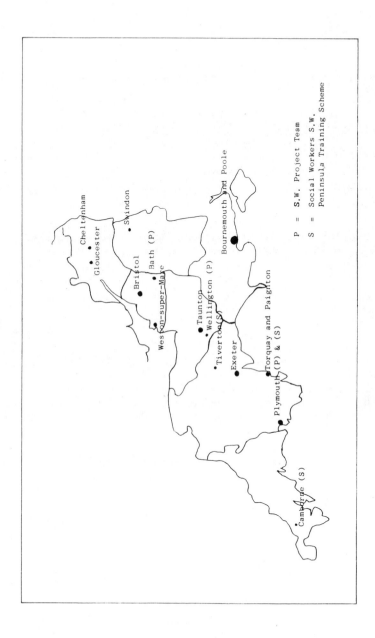

Figure 1. *The South West Region*

Outside organizations
3. Remote interactive learning (RIL)
4. Mediated learning (ML)

Overall management
5. Management of learning and teaching support (MLTS)

Resource assisted teaching is conventional teaching where the trainer talks to the groups using a range of resources such as chalkboard, television, and/or computers.

Resource based learning occurs where trainees work singly or in pairs with resources such as books, worksheets, laboratory equipment, video recorders, and/or computers. The trainer is present or easily accessible.

Remote interactive learning occurs when trainees are remote from the organization but contact is available at a distance. Such contacts may be by means such as the telephone, or interactive computer terminals.

Mediated learning occurs when trainees obtain materials and work on their own without tutorial contact, for example: TV programmes, radio, and the personal computer.

Management of learning and teaching support includes the management and organization of resources, assessment procedures, preparation, production, maintenance, supplying of learning and teaching resources, and the evaluation of the system. It is the vital element to enable the four approaches to function.

The Organization

There were two regions initiated with funding from CET. One region was urban, the other in the rural South West. The purposes were:

☐ Identification of the needs existing for training trainers within the five approaches.
☐ Identification of existing material on training within these approaches.
☐ Defining the needs felt to be of the highest priority.
☐ Identification of 'good practice' and recommendation for deriving case studies.
☐ Adaptation of existing materials for highest priority needs.

The strategies were left to each region. In the SW there were three people involved based at Bath (the director of the project), Wellington (the co-ordinator) and Plymouth (the liaison officer), each shown with a (P) on the map. All were part-time, the co-ordinator having the most time with two days each week over a six-month period.

The first task seen was to identify the needs of the trainers of practitioners in the region. The identification of practices adopted and the use of recent technologies were also seen as early tasks. Within the time scale a variety of strategies were possible, for example: (i) questionnaires sent to a wide range of trainers; (ii) interviews with a selected range of trainers; (iii) meetings with groups of trainers.

The potential range of trainers included those from industry and commerce (private and public sectors), education (at all levels), the Armed Services, and public administration (at national, regional and local levels in government departments: in local authorities).

It was clear that in six months a limited range of trainers could be followed. The use of a questionnaire would have entailed the design and piloting. With a large sample for ease of processing it would have been necessary for us to prejudge the key needs and problems of trainers.

An alternative strategy was used based on strategies (ii) and (iii). The strategy attempted to use a chain sequence (Figure 2).

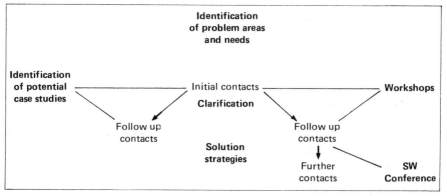

Figure 2. *South West training programme*

The initial contacts were made through names already known by CET or the project team, and by contacting organizations and asking for contacts. The co-ordinator visited the initial contacts identified. From the interviews, problem areas, needs and existing practice were identified. Often further contacts in other organizations were also followed from leads given during interviews.

The first workshop was an invited group covering the spectrum of the range of trainers identified earlier in the paper. The workshop focused on raising needs and problems and sharing some existing and potential practice. One idea brought into the workshop by the team was telephone conferencing which proved to be a good choice. (More details are given later in the paper.) One of the case studies used in the workshop was also popular later in the project because of its simplicity and its limited use of expensive resources. The trainers present were not enthusiastic about the use of modern technology.

The Problems and Needs of Trainers

From the personal interviews and the initial workshop a range of problems and needs were raised. The common ones were:

☐ the geographical nature of the SW Region, with resulting problems of communication, travel and time loss in training,
☐ the need for alternatives to bringing practitioners to a centre for training (for example, trainees working on remote sites, students on placement),
☐ the need for time (resources/assistance in preparing suitable materials relevant to specific organizational needs),
☐ information on how new information technology can assist (or hinder) the training strategies to be used in the future.

In addition the initial workshop identified a desire to:

☐ exchange ideas and information between education and training.

Many other issues were raised, but with less agreement with those consulted.

The Strategy

In the second three months the problems and needs were followed to the limits of the resources. It was clear that the co-ordinator was proving to be a catalyst as a result of meeting trainers and passing on ideas and information and is responding in writing to requests for information. The liaison officer at Plymouth not only produced a tape- slide sequence on the five approaches, but also identified several examples of current practice to add to those already found by the co-ordinator. The examples of current practice were developed as case studies. The remaining workshops and the conference used the case studies as bases for small group activities. A typical workshop had the following framework:

a.m.   Introduction to CET Training Programme
       Tape-slide sequence on five approaches
       Small group work on trainers' needs
       Case studies on current practice

Lunch

p.m.   Detailed example with participation (eg telephone conferencing)
       Discussion on example
       Suggestions for further work
       Evaluation of workshop.

The case studies were presented, wherever possible, by the original person involved in the development of the practice. Case studies used included:

- [ ] An open learning scheme on technician training.
- [ ] SW peninsula scheme for Certificate in Social Service.
- [ ] An open learning scheme for a Diploma in Acoustics.
- [ ] Flexistudy.
- [ ] A marine microcomputer and audiovisual instructional system for use in oil tankers.
- [ ] Use of peer group assessment of trainers.
- [ ] Use of resource based learning and PLATO for courses run under the auspices of Manpower Services Commission.
- [ ] A resource pack: 'Signposts for Evaluating'.
- [ ] Teleconferencing.

Ultimately it is to be hoped that many of the case studies will be written up to enable ideas to be transferred over a wider area.

The area of least familiarity was that of teleconferencing. A brief outline of two case studies is given below.

Teleconferencing

Teleconferencing is a method of holding a meeting for training purposes over the telephone. Advantages include:

(a) Time saving (no need for travelling).
(b) Cost saving (travel costs and opportunity costs of further time available to participants when they would have been travelling).

The disadvantages include:

(a) Lack of face-to-face contact (there is a television version called confravision which practically overcomes this).
(b) Potential problems with bad lines (winter weather often precludes travel; more expensive teleconferencing systems reduce the problems of bad connections).
(c) Limited number of participants (limits are about nine to 18 locations depending on the system used).

Details of the system, its costs and a comparative costing with meetings is in *CET News* Number 15. (Copies are available either from the Council for Eduational Technology or from the authors.) A simple summary of the costing is:

Costs of Meetings

T + S + O

T	Travel costs	— rail fares, car mileage allowance, taxi fares, parking etc,
S	Subsistence costs	— meals en route, overnight stays,
O	Opportunity costs	— travel time is wholly or partially lost time — use relevant salary costs per hour or day.

Costs of Teleconference (operator connected)

C + T + E

C	Connection charges	— charges levied per caller,
T	Telephone call charges	— charges levied per caller,
E	Extra costs	— administrative, secretarial, postage costs incurred in circulating documents prior to teleconference which would not have been used for a meeting.

Other factors to consider include:

☐ Teleconferencing is more likely to be effective if participants know one another.
☐ Cost comparisons do not take account of any effects on morale compared with face-to-face.
☐ A chairman is essential; different styles may affect the benefits of teleconferencing (or meetings?).
☐ Teleconferencing is limited for applications to training sessions compared with face-to-face.
☐ Poor reception reduces effectiveness (bad weather and stuffy rooms affect meetings).

Teleconferencing has been used in the SW region for the following purposes:

Contacting students who are on placement.
Editorial meetings for a journal.
Reporting progress on a training programme.
Exchanging ideas on potential training materials.

As far as we can determine all these meetings have developed from the project's initiatives.

South West Peninsula Scheme for the Certificate in Social Work

The scheme has as its main features:

☐ The combination of attendance at a training centre (college) with independent guided learning at the place of work.
☐ The involvement of college academic staff, study supervisors at the place of work and line managers in the operation of the training scheme.
☐ The use of continuous assessment by job-related assignments within the place of work.

The certificate is a nationally-approved and accredited scheme. The courses are open to a variety of staff working as managers, senior staff and instructors in day-care units; organizers of volunteer specialist work; social workers. The course is modular in structure, enabling a choice of units according to individual needs.

The attendance at training centres is made up of block residential periods at the beginning and end of each term over two years, weekly bridging days at one of three colleges: Camborne, Plymouth, and Tiverton (marked (S) on Figure 1).

The scheme has had the following benefits when compared with previous training:

- [ ] Improvement in the attitudes of trainees, tutors and study supervisors to training, now seen as job-related.
- [ ] Improvement in the attitudes to training by senior line managers who participate in the scheme, and are involved in the development of the scheme.
- [ ] Feedback loops between staff and trainees providing better monitoring of the progress of the scheme.

Telephone tutorials and telephone contact between the trainers, managers and supervisors are important when such large distances are involved. Teleconferencing may feature in the next stage of development.

View from the End of the Journey

Considering the small total time available on the project the progress has been beyond original expectations. The role of catalyst, played by the co-ordinator and liaison officer, has not only initiated new solutions to existing problems, but has enabled a large amount of transfer of ideas within the region. New information technologies were not received enthusiastically in the region. Not only do new technologies involve expenditure, but they also threaten trainers' present roles. The difference between what trainers do and what trainers should aim to do is highlighted. The only technological development which showed potential for rapid transfer was teleconferencing. The use of a mixture of institution-based self-study, and meeting together, which has been achieved in the social work scheme, was also seen as having much potential for transfer. Several other distant study schemes generated interest too, with printed materials as the basis.

Assessment and evaluation were two further issues which provided bases for discussion. The use of peer assessment was recognized as having considerable training potential for training trainers. Little formal work seemed to have been carried out on cost analysis.

The problems of the development, design, production, assessment and tutorial contact in distance learning was the ultimate focus. The resources and expertise were very limited compared with the Open University, which was felt to be an ideal (but impossible) model to emulate in the current financial climate. The smaller scale models being used from Plymouth Polytechnic and Camborne seemed to have more potential.

Many of the problems raised may have potential for transfer to urban areas too, where travel can be even more time-consuming than in areas well served by motorways and trains.

There is a large potential for the development and continuation of the role of catalyst to enable the continuing transfer and diffusion of ideas. After the conference being held in March a further conference has been initiated by CET in July to follow up developments in the SW region.

2.2 Making a Development Sector Package

K J Ogilvie and W S Telfer
Paisley College of Technology

Abstract: The Physics Learning Unit was set up at Paisley to overcome difficulties relating to a particular class. The result was a distribution of teaching material into three different sectors, these being Basic Sector, Course Sector, and Development Sector. The Basic Sector was mainly remedial in character; the Course Sector was the major sector upon which the final examinations were based.

The Development Sector, like the Basic Sector, is voluntary and is used to develop some topic or theme introduced in the Course Sector. The use of a series of Development Sector packages to motivate the student, and especially to increase the effectiveness of the student's learning in important and historically difficult sections of the Course Sector, is described.

Some subjects have been found to produce more ideas for Development Sector packages than others, so with a proposal for a package to develop magnetic effects, we started work immediately. K J Ogilvie describes the problems associated with making a three-programme package entitled 'High Energy Particles'.

This Development Sector package was offered to the students for the first time in January 1982 and, although no usage figures exist at the time of writing, the interaction between the Development Sector packages, with special reference to the one described and the Course Sector, and also the response of the students, will be discussed.

General

Five years ago, in order to overcome the difficulties encountered by accepting into a first-year physics class students with a wide variation in background qualifications, a pre-recorded, three-tier, audio-tutorial system (Postlethwaite, 1972) was introduced for a physics class at Paisley College (Telfer, 1978).

The teaching material was split into three sectors, the major one being the Course Sector, comprising the main burden of a biology or chemistry student's physics syllabus.

The major subject headings found in a first-year physics syllabus were placed here, and the final examinations were based on this sector.

Each subject heading was divided into specific subject programmes and on average there were 20 in each subject heading. Each programme consisted of (i) a tape and accompanying print when used as an audio-tape, and (ii) tape, print and slides when used as a tape-slide programme. The print was issued at the time the programme was studied. The student found this most useful and used it as the basis of his permanent set of notes. Sometimes this print was a full record of the programme; on other occasions only a skeleton structure. Some elementary attempts have been made to study the student's note-taking habits using this print (Hartley, 1976).

Four programmes are studied each week; initially a fifth specific tutorial tape devoted to the questions on the previous week's print was also provided. However, the alternative of a simple solutions print has been found by most students to be a satisfactory introduction to replace this solutions programme.

The Basic Sector was initially intended to give a short, concise introduction to some basic ideas, mainly in elementary mathematics. Four such programmes were used to introduce the course during the first week of the first term. However, it has been found necessary to increase the Basic Sector considerably; there are now over 20 programmes ranging from topics in elementary mathematics to the analysis of experimental results.

The Development Sector

Individual Development Sector packages are available to the students, each package designed to develop some topic or theme introduced in the Course Sector. Initially there were six packages but soon this was reduced to five owing to amalgamation.

These packages have had a mixed reception, their popularity varying from package to package and also from year to year. Four have generally found favour and have been used extensively by students.

The objectives of the Development Sector packages have, naturally, a different priority from the programmes of the Course Sector. They can be much more entertaining and broadly-based in concept, but they must still stimulate and motivate the student, and preferably lead him or her to a better understanding of the related subject matter. Such programmes should also endeavour to show the student, where possible, major applications of the fundamental physics being studied.

Unfortunately some subjects lend themselves to obvious and interesting Development Sector packages, and some do not. For example, in optics there are microscopes and photography; in modern physics, nuclear power and health physics. In other subjects it has been less easy to find topics which would be at the correct scientific level and at the same time meet the Sector's objectives. One is therefore always looking for new titles to add to the Development Sector in areas such as mechanics and electricity.

A New Development Sector Package

During the summer of 1981 the production of a package of three programmes related to concepts in the course on electricity was begun. The subject of the package, 'High Energy Particles', grew out of a contact one of us had with the CERN organization, in Switzerland.

Much information was obtained from CERN. This came in the form of slides, mainly photographs of accelerator, detectors and a few diagrams, with additional data related to the visuals. Without this material the making of the package would not have been possible.

We knew the areas of electricity we wished to develop, which were the following:

(a) The interaction of particles with magnetic fields both from the point of view of the accelerators and also from an analysis of particle tracks.
(b) Stress of the unit of energy used in this field and its relationship with other units met in the Course Sector.
(c) The use of AC fields to accelerate particles.

It was known that other subjects would appear, for example the use of computers, but a specific layout and individual programme headings for the package had to be decided first.

A great deal of time was spent studying the slides that were received from CERN, categorizing them, and selecting those that would be used. It became apparent from a very early stage that an initial, fairly comprehensive programme describing the particle families would be necessary, if a description of the CERN accelerators and experiments was to have any meaning. Thus three individual programme titles were chosen:

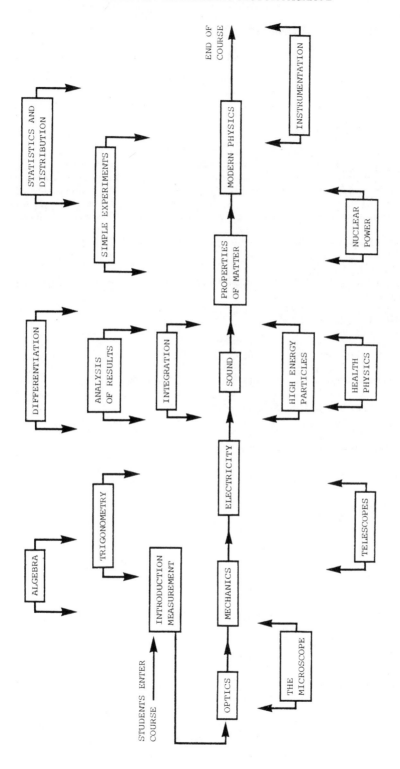

Figure 1. *The relationships between Development Sector topics and Course Sector topics*

    (a) Building Particle Families.
    (b) The CERN Organization.
    (c) Some Experiments in Particle Physics.

Many additional graphics, especially for the first programme, were required. Fortunately, at Paisley College of Technology this presents no serious problems. The number of visuals in the package eventually totalled 119.

Building Particle Families

Most of the additional graphics were used in this first programme, which had a total of 33 visuals. The programme was designed to show that there are two fundamental types of elementary particle, and that they can be put together in various set combinations. This ultimately leads to a description of the SU(3) model and the discovery of the Ω^- particle. Emphasis was placed on the fact that there was some collaboration between theoretical mathematics and particle experimentation to find some of these particles (*viz* Ω^-). A great deal of time was spent studying the problem that would best describe the concept of anti-matter to a first-year student. It was found that the most satisfactory way of overcoming this would be to return to a classical experiment by Anderson and to amplify this by bringing back a concept discussed in the Course Sector, describing the motion of charged particles in a magnetic field.

The CERN Organization

This was the longest of the three programmes, running for about 32 minutes with 49 visuals. The programme was longer than the others as it was mainly descriptive, discussing the running of the CERN Organization, its collaboration with other scientific institutions, and the experimental machines in use. It was found most convenient to discuss the development of CERN chronologically in relation to the building of the accelerators. This made it possible to discuss the various types of detection apparatus, methods of data collection, analysis and transfer.

Some Experiments in Particle Physics

As it would be impractical to discuss all the work done at CERN, it wad decided to mention two specific areas in some detail, these being (i) Neutrino Physics, and (ii) The LEP Project.

These subjects were chosen deliberately, as techniques dealt with in the second programme could be reintroduced. This in turn led to a continued discussion of the concepts met in the first programme.

The programme was also designed to inform students that CERN is involved in pioneering work to obtain the cheapest and most efficient methods of accelerating particles to high energies on such a large scale. Efforts are being made to use heat energy dissipated in the system to the advantage of the Swiss and French public, for example for domestic water heating systems or fish farms.

It was also stressed that CERN is purely a research establishment and is in no way connected with nuclear power or arms.

The Electron Volt

It was decided that the electron volt, the unit of energy used extensively in particle physics, should be defined. This unit had already been defined in the Course Sector at the beginning of the second term, three weeks earlier.

An introductory course on electricity always starts with electrostatics, as this saves struggling through Ohm's Law. Electrostatics can then immediately define the electrical unit of potential in terms of the mechanical unit of energy. Students find this programme hard to come to terms with, and to lessen the strain a little, the electron volt is defined and its applications mentioned.

The subject is reintroduced in the Properties of Matter course during the second half of the second term, showing that it is a very convenient size when studying chemical reactions, and again when Modern Physics is reached in term three. Therefore, although the electron volt has already been defined and is met twice more in the Course Sector, it was decided to define it again for reinforcement purposes, since it is of vital importance to the package.

Magnetic Effects

The major topic in the electricity course which stimulated the making of the package was the section on magnetism. In the past there has been criticism for including the two programmes on magnetism in the Course Sector, but it is believed that students should be acquainted with Faraday's Law if they claim to have a first-year physics pass of a Scottish College. Nevertheless, the students find these two programmes difficult, although applications of electromagnetic induction make up a further two programmes in the course. The inclusion of this package was therefore considered to be a significant improvement on the existing structure.

The similarities between a current carrying conductor and a free charged particle in a magnetic field had already been established mathematically in the second programme on magnetic effects in the Course Sector. No further attempt was made to do this, but it was possible to have some stimulating graphics made to emphasize the path of charged particles in a magnetic field. This was done by developing a diagram on the print of the second programme on magnetic effects. It showed the paths of an electron and position beam being split in a magnetic field, encouraging the student to review the fundamental physics of the interaction. Extensive use of this application was made both when discussing the accelerators and describing the analysis of experimental results.

AC Theory

Application of the alternating current theory section of the electricity course is mentioned when discussing the operation of the Cyclotron, where it is relatively simple to describe the use of a varying radio-frequency field to achieve acceleration. However, the decision was made not to labour this application on the grounds that it might overstress the technique.

Computing

To complete the second programme, it was necessary to describe the role of computers at CERN, concerning the transfer of data with other international centres and control of the machinery. The students know a minimum about computing, and so careful use of words had to be made when explaining the flexibility of the powerful computer network. To stimulate student interest further, it was decided to discuss a pioneer programme of high speed international data transmission. The data is transmitted via satellite and dish aerial, both illustrated using slides.

Usage and Results

The development sector package on High Energy Particles was offered to the class for the first time during February 1982. Two other Development Sector packages were offered during the first term, in November 1981, and a final two during term three in April 1982. Table 1 shows the number of students, as a percentage, who picked up programmes from the three development sector packages discussed here.

Development sector	Student pick-up %
Microscopes	50
Telescopes	50
High Energy Particles	43
All three	25
Nil	25

Table 1. *Student pick-up of Development Sector packages*

Results for three parameters are available:
  (a) Test and examination results.
  (b) Pick-up of the Optics Development Sector packages for November and
       of the High Energy Particles Development Sector package for February.
  (c) The student's pick-up of the Course Sector programmes for the same
       two months.

Figures 2 and 3 indicate the results for the pick-up of the Development Sector
programmes as a function of the students' use of the Course Sector programmes
during the first month that the particular package was first offered to the class.
In Figure 2 the two Optics packages are taken together, with High Energy Particles
in Figure 3.

All points to the right of the vertical line indicate students who repeated Course
Sector programmes. There is a suggestion that if a student feels the necessity to
repeat a Course Sector programme he is less likely to go into the Development
Sector; this allows for a definite choice of the best way to allocate the time
available to the study of the subject. From an examination of Figure 3 it seems
that here it was the harder-working students who were picking up the package.

Figures 4 and 5 show the Development Sector pick-up as a function of the
examination results which immediately preceded the introduction of the package.
These were the mid-term test for the Optics packages, and the first-term
examination for the High Energy Particles package. In spite of the mid-term test
score being ragged, Figure 4 shows that the students' pick-up of the Optics package
closely follows it.

This result was repeated with the High Energy Particles package (Figure 5).
Interestingly, for both results, there is no evidence of any skew in the pick-up
curve towards the higher achievers.

Conclusions

A pick-up of the new Development Sector package on High Energy Particles of
43 per cent is considered very successful, especially as the Course Sector in use at
the time is the difficult Electricity course. Any positive contribution to an
improvement in the final results of the class, especially in electricity and
magnetism, must await the second term and final examination results. However,
taking into account that the Development Sector is not compulsory, the enthusiasm
with which this testing package has been received by the students, and the interest
generated by it, is most encouraging.

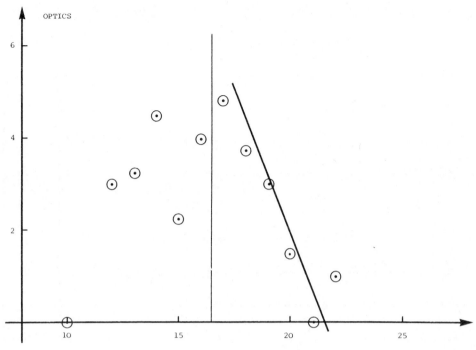

Figure 2. *Course Sector programmes*

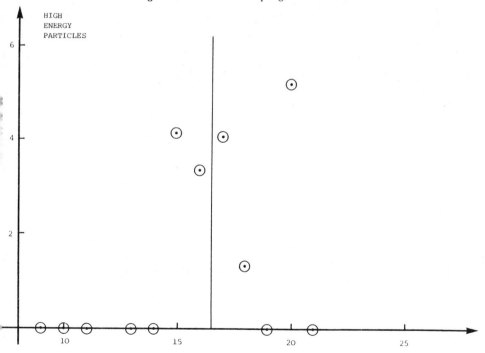

Figure 3. *Course Sector programmes*

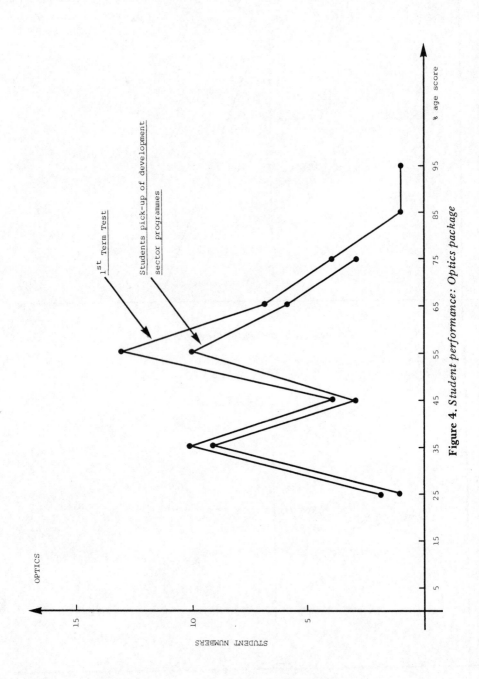

Figure 4. *Student performance: Optics package*

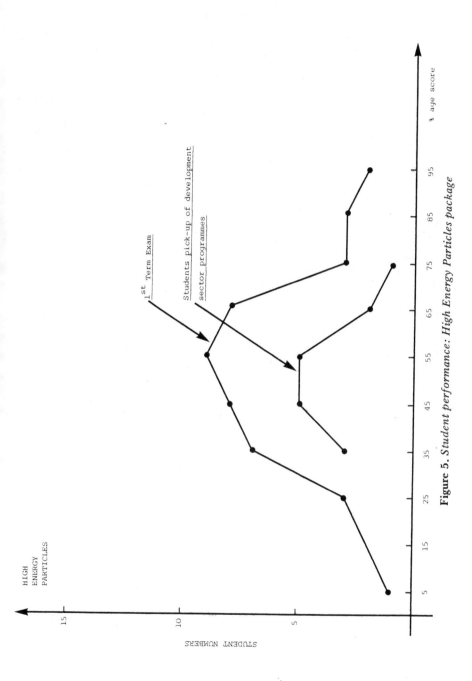

Figure 5. *Student performance: High Energy Particles package*

References

Hartley, J (1976) Lecture handouts and student notetaking. *Programmed Learning and Educational Technology*, 13, 2, pp 58-64.

Postlethwaite, S N, Novak, J and Murray H T (1972) *The Audio-Tutorial Approach to Learning* (3rd edition). Burgess, Minneapolis.

Telfer, W S (1978) A three-tier approach to first-year physics. In Race, P and Brook, D (eds) *Aspects of Educational Technology* XII. Kogan Page, London.

2.3 A Resource Pack to Enable Schools and Colleges to Consider the Effectiveness of their Education

N D C Harris, C D Bell and J H Carter
University of Bath

Abstract: A Resource Pack 'Signposts for Evaluating' has been developed with funding from the Council for Educational Technology and the Schools Council. The pack is intended as a basis for enabling schools and colleges to carry out evaluation within their own establishment.

The emphasis of the presentation will be to identify the premises on which the pack was designed, its purposes and its intended use. A brief outline of its content will be made with supporting hand-outs.

A set of regional workshops is now being initiated. The workshops are funded by the Council for Educational Technology. The strategy being used and the state of progress are outlined.

Introduction

'What schools desperately need is help in the techniques of self-evaluation and consultation, a totally different mode of giving account of themselves. Teachers are amateurs in self-evaluation where they should be professionals, able to carry out mutual assessments and able to teach the techniques to their students.' (Delves and Watts, 1979)

Increasing interest is currently being shown in a mode of evaluation variously termed 'small-scale', 'institution-based', 'self-evaluation'. Possible reasons for this interest are explored elsewhere (see for example, Elliott (1979); Shipman (1979); Elliott (1980); Harris, Bell and Carter (1982)).

A project based at the University of Bath aimed to respond to this interest, was initially funded jointly by the Council for Educational Technology and the Schools Council, and subsequently by the Council for Educational Technology only. The first phase of the project, between September 1980 and August 1981, was to develop a resource pack of materials designed to aid teachers and others in the techniques and processes of small-scale, institution-based evaluating. The second phase, between January and June 1981, was a dissemination and training exercise, using the pack of materials.

The pack 'Signposts for Evaluating a Resource Pack' is published by the Council for Educational Technology (Harris, Bell and Carter, 1981).

This paper comprises four sections, describing:
1. the structure of the Resource Pack;
2. the process engaged during development of the Pack;
3. some of the assumptions underlying the production of the Pack;
4. the dissemination and training phase.

Structure and Content of the Pack

The Pack is a collection of material which provides information about small-scale evaluating. It is intended that the material will provide an initial and basic guide for people wishing to become involved in the process of small-scale evaluating.

To allow for use in various ways by various users, the Pack has been developed and assembled with flexibility as a prime concern. It may be read in its entirety, or 'dipped into'; users may extract whichever parts they consider applicable to their needs.

The Pack comprises three distinct but related parts:

(a) Part 1: Introduction to evaluating
(b) Part 2: Collecting and analysing information
(c) Part 3: Some theoretical aspects of evaluation

Each part is further divided into sections and sub-sections, and contained within a folded booklet of loose papers. In addition, each booklet contains advanced and post organizers to assist in the preparation and conclusion of each section or sub-section.

Part 1

Part 1 outlines the aims and assumptions of the Pack, identifying possible users of, and uses for the material. Issues raised by such questions as What is evaluating?, Who does it?, Why do it?, Where can help be obtained?, and some ways of planning are considered briefly. Some paths through the material are described, from both problem-centred and techniques-orientated perspectives. A glossary of terms used in the evaluation literature, and suggestions for further reading, are also given.

Part 2

Part 2 forms the bulk of the material. It makes the assumption that collecting, analysing and judging information are central activities in the process of evaluating, and focuses upon techniques which are applicable to a wide variety of situations, such as the use of:

☐ Conversations and interviews.
☐ Group discussions.
☐ Delphi techniques.
☐ Questionnaires.
☐ Diaries.
☐ Personal constraints.
☐ Sound and video recording.

Each technique is described, and its range of convenience, limitations, advantages and disadvantages are explored. The aim is not to present 'comprehensive' or theoretical coverage, but to provide 'signposts' towards some pragmatic possibilities. For those who wish to find out more, references to easily available texts are given.

Specific aspects which often form the focus of small-scale evaluating are described in more detail:

☐ Observing inside 'classrooms'.
☐ Aims and practices.
☐ Diagnostic assessment.
☐ Profile recording.
☐ Interpreting and analysing information from assessments.
☐ Analysis of materials and resources.
☐ Analysis of the 'institution'.

Part 3

Part 3 may be viewed as an 'appendix' to the bulk of the material. Although theoretical and conceptual issues are obviously of the utmost importance; for the practising educator, involved in systematic planned evaluating, they are likely to be secondary. Issues briefly considered include:

☐ What is evaluation?
☐ Historical perspectives of evaluation.
☐ Scales and styles of evaluation.
☐ Some underlying assumptions of 'evaluators'.

Once again, the aim is to provide 'signposts', reference being made to more detailed texts.

Developmental Process

The project had, as its initial brief: 'To produce in-service training materials on course evaluation for schools and further education colleges for use on an individual or group basis.'

Very soon it became clear that 'grass roots' interest was high, and that the initial brief was too limited in scope. Consequently, a wider aim was negotiated between the developers and funding agencies, to produce a broad-based resource pack of use to teachers and others involved in, or interested in, small-scale institution-based evaluating.

Two distinct related phases of the developmental process are evident.

Needs Analysis and Research

Many individuals were contacted, with the aim of:

(a) Identifying and qualifying the type of help which it was considered a resource pack could provide.
(b) Establishing a network of members willing to read and comment upon draft materials.

The range of contacts thus made was wide-ranging, and included:

☐ Teachers from primary, middle and secondary schools.
☐ Teachers (including those studying for an advanced degree in education) within a university.
☐ Representatives from various levels within local education authorities.
☐ Representatives of the Technician Education Council, Business Education Council, City and Guilds of London Institute and other training organizations.
☐ Her Majesty's Inspectorate.
☐ Leaders of teachers' centres.

Information thus generated was developed into a framework for the subsequent writing of the materials. The process was aided by a short intensive workshop, at which the framework was discussed, further ideas and possibilities generated, and initial draft material studied and criticized. The needs analysis was, by contractual necessity, focused upon those needs which could be satisfied by the development of a resource pack of materials. It has been evident from the start of the project that materials alone could not completely satisfy the needs of would-be evaluators. It was from this 'finding' that the dissemination and training phase developed.

Production and Evaluation

Initial production of materials was organized around a series of write-trial-assess-rewrite cycles. Primary focus in trials was not upon content but upon style and presentation, these aspects appearing of major concern to the target audience. Simplicity of syntax, lack of 'jargon' or esoteric terminology, and flexibility and ease of use were all concerns of paramount importance.

Production to final format occupied the last stages of the one-year project,

and was aided by one of the present authors, who was not involved in the initial
needs analysis research or production and who acted as critical editor.

(A full description of the developmental process of this project, from the
perspectives of the funding agencies and the development team, is to form the
basis of a subsequent paper.)

Assumptions

A number of assumptions about the users of the Pack and about the process of
evaluating are implicit in its development.

Users

A major assumption in the development of the Pack has been that the majority of
users will consider themselves to have little knowledge of evaluating, and will, at
least initially, not wish to enter too deeply into theoretical or philosophical issues.
Such users may be people:

- ☐ interested in systematically improving their particular area of education,
  whether it be teaching or administration;
- ☐ individuals or groups, involved in the monitoring of curricula or curriculum
  materials;
- ☐ who wish to present information about what they are doing, why they are
  doing it, and the effects of their actions;
- ☐ who have a special responsibility within their institution for evaluation, or
  the professional development of staff;
- ☐ organizing in-service courses about institution-based evaluation.

It is acknowledged that such users will have limited time and resources. The Pack
has thus been designed for ease and flexibility of use. Each section forms a more-or-
less self-sufficient set of information, allowing the materials to be 'dipped into'.

The Process of Evaluating

The Pack has been developed in the belief that evaluating should be a normal, and
necessary, part of the professional practices of educators, and not an activity
separate or detached from everyday curricula or management processes.

More precisely, evaluation is seen as one way in which to 'improve' the quality
of educational provision in a planned way, there being professional, social and
economic reasons for so doing.

Professional Reasons

Evaluating may help in the choice of curriculum, curriculum materials, and policy.
It may provide evidence to explain and justify such choice.

Evaluating may highlight problems and difficulties experienced by learners and
may suggest solutions to such problems.

Evaluating may allow individuals to become more aware of what they are
doing, why they are doing it, and how it compares with what others are doing. Such
increased awareness may lead to professional development and increased
satisfaction.

Evaluating may develop understanding and increase communication between
individuals.

Social Reasons

Educational institutions are part of a larger society. Evaluating may enable institutions to provide evidence of what it is they are trying to achieve, and whether or not they are succeeding. It may also enable them to justify and explain their intentions.

Economic Reasons

Evaluating may indicate areas where resources are lacking, or where they are used uneconomically; it can provide evidence to support such indicators.

Evaluating can demonstrate effectiveness, perhaps in terms of 'value for money'.

The view of evaluating taken in the Pack is that it involves the intentional and planned collection of information, so that informed judgements can be made about the worth of something.

Evaluating based within an institution, may include:

(a) Identification of issues of interest and concern.
(b) Collection of information.
(c) Sorting, analysing and presenting information.
(d) Using information to make informed judgements about whether or not the changes are worthwhile.

These aspects of evaluating are not necessarily separate and are often related. Some may be carried out simultaneously.

Evaluating must be regarded as a long-term activity. It is not a process which will normally allow an instant judgement to be made at the end of a brief period of intense work, and some issues may be resolved only after months or even years of careful effort.

In the Pack, evaluating is not considered to be something with a starting point and an end point. It is seen as an ongoing activity, part of a teacher's normal professional practice.

It may be useful to consider evaluation going in cycles, with some, or all, of the above parts being in the cycle (see Figure 1). The cycle should not be taken as fixed. Those evaluating may select the parts which suit their own situation and use them in whatever order and/or combination is appropriate.

The Dissemination and Training Phase

Although the Pack may give an initial impression of being a self-instructional pack for novice evaluators, and has, in fact, been referred to as 'The Amateur's Guide to School Evaluation' by one correspondent, the materials were never intended to stand on their own. Rather, they were seen as forming the basis of support for a group of people who were involved, or were about to become involved, with planned evaluation. For this reason, it was thought that the materials would be used more profitably if they were introduced and demonstrated to potential users by someone who was already familiar with them. It was also hoped that the impact of the material might be greater if disseminated by 'practical' means and by way of people who had personal experience of its use, rather than by the more usual methods of circulars and abstracts in publishers' catalogues. Consequently the Dissemination and Training phase of the project was set up, and was designed to run for six months, from January to June 1982. Within this time, it was thought reasonable to organize lectures and workshops in 10 different regions of the United Kingdom. The stated aims of the workshops are:

☐ To enable participants to see the materials.
☐ To enable participants to identify the potential of the material for school or college-based evaluation.

☐ To propose follow-up workshops within the region.
☐ To identify people who would be available to assist schools and colleges
  with evaluating.

When considering potential participants for workshops, two contrasting points of
view emerged:

1. To gain the widest possible dissemination, workshop participants needed to
   be people in posititons such as LEA advisers, who would come into contact
   with many institutions and be well-placed to run 'follow-up' workshops as
   part of 'in-service training days' etc.
2. The material would have far more impact, and the ideas behind institution-
   based evaluating be more widely accepted, if they were introduced at a
   'grass roots' level, rather than being thought of as being 'imposed' from
   above.

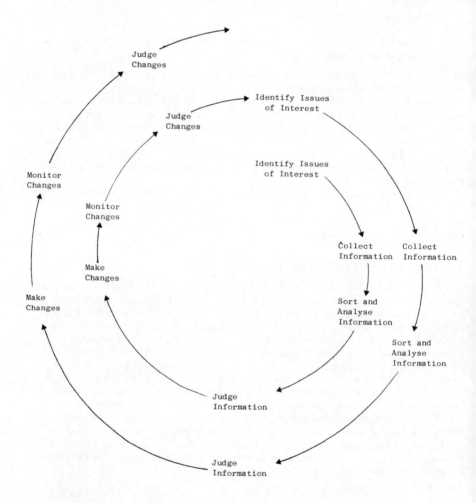

Figure 1. *Evaluation cycle components*

In practice, we have attempted to accommodate both points of view, but because of the time constraint and a desire to reach as large an audience as possible, we have tended to concentrate on the former.

Strategy for Setting up Workshops

☐ The United Kingdom was divided (arbitrarily) into 10 regions, having as broad a geographical spread as possible.

☐ One or two initial contacts were identified in each region, and approached with a request for help, either in setting up a workshop. or by providing the names of other people who might be able to help or who would be interested.

☐ The main sources of contact have been through:
  — An initial list supplied by CET.
  — A list of interested people compiled when the material was being produced.
  — Personal contacts made at conferences, meetings, etc.
  — Schools Council Programme groups.
  — Teachers' Centres.

Workshop Format

A typical one-day programme would incorporate:

☐ An introduction explaining the aims and structure of the Pack.
☐ A familiarization exercise taking the form of a directed exploration of the whole Pack.
☐ A detailed examination of selected sections of the Pack.
☐ An explanation and discussion of the underlying theory.
☐ An explanation of the supporting 'network'.
☐ An evaluation of the workshop (with comments from participants).

Post-Workshop Strategy

Although no formal evaluation of the dissemination phase is planned, it is hoped to obtain some indication of the impact of the workshops by sending out a 'follow-up' questionnaire to participants about six weeks after any particular workshop. This might give some indication of whether participants have passed on to colleagues any ideas or information gained in the workshops , whether they have been able to put any of the workshop ideas into practice, whether they have persuaded their institution to buy a copy of the Pack, etc.

Also, with each questionnaire will go a list of names and addresses of people in that particular region who are known to be interested in evaluating and who may be able to offer support and advice if needed. In this way, it is hoped that after the formal 'dissemination and training phase' is over, there will remain the basis of a regional network of people who are able to exchange ideas and offer mutual self-help.

This supports the view of evaluating that is promoted in the Pack: that it is not something that can be done in isolation but that it thrives on discussion and an exchange of information.

References

Delves, A R and Watts, J (1979) A year of evaluation. *Forum* 22, 1, pp 27-29.
Elliott, G (1980) *Self Evaluation and the Teacher.* Schools Council, London.
Elliott, J (1979) The case for school self evaluation. *Forum* 22, 1, pp 23-25.
Harris, N D C, Bell, C D and Carter, J E H (1981) *Signposts for Evaluating: A Resource Pack.* Council for Educational Technology, London.
Harris, N D C, Bell, C D and Carter, J E H (1982) Towards internal evaluation: a strategy for coping with change. *Programmed Learning and Educational Technology* (to be published shortly).
Shipman, M (1979) *In-School Evaluation.* Heinemann, London.

Section 3:
The Applications of Interactive Video Systems

3.1 An Interactive Video System for Education

Peter Copeland
West Sussex Institute of Higher Education

Abstract: This paper describes the CAVIS interactive video system. CAVIS is an interactive teaching system that mixes video-cassette pictures, text and videotex diagrams and presents these via a single TV screen and with sound. The student uses a keypad to respond to questions asked via the TV screen or narrative and, interactively, CAVIS adapts its presentation according to the responses given. Existing learning materials on VHS video-cassette can be made interactive by CAVIS and have text and branching video segments integrated into their presentation. Material which has been originated on film, slide and video can be transferred on to the system. Information processing techniques are provided for the teacher to enable the generation of text and diagrams, and the mixing of text, diagrams, video-cassette pictures and sound. Student performance and the effectiveness of the teaching materials used are automatically monitored, and can be displayed graphically using the colour videotex display. CAVIS was designed to meet certain training needs within BP International. These are discussed, along with research relating to its development.

The Development of CAVIS

The development of CAVIS began at the West Sussex Institute of Higher Education four years ago as a research project undertaken for the Training Division of BP International. Self-instructional materials were already in use within BP Training, but the project was initiated following the general requirement for more effective and efficient facilities.

An analysis of needs was undertaken, and the resultant development brief identified nine key requirements. These were regarded independently of any specific hardware solutions at this stage.

The development brief required the system to:

1. *Teach a wide range of subjects efficiently.* Subjects to be taught ranged from accountancy and budgetary control to refinery operations and safety at work. Efficiency was regarded as 80-100 per cent mastery of content.
2. *Provide a cost-effective learning system.* Measurement of cost-effectiveness was to be judged in comparison with the costs of achieving training using existing procedures.
3. *Provide a simple means for the trainer to prepare and assemble learning materials.* Computer-aided design, work processing and portable video recording were seen as good examples of where technology was being applied to assist the processing of specific forms of information. It seemed reasonable to assume that the production of learning materials could also benefit from these advances and the trainer would be more likely to create effective learning materials as a result.
4. *Evaluate the level of learning success.* Many of the teaching procedures used in education and training do not readily enable student achievement to be monitored. This is especially true of self-instruction procedures which use tape-slide, film and video-cassette. As a result, judgements of learner-performance and the efficiency of learning materials are often made on

evidence which is unreliable and incomplete. To remedy this it was thought desirable that the system should simultaneously monitor individual student performance levels and the effectiveness of training materials.

5. *Provide an accessible and continually available training facility.* Often it is difficult to provide training as an integral element of work because of the disruption it causes to the work schedule. Typically, for instance, a training course may last several days or operate over a number of weeks on a daily basis. When a pattern of shift work is in operation and/or work is taking place in geographically isolated situations, such as drilling platforms and oil tankers, providing training support is especially difficult. A system which could provide training at any time 24 hours a day, seven days a week, was seen to be the ideal solution.

6. *Provide a means of learning with or without supervision.* The problems identified above implied the need for a stand-alone facility which could be operated without supervision. Two other factors endorsed this as a requirement.

   (a) Students were not always adept at using audio-visual equipment and would often not use it because of operating difficulties or the organizational problems involved.

   (b) Students, particularly those engaged in in-service training or retraining, often preferred to make mistakes in private.

7. *Pace and adapt what is taught to suit the needs of each student.* A system was required that could adapt its teaching to suit the individual, allow the individual to vary the pace and be selective over what was learned.

8. *Tailor what is to be taught to suit local training requirements.* A method was sought of using the programmes available from commercial suppliers. The general nature of these usually meant in-house support materials had to be provided in order to set the commercial materials in the context of local training tasks. A system that could use these programmes and integrate additional information was required.

9. *Enable revision and updating of what is taught.* Revision was regarded as essential in order to increase the effectiveness of materials using the evidence gained from their use. In view of current rapid technological change, updating was considered an important requirement and one which was not easily achieved using non-book materials such as film, slides and video.

Related Research

The design brief emphasizes that the project was driven from a user-needs approach rather than from any preconceived notions of hardware. The starting point of the brief, and fundamental to many of its elements, was the teaching and learning encounter itself. A literature search in the area of educational media identified two factors which were seen as essential to its improvement: (i) establish a presentation mix, and (ii) provide interaction.

The attributes possessed by media give rise to different presentation characteristics, eg colour, moving images, sound, text, etc. These have been identified but labelled differently by several researchers in the field (Tosti and Ball, 1969; Levie and Dickie, 1973; Salomon, 1979). When these attributes can be matched with the information to be communicated, the mental encoding and decoding of the information is simplified.

For instance, for the teacher it is often difficult encoding practical tasks using text and diagrams. Equally, it is often difficult for the learner translating words and diagrams into actions. A film would probably perform this task better. On the other hand, film does not always lend itself to the teaching of high order concepts.

It might do the job eventually, but words would probably do it more efficiently.

The problem is that many teaching tasks are not solved simply by using, say, film *or* text. Teaching a given subject might require the static presentation of text at one point and then require a filmic sequence at another. Unfortunately, media have had fixed characteristics in this respect. Their attributes have either allowed transience, as in the case of film and TV, or inhibited it as with print.

The author has previously presented a theoretical model to illustrate this relationship (Copeland, 1981). In developing this it became clear that an effective medium would be one which could enable its presentation characteristics to be altered to suit each specific information element of the subject being taught.

CAVIS was designed on the basis of this model. It allows the teacher to pre-programme any combination and sequence of text, diagrams, video-cassette pictures, dynamic diagrams and audio.

Interaction

In many of the procedures used in education and training the transfer of information is one direction only: from teacher to learner. This is true of much classroom teaching and also of many forms of mediated learning such as film, tape-slide, broadcast television, etc.

Research into the use of interaction within the teaching/learning encounter has mostly focused on the use of the computer to ask questions, establish dialogue and adapt the teaching according to the responses given by students (Campeau, 1966; Anderson, Culhavey and Andre, 1972; Klausmeier, 1975; Levie and Dickie, 1973).

Certain studies have shown this interaction to have significant benefits in terms of time to mastery and overall achievement (Tennyson and Tennyson, 1977). The use of adaptive computer presentation strategies to suit differences in study procedure (Pask, 1969) and learning characteristics (Bunderson, 1973) has also indicated certain benefits.

Computer-assisted learning has mostly developed on the basis of this interaction. Its greatest limitation, however, has been that its delivery of information predominantly has been by using text. This has narrowed its effectiveness to a limited range of teaching tasks.

The ideal teaching medium was seen to be a system that could respond interactively to the responses made by the student and, at the same time, provide a mix of presentation characteristics. CAVIS provides interaction by asking questions using text on the screen or by using the spoken narrative. The presentation can be programmed to adapt to these responses with text and additionally with video branching sequences. The student can return or manually interrupt the courseware at any point.

In addition to this interaction, the presentation mix enables text, text and VCR picture, VCR picture, videotex diagrams and dynamic diagrams to be presented in sequence. Furthermore, any of these elements can be mixed to make the delivery of information more effective For instance, an audio narrative when accompanying a diagram can be used to establish sequence. A dynamic diagram overlaid on a video-cassette picture can give emphasis to certain parts or explain the content of the picture.

How CAVIS Works

CAVIS uses a TV screen which is used in conjunction with a keypad to present information. The information is stored on video-cassette and magnetic disk and this combination of media is referred to as CAVIS courseware. This labelling eliminates the problems which arise when the words 'program' and 'software' are used to describe elements of video, computer and training technologies.

The video-cassette stores audio and video information and the magnetic disk stores all the text and diagrams. This arrangement enables all text to be updated and revised easily. Additionally, different disks can accompany the same video-cassette to accommodate different learning applications or provide text in alternative languages.

In addition to the text pages the disk stores the pattern of interaction built into the courseware and the presentation of the courseware itself; for this reason it is called the 'presentation' disk.

A typical sequence of student operation might be as follows:

☐ The student switches on the power.
☐ CAVIS starts-up automatically and tells the student what to do next.
☐ A video-cassette is inserted at the top of the control cabinet and a presentation disk is pushed into the slot at the front.
☐ The student pushes a button on the keypad and CAVIS displays the title of the courseware and, after a short delay of about 20 seconds, displays the video pictures, and/or text and audio.
☐ After a short exposure to this, the video-cassette automatically stops, a question is asked and the student keys in a response. The answer given is wrong!
☐ CAVIS presents some more information using text and diagrams to help the student's understanding. The student takes a hard copy print of this information for later reference and CAVIS invites the student to branch to another part of the courseware for some more background information. The student elects to do this and CAVIS automatically finds the relevant sequence.
☐ After three or so minutes of this sequence, the student realizes his or her misunderstanding and presses the 'return' key. CAVIS returns the courseware to the question point from which the student branched. The question appears again; this time the correct response is made.
☐ The courseware continues.

At any time the student can press the 'index' key to see the contents of the courseware. By keying in the appropriate number, any section of the courseware can be accessed quickly and accurately. Other manual controls are provided.

The 'skip' key allows the student to proceed 20 seconds forward and the 'recap' key enables the last 20 seconds of the courseware to be repeated. The frame button displays the courseware location in the top left corner of the screen.

All the student operations performed on the keypad are stored in CAVIS for future analysis by the teacher.

Creating CAVIS Courseware

The information processing facilities built into CAVIS enable the trainer to create and revise training materials. No knowledge of computers or typewriting skill is assumed, and indeed CAVIS displays guidance and help messages to assist authoring and editing.

Text and diagrams are typed into the system using the colour-coded keyboard and screen editing facilities. A screenful of text and/or diagrams is called a 'page' and 200 such pages can be stored on one presentation disk. Subsequent retrieval of any one of these pages, either within the presentation of courseware or during editing, is within half a second. This facility enables slow animation to be presented.

Compatibility

The video component of the system is based on the VHS format cassette. This allows video materials to be created economically using low-cost portable equipment. Alternatively, any existing programme already on VHS cassette can be made interactive. Without any physical alteration to the original video and narrative, text, diagrams and interaction can be added and indeed the video sequences can be re-ordered automatically if required.

The videotex format is used for the pages stored and presented by the system. This feature enables CAVIS to receive from and transmit to other videotex compatible equipment. One such piece of equipment allows high contrast artwork to be captured by a television camera and converted into a videotex image. CAVIS can receive this image and store it as a 'page'.

Evaluating Trainee and Courseware Performance

The responses entered on the student keypad are stored in the system and used in conjunction with an analysis package. With this the teacher is able to have presented a detailed graphical analysis of student performance and a profile of the effectiveness of the cassette. This information includes the number of questions answered correctly, the number of attempts made on each question, the study session duration, courseware sequences viewed, etc.

This information is stored either anonymously or with a student code depending on the option selected by the teacher. The student is always made aware that his or her performance is being monitored by the request to enter a pass number before the courseware starts.

Using the evaluation facility, accumulated records can be processed to provide a detailed analysis of how a number of students studied specific courseware. This analysis enables courseware to be checked, sequence by sequence, for deficiencies. When a certain sequence of questions yields consistently low scores, for instance, then a decision can be taken to revise the previous courseware content.

CAVIS thus provides an objective indication of courseware efficiency. The teacher can have printed records of this data from the printer unit. Using the editing and authoring facilities, deficient courseware can quickly be revised and repeatedly recycled until a defined performance level is achieved.

The systems model can be implemented in a microcontext by using CAVIS to develop, teach and evaluate courseware. The mix of colour moving pictures, audio, text and questions, provides a learning experience quite different from other teaching procedures. In the longer term, the analysis of this experience should provide valuable insights into how the arrangement of information and the presentation attributes used can effect and relate to learning performance and patterns of study.

References

Anderson, R C, Kulhavy, R W and Andre, T (1972) Conditions under which feedback facilitates learning from programmed lessons. *Journal of Educational Psychology* 63, p 186.
Bunderson, C Victor (1973) *The Ticcit Project: Design strategy for Educational Innovation.* ERIC ED 096 p 996.
Campeau, Peggy L (1966) Selective review of literature on audio-visual methods of instruction. In Briggs, L J, Campeau, P L, Gagné, R N and May, M A (eds) *Instructional Media: A Procedure for the Design of Multimedia Instruction.* Pittsburgh, pp 99-142.
Copeland, P (1981) The educational significance of electronic media. *Aspects of Educational Technology* XV *Distance Learning and Evaluation.* Kogan Page, London.
Klausmeier, H J and Feldman, K V (1975) Effects of a definition and a varying number of examples and non-examples on concept attainment. *Journal of Educational Psychology* 67, pp 174-178.
Levie, W H and Dickie, K E (1973) The analysis and application of media. In Travers, R M W (ed) *Second Handbook of Research on Teaching.* Rand McNally.

Pask, G (1969) Strategy, competence and conversation as determinants of learning. *Programmed Learning and Educational Technology* 6, pp 250-267.
Salomon, G (1979) *Interaction of Media, Cognition and Learning.* Jossey-Bass.
Tennyson, R D and Tennyson, C L (1977) Computer-based adaptive instructional strategies for the improvement of performance and reduction of time. ERIC ED 140, p 782.
Tosti, D T and Ball, J R (1969) A behavioural approach to instructional design and media selection. *Audio Visual Communications Review,* 17, 1, Spring.

3.2 Interactive Video in Distance Education

D Wright
Felix Learning Systems Ltd, London

Abstract: The contribution that distance learning can make towards the achievement of educational and training objectives is becoming increasingly recognized. The prospect of cost-effective learning, carried out on a distributed basis, possesses attractions which will become even more apparent as the costs and inconvenience of conventional group-based learning continue to multiply.

Companies and colleges alike have an interest in providing open learning systems within which effective training and educational resources are made easily accessible to as wide a range of students as possible. It is important, however, that such provision should be carefully structured and controlled. Students should be able to achieve access only to courses which are appropriate, and course administrators need to be provided with essential information on the performance of the students and the efficiency and effectiveness of the course material. When open learning is taking place at locations remote from the administrative function, controlling and monitoring the educational process can be extremely difficult.

The two major obstacles to providing distance learning are the creation of effective learning materials and the management of their use. In this paper, I will look at a new training medium which, by combining established training technologies, provides a means of confronting both of these problems. This new medium is interactive video which combines the techniques of computer-aided learning (CAL), computer-managed learning (CML) and passive video.

Distance Learning Methods

If we examine the use of distance-learning techniques we find a disparate range of applications with a correspondingly disparate range of media employed. Distance-learning packages have been introduced in response to the problems raised by the alternative methods of training. Clerical grade workers are being taught basic office procedures from crude manuals or programmed instruction texts, because the expense of sending such personnel on group-based courses is not seen as justifiable. At the other end of the scale, senior management and professional grade staff are being trained via more elaborate tape-slide packages and video films, not necessarily because courses for these people are too expensive, but because they are (or at least they think they are) unable to leave their work for long enough to attend conventional courses.

Therefore, there is already an established need for distance or independent learning packages and we can expect the demand for such packages to grow considerably. In a highly competitive market place with an emphasis on productivity, more enlightened organizations are realising the value of effective training. But they want value for money and will look seriously at alternatives to the increasingly expensive centralized group-based courses.

Print-based packages have been used with varying degrees of success for many years. More recently, however, attempts have been made to provide learning material which is more stimulating and hence more attractive to the student — and, it is to be hoped, therefore more effective in achieving its objectives. This approach is typified by the increasing number of audio-visual tape-slide packages available.

These packages, working on the proven principle that the more senses you bombard with a piece of information the more likely it is that the information will stick, include printed 'guide' books, spoken commentaries and visually stimulating pictures.

There seems little doubt that, in many areas, the most effective means of training is by example, showing 'how it is done', and also, quite often, 'how *not* to do it'. Picture stills, with commentary, can often go some way to achieving these results but are necessarily restricted to showing crude time-slices of the action. This is not adequate for imparting, for example, many complex technical skills. Communication skills are even more problematic. It is impossible to capture the essential subtleties and nuances of, say, a disciplinary interview, by a series of projected stills. It is in areas like these that video comes into its own. The realism and drama, and the entertainment value of video, make this medium more acceptable to the student, but how effective is it in fact?

Although stimulating and maybe entertaining, video training films, like other distance learning media, merely require the student to be a passive onlooker. They cannot demand the attention of the student, nor can they monitor or adapt to the student's problems in assimilating the information presented. Video films are typically restricted to establishing perhaps five or six main teaching points repeating them once or twice, and then finishing without knowing (i) whether the student's attention was maintained, and (ii) whether what was said was finally understood. The learning experience is typically inflexible and uncontrolled.

The initial production of a distance learning package, video or otherwise, is an expensive procedure. Once produced there is a temptation, if not a requirement, to use that package with as many students as possible — however inappropriate that may be. Students with widely varying backgrounds and abilities will often study from the same package of material. Under these circumstances the issues of flexibility and control achieve a certain prominence. To cater for individual needs, the material should ideally have various paths running through it. The students should receive immediate feedback on their standard of performance, and the training administrators need that same information to assess the efficiency and effectiveness of the training provision.

A powerful tool for distance learning which helps to deal with these problems is the computer, via the techniques of computer-aided learning (CAL) and computer-managed learning (CML). Highly interactive and adaptive CAL can be developed, incorporating frequent checks of student understanding and controlling the path of the student through the material according to his or her needs. CML systems provide automatic means of registering students, organizing the most appropriate courses of study for them, recording their performances and finally providing the administrators and training designers with invaluable information in the form of analyses of the students' combined performances.

But the computer alone does not have the power of presentation of some of the more passive training media. Even using advanced computer graphics it is impossible to create CAL material which could match the visual impact, the realism and drama of video. The ideal solution would appear to be an integration of CAL, CML and video. This we now have in what is known as *interactive video*. Interactive video systems combine the power of presentation of video, the flexibility and adaptability of CAL, and the training management and control capabilities of CML.

Neither CAL/CML nor video are fundamentally new techniques but both have gained considerably increased acceptance in the last few years, largely as a result of advances in electronic engineering and microtechnology, bringing computing and video within the reach of many more people and organizations. It is not surprising, therefore, that the natural progression to interactive video is a relatively recent move. In this context it is important to note that interactive video is not a new technological solution in search of a problem. Interactive video has been developed, from the proven techniques of CAL and passive video, as a solution to training problems which these other techniques alone have been unable to solve.

Interactive Video Systems

There are now available a number of 'intelligent' video systems which have been labelled 'interactive'. At one end of the spectrum we have video players with enhanced functions such as variable speed play, random access searching, and so on. At the other extreme there are fully integrated microcomputer and video systems which allow operation of the video player functions by program control and which can switch between computer-generated displays and sequences from the video player. Only these latter systems have the ability to provide the full facilities of a truly interactive system.

Figure 1 illustrates a schematic diagram of a typical interactive video configuration. The microcomputer is the intelligence of the system, controlling by program the information and question presentation, whether via its own text and graphic display capabilities or by 'remote' operation of the video player. The microcomputer also handles the analysis of the student response, the consequent branching, and the overall record keeping and course management.

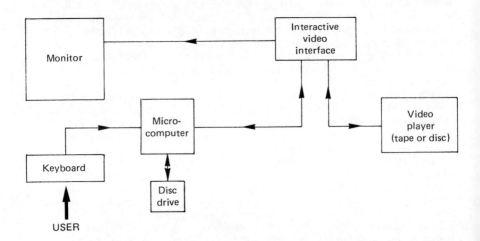

Figure 1. *Schematic diagram of interactive video system*

The interactive video interface carries out four functions. First, it translates control pulse output from the computer into a form which can drive the video player through its remote socket. So, for a typical player, the computer will be able to set the player into any of the standard modes: play, fast forward, rewind, stop and pause. The interface also monitors the status of the video player and is able to pass information to the computer, such as that a tape cassette has been loaded and rewound to the beginning. A third function of the interface is to switch, as instructed by the program, between picture and/or audio from the computer and the video player.

One of the more problematic areas when using a computer to control a video-tape player is in accurately monitoring the position of the tape so that specified video sequences can be 'randomly' selected for presentation to the student. A basic method frequently employed is to count 'control track pulses' as the tape moves (in any mode). These pulses are recorded on a special track on the tape whenever a video recording is made. Unfortunately, counting these pulses in fast-forward or rewind modes is not absolutely reliable, and cumulative errors build up causing inaccuracies in identifying the positions of video sequences. Various techniques have been employed to overcome this problem, either by frame coding the control track pulses or by adding frame markers, typically on the second audio track on the tape.

Many of these problems associated with interactive video are, of course, a function of current video-tape technology. People often ask, therefore, whether tape-based interactive video is worth pursuing, when video-disc systems, with their accurate and almost instant random search capabilities, are just around the corner. To conclude this paper I will examine briefly the question of video-discs and, in particular, their suitability for training applications.

First, it has to be said that at the time of writing there is no commercially-available UK standard video-disc system. We are relying for our prognostications on the experience in other countries, notably the US, and on the promises of manufacturers and distributors. One of the major problems faced by manufacturers has been the production of discs. Estimates of the rejection rate for disc pressings are as high as 90 per cent. Nevertheless, it is a new technology and we can expect many of the initial difficulties to be overcome.

There are strong arguments, however, to support the view that the advantages of video-disc technology are not such that it will replace the need for video-tape in training or elsewhere.

The initial cost of producing a 'master' disc is high. Although the cost of disc copying is essentially cheaper than with tapes, enough copies must be required to cover the initial mastering costs. It is currently stated that disc production is only worthwhile in quantities of around 100 or more. These quantities are normally only required for published material. Also, the disc mastering and copying process takes some weeks, while for urgent requirements tape copies can be produced within days.

For these reasons alone, most organizations will want to retain the use of video-tape; hence they will seriously question whether the *addition* of video-discs would be justifiable. For intensive video training one further issue favours tape technology, and that is the relative ease with which the training material can be changed. At the moment a video-disc package will be a very permanent proposition.

The real advantage of video-disc systems is their ability to select (smoothly, accurately and immediately) required video sequences. This would seem to be a major advantage over tape systems for use with 'branching' training packages. However, in practice, training material is usually sequential and the need for random access over large amounts of material is minimal. Tape systems have shown themselves to be perfectly adequate for the task.

I think it is clear that video-tape systems will be in demand for many years to come. The smoothness of operation of the video-disc will cause this new technology to appeal to some people, but both the video-tape and video-disc systems can live quite comfortably together. In either case, the role of interactive video in training will become increasingly apparent and compelling.

Section 4:
Computers in Learning

4.1 Computer-Based Trainers: Aspirations and Expectations

Anne Howe and Nick Rushby
Imperial College, London

Abstract: Over the past two years there has emerged a need for courses to introduce trainers to the techniques of computer-based training. In the absence of historically established norms for the content of such courses, the course organizers have developed materials in the light of their understanding of what is required and what is feasible. The results do not necessarily match the expectations and aspirations of the course participants.

Given that it is difficult, as yet, to carry out a sensible job analysis for the archetypal computer-based trainer, his or her own perceptions of what he or she needs to know and be able to do are very relevant. Based on the experience of running a series of such courses for trainers, this paper will examine the relationships between the different aspirations and expectations of the teachers and the students on the course.

Introduction

The rapid development of microcomputers has encouraged their possible use in the training world. Like the rest of us, trainers hear a lot about how micros are going to change the whole way we do things, and computer-based training (CBT) has been in the air long enough for it to have become a familiar idea to many people — even if its actual use seems rather remote and difficult to achieve. Trainers are now the focus of considerable marketing efforts regarding CBT, and are exposed to a good deal of publicity about what others are doing in this field and about the possibilities it offers for improving various aspects of the training function. There is thus quite a considerable demand for courses on CBT to help trainers to find their way round this new subject.

This paper relates our experience in designing and running such a course. At the time, about 18 months ago, when the original design was being developed, we knew that there existed, in the training world, a demand and a need for information about the possibilities of CBT.

Generally speaking, the demand was not well-formulated; trainers wanted to know *something* about CBT but their expectations varied widely and were rather vague.

As prospective providers, we had fairly clear but untested views about the nature of the needs that the course should meet, and how these might marry up with what we knew about the nature of the demand.

But the prospective students and course leaders were not the only parties whose expectations needed to be considered. Providing courses for industry is like selling children's books: the consumers are not the purchasers. So the course had to meet not only the perceived requirements of the trainers who came on it, but also those of the managers who sent them and who might be expected to have views on the nature of the skills to be acquired and their subsequent deposition within the organization.

Constraints

The curriculum of any such course is bound by a number of constraints. In this case the most important were:

(a) *Time.* It is not usually very easy for training officers to get away from their jobs for long periods, and so we settled for a three-day course.

(b) *Equipment.* We thought, and experience supports the idea, that hands-on experience would be an important element of the course. To ensure that all course members get a reasonable chance to use machines, we have needed to provide one microcomputer for every four or five course members. In practical terms this has meant limiting course numbers to about 20.

(c) *Pre-knowledge.* Exactly what the course members know beforehand is a most important constraint for obvious reasons. It is not predictable in a general sense, though with any particular group it can be established. Unfortunately, this is not much help when embarking on the design of a first course with a general audience in view.

The other constraints were *our* perceptions of the expectations of the people involved:

(d) the trainers who wanted to learn something useful for themselves and their organizations;

(e) the training managers who wanted the course to provide something useful for their organizations and their training staff;

(f) ourselves as trainers, aware of (some of) these other constraints and also, in a sense, as arbiters of what the outcomes 'should be'.

Course Design

It was our intention to devise a framework for the course that would be flexible enough to provide for the requirements of a range of different sorts of course members, including training managers, training officers and instructors from all types of organizations, dealing with most types of training problems. We hoped, also, that there would be a significant amount of common ground and shared material with a parallel course on using computer-based learning that we were developing for teachers in the education sector. The general intention was that the course should be fairly intensive, although we presumed that it might sometimes be spread more thinly over a few weeks. It was also probable that several course tutors would be involved. It was therefore essential that the course should have an explicit underlying structure with clear objectives which could be modified to meet particular needs, without losing the shape of the course as a whole. The detailed objectives associated with each course component have not usually been discussed with the course participants — as well as enabling us to design a structured course they have provided us with the criteria against which to assess the feedback we have received.

The overall design of the course and a more detailed discussion of its rationale are given elsewhere (Rushby, 1981; Rushby *et al*, 1981). Our overall aim, an aspiration which we hoped would be shared by the course participants and their managers, could be summed up as: 'to help trainers make *informed* decisions about whether, when and how, to use computer-based training'.

Expectations

As we ran the course for a variety of different groups of trainers, and elicited their views and comment through course diaries and feedback sheets, it became clear that there were a number of mismatches between our expectations and theirs.

Although we had designed a modular course that could be used in different ways with the emphasis on different areas, our inclination was to concentrate on the *training* rather than on the *computing* aspects of CBT. We therefore included some background material on instructional media and methods and on course design, and related the new media and methods of CBT to this existing framework. But the trainers expected much less about training and wanted more information and experience of computer technology. They were not in a position to know precisely what they wanted to know, but they thought that computer hardware should be given more attention.

At the beginning of each course we ask the trainers to specify their expectations from the course. Typical responses specified 'a greater understanding of computers', 'a knowledge of computer applications to training procedures' (often specifying the subject matter or the target population the individual trainer has on his or her mind), 'evaluation of computers in training so as to exploit existing resources', 'a knowledge of materials that already exist', and, most frequently mentioned, 'an understanding of the jargon'.

Many trainers also come on the course expecting to learn a programming language. In most of the courses there has been an unprompted demand for a session on choosing a personal computer for use at home. We responded quickly and now this is, almost against our 'better judgement', an integral part of the course.

In contrast, the parallel version of the course run for teachers has needed to evolve in an opposite way. Perhaps it is reasonable to expect that, by self-selection, the teachers coming on this course will be enthusiastic and knowledgeable about computers. Certainly we have had to include more basic educational technology and have been able to reduce the time spent on computer literacy for this other audience.

It is quite interesting to note the very marked difference between these two groups in their grasp of the basic ideas of educational technology. The trainer groups usually take for granted the concepts of using objectives, the need to study the training population, the tasks to be studied, and, of course, development and evaluation. Generally, much more time has to be spent on educational technology with the teacher groups.

The trainers lacked interest in generalized models of CBT, being much more interested in direct applications of models they saw to well-defined problems in specific subject areas. It was also very obvious that trainers were less concerned with innovation studies than are educationalists generally, which possibly reflects as much on the relative ease of adopting and using new methods in industry as it does on the pronounced lack of interest of most of our trainers in any theory for which they could not see an immediate practical application.

We also underestimated the significance of the practical work in which small groups of trainers criticize existing CBT material. This has now evolved into the focus of the course, developing their critical facilities about CBT and providing the stimulus for much deeper discussions than we expected. On the whole, the discussions are particularly sophisticated when it comes to analysing teaching styles and strategies and relating the material to the supposed learning process, most participants using convenience of use and elegance of presentation as their prime criteria for evaluation.

Our expectation is that the syndicate work should be related to the course participants' own problems in their own organizations and that they should come away with something, if only an initial design and an action plan, that will be of use to them later. The purpose of this exercise is to force participants to put what they have learned into a real life context, and to consider what may be real possibilities for them. Perhaps our expectations are too high, or perhaps, in their enthusiasm, the syndicates are too ambitious; for whatever reason, the syndicates are often over-extended and our expectations are not always satisfied.

Turning to the less obvious expectations concerning the role of CBT in the organization, we come to a problem of evidence. We are aware of our own aspirations and expectations, even though they may have been compromised (or at least tempered) by experience. We have sets of feedback questionnaires from trainers who have come on the courses, to supplement our personal experiences of working with them. But the aspirations and expectations of the training *managers* are more difficult to elicit.

Prior to each course, we have had extended discussions with the training managers in the client organizaton to negotiate the course content and to establish specified desired outcomes. In most cases the organizations' aims, as expressed by the training manager, are much less well defined than are those of their staff. From our interviews we have pieced together a picture of concern with the impact of CBT on training in specific areas, together with the cost implications. We would have preferred to take a rather broader view of organizational development, and the impact of CBT on the training department as a whole, but, in practice, managers do not yet seem to be thinking of CBT as a radical alternative to existing training methods, but rather as something much more like the media-based innovations of the past such as television, which has been used to extend, but not to reform, the traditional pattern of training.

Conclusions

Like most evaluations, our study of the aspirations and expectations of those involved with the course 'Using Computer-Based Training' has not produced any startling recipes for success. It has made us aware of the different perceptions of the purchasers, consumers and providers of courses, and has highlighted a number of dimensions on which the content of such a course can be plotted. The four most significant of these are:

1. general educational technology *vs* specific to CBT
2. computer technical *vs* non-technical
3. theoretical *vs* practical
4. organizational development *vs* CBT in isolation

Acknowledgements

We would like to thank all those consumers and customers who have provided the evidence for this study.

References

Rushby, N J (1981) Computer-based learning: what will we teach the teachers? In Percival, F and Ellington, H (eds) *Aspects of Educational Technology* **XV**, *Distance Learning and Evaluation*. Kogan Page, London.

Rushby, N, Anderson, J, Howe, A, Marrow, F and Warren Piper, D (1981) A recursive approach to teacher training in the use of CBL. In *Conference Proceedings of Computers and Education*. IFIP North Holland.

4.2 Uses and Abuses of Computer-Assisted Learning

J Mooney and J Stoane
Department of Learning Systems and Microtechnology,
Kingsway Technical College, Dundee

Abstract: Computer-assisted learning (CAL) is probably the most important development in education since the teacher. Every year more microcomputers appear in schools and colleges. Yet much of the small amount of available software is educationally unsound, dated or expensive, so many teachers will be attempting to write their own software.

This paper provides some guidelines for such writers as to what is, and what is not, suitable for CAL, and describes two experiments in interfacing the computer interactively with external devices to provide CAL.

Some programming hints which inexperienced programmers may find useful in making CAL software more acceptable and student proof are given in this paper.

Uses and Abuses of Computer-Assisted Learning

The microcomputer is probably the most powerful teaching aid yet devised (apart, that is, from a teacher). New strides are made in hardware every few months. Programming techniques are becoming rapidly more sophisticated. Yet CAL software lags far behind as regards availability, up-to-dateness, educational quality and topic coverage.

Producing *good* CAL programs is very time-consuming and therefore expensive. Wright (1981) quotes a figure of around 100 hours to produce one hour of CAL material. So, while the cost of hardware decreases steadily (the BBC microcomputer is a very rare case of an *increase* in computer prices), the cost of software increases rapidly.

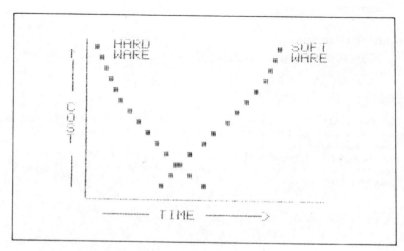

Figure 1. *Relative costs of hardware and software*

Commercial CAL software is thus unlikely to be viable on any great scale. So most CAL programs are going to be written within schools and colleges and often by individual teachers. (There are close parallels between this situation and the situation following the introduction of teaching machines, programmed learning and feedback classrooms.)

In many ways it is probably fortunate that teachers will write their own material. They will do it in their own time and get little thanks or recognition for it; but at least it will be exactly what they want in their own classroom.

Many authorities are aware of the need for development in the educational uses of computers to come from the grass roots.

'Previous experience with many forms of educational innovation, including educational computing, have shown that the 'successful' innovations are those driven by the teachers themselves, rather than those imposed on them from above, either by administrators or detached research and development teams.'
The CEDAR Project 1980

'There is a real need for *teachers* to become program writers; otherwise there is a danger that the market will be flooded with badly prepared software which could ruin computer-assisted learning.'
CAL Consortium 1979

'Programmed learning died because teachers did not realise its potential. If micro programs fall into the hands of professional writers, could the results be similar?'
C A Nichols 1980

It is vital that the *educational quality* of the CAL programs is high. It does not matter too much if the programming is amateurish, so long as it works, although, obviously, some assistance from a professional programmer to make the program student-proof, improve screen layout, etc is desirable. Some standard programming techniques to improve 'home made' programs will be described later in this paper.

Ideally, to produce a good CAL package requires the input of three experts:

☐ *The subject expert* who initiates the project. He perceives the need and describes the topic to be taught.

☐ *The educational technologist* who designs the learning system in conjunction with the subject expert.

☐ *The programmer* who designs the program in conjunction with the educational technologist.

There will also be, of course, a great deal of discussion between all three, and each should have at least some knowledge of the areas of expertise of the other two. It will be the subject expert, the one who will use it, who will decide when the package is acceptable.

It is very important that CAL should be used properly, that is, only where appropriate. It is perhaps the educational technologist, with the expertise in designing interesting, efficient learning systems, who is in the best position to say what is an appropriate use of CAL and what is not. He believes that the medium should be appropriate to the message. The computer should be used to do only those things it is good at and not used just for its own sake.

We will now consider some *abuses* of CAL — instances where the computer is not a good method of teaching.

1. Linear programmed learning material is sometimes presented via the computer. We believe that the computer is an unnecessarily elaborate and expensive way of presenting such material and for this purpose is inferior to paper. Also, it is very tiring to read large chunks of text from a VDU.

2. A popular exercise by, for example, science teachers who have begun to learn programming is to write programs to carry out routine calculations. There is no point to such programs as the students must be able to do the calculations for themselves on paper.

3. Although computers are good at simulating some kinds of laboratory experiments, there are pitfalls. One program simulates a simple chemical titration using POKE graphics. On pressing a key the level in the burette goes down and liquid drops into the flask. At the end point the liquid in the flask changes from green to red. This is clever programming, but is it useful? The experiment simulated is very simple and employs cheap, safe apparatus and chemicals. It is surely much sounder educationally to let pupils carry out a *real* titration. Another pitfall with simulating experiments is using a simulation to 'prove' something when the law in question was assumed to write the program. For example, a teacher wrote a program to calculate the ratio of voltage to current for varying currents passing through a resistor, thus 'proving' Ohm's Law. If the program (see Figure 2) itself is examined it can be seen that, to write the program, Ohm's Law was assumed (in line 150) in the first place.

```
130 PRINT
140 INPUTI
150 V= I * 10
160 PRINT
170 PRINT
180 PRINT"THE VOLTAGE DROP ACROSS THE RESISTOR"
190 PRINT"IS " V
200 PRINT
210 GET A$: IF A$ <> "C" THEN 210
```

Figure 2. *The 'proving' of Ohm's Law*

Having described some abuses of CAL we will now be more positive and suggest some more appropriate uses.

These examples are based on what we see as the *strengths* of the computer, ie:

1. infinite patience
2. the ability to generate endless examples and practice situations
3. carrying out calculations quickly
4. simulations
5. responding to and controlling external devices through interfacing

1. Infinite patience.
   This program (see Figure 3) forces pupils to learn Latin vocabulary. It will keep asking them the words all night if necessary, without losing its temper, until they know them thoroughly.
2. Generating an unending succession of examples upon which to practice a set of rules.
   This chemistry program generates examples of salts to be made by five possible methods. The student chooses what he thinks is a correct method and the computer tells him if he is right. If he is wrong, he is told why he is wrong and he is given the correct method(s) — see Figure 4. Where appropriate, the program (see Figure 5) guides him towards the correct method.

```
REMEMBER:

    TO SEE THE ANSWER ...........A

    TO RETURN TO THE MENU .......M

    TO FINISH ...................F
_____

              ENGLISH TO LATIN
    _____

I LOVE ✳ AMO-AMARE-AMAVI-AMATUM

CORRECT

DITCH ✳ VALLA-AE

NO, TRY AGAIN

    ✳
```

Figure 3. *The 'patient' computer*

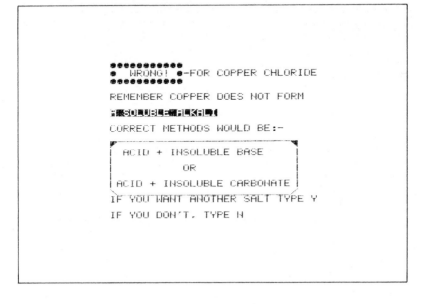

Figure 4. *The computer as prompter*

```
OOPS! YOU CAN'T MAKE A SOLUTION OF

        LEAD CHLORIDE

AS IT IS INSOLUBLE!

TRY AGAIN TO PRECIPITATE

    *** LEAD SULPHATE ***


TYPE IN THE NAME OF THE FIRST SUBSTANCE


LEAD NITRATE

OK SO FAR. NOW TYPE IN THE NAME

OF THE SECOND SUBSTANCE
```

Figure 5. *The computer as correcter*

3. Carrying out calculations quickly.

   We have said that there is little point in doing calculations by computer when pupils must be able to do them for themselves. A valid use is to remove the burden of calculations which would otherwise prevent, say, less able pupils from carrying out a scientific investigation. The example given is taken from an elementary integrated science experiment on analysis of soils. Pupils are asked to find the percentage of water, humus and various sizes of rock particles by heating and roasting soil samples and passing them through graded sieves. The sample is weighed at each stage. Less able pupils can usually manage the weighing and manipulation of the sieves, etc but are unable to calculate the percentages. If they can feed their results into a computer (which they enjoy doing) and be presented with all the percentages for their sample, then the main objectives of the lesson (the use of apparatus, discussion of what makes up soil and the differences between various types of soils) can be achieved — see Figures 6 and 7.

4. Simulations.

   It is valid to simulate experiments which cannot normally be performed as they are dangerous, expensive, difficult or time-consuming. It is also useful to simulate industrial or natural processes. The effect of changing parameters can be seen at once. This is particularly useful in biology. The program shown in Figure 8 simulates the effect on natural water of several varying factors.

5. Interfacing with and controlling external devices. Two examples will be described.

Example A

In this example the technologies of video and microcomputing are merged to demonstrate the potential of what is referred to as 'interactive' video, in creating a learning environment in the field of technical training as carried out at the Microtechnology Centre, Kingsway Technical College, Dundee.

```
        ┌─────────────────────────┐
        │    Soil Analysis        │
        └─────────────────────────┘

  Type in the weight of fresh soil you
  started with; then press RETURN
   45
  Now type in the weight of your soil
  Sample after drying, then press RETURN
   38
  Now type in the weight of your soil
  after roasting, then press RETURN
   29
```

Figure 6. *The computer helps with calculations. . .*

```

  Your soil sample contained
        16 % WATER
  and   20 % HUMUS

```

Figure 7. *. . . and provides the answers*

```
  A.  THE KIND OF BODY OF WATER
        1.  LARGE POND
        2.  LARGE LAKE
        3.  SLOW-MOVING RIVER
        4.  FAST-MOVING RIVER

    2

  B.  WATER TEMP. IN DEGREES C (1 - 30)

    12

  C.  TYPE OF WASTE DUMPED INTO THE WATER
        1.  INDUSTRIAL
        2.  SEWAGE

    2
```

Figure 8. *The computer as simulator*

The objective was to evaluate the effectiveness of such a set up in a didactic situation and to explore the possibilities of computer-assisted training of trainees in the early weeks of short courses. To this end the following equipment was used. The selection was determined by that which was available at hand, and such expertise as was available to 'interface' them through hardware and software.

Microcomputer	— CBM
Floppy disk unit	— CBM
Electronic interface	— college devised
Video-recorder	— Hitachi
Domestic TV	
Video-recording	

The particular aims were to:

(a) Allow the trainee to select the lesson.
(b) Present learning material through pre-recorded video-recording.
(c) Evaluate the trainees' knowledge of subject material after viewing.
(d) Record on disc the results of such evaluation.
(e) Direct the trainee to a suitable next stage.

The equipment was arranged as in Figure 9.

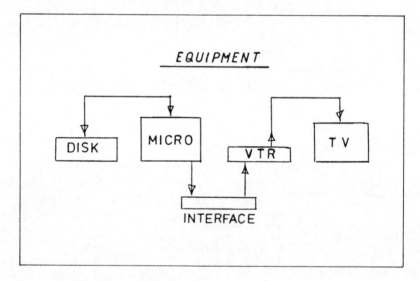

Figure 9. *The interfacing of computer and video*

The hardware interface shown between microcomputer and VTR was a simple series of transistor switches connected between the remote control socket of the VTR and the user port of the microcomputer. The circuit is shown in Figure 10. This arrangement allowed a 'bit' sent high at the user port of the micro to activate the switches on the VTR thus allowing the micro to assume control over the VTR through software within a computer program and hence enable a program to control the sequence, repetition and viewing time of the learning material as presented to the trainee and, more important, to allow these variables to be determined by the trainees' responses (see Figure 11).

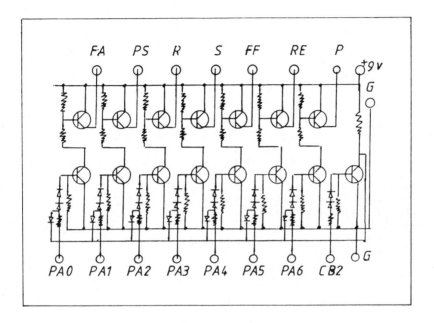

Figure 10. *The circuit of an interface between a microcomputer and a VTR*

```
 5 REM TEST INTERFACE
10 PRINT"SELECT FUCTION"
20 PRINT"0)FRAME ADVANCE"
25 PRINT"1)PAUSE"
30 PRINT"2)RECORD"
35 PRINT"3)STOP"
40 PRINT"4)FAST FORWARD"
45 PRINT"REWIND"
50 PRINT"PLAY"
60 INPUTA:B=2↑A:REM..SELECT FUNCTION
70 POKE59459,255:REM..SET ALL PORTS TO OUTPUT
80 POKE59471,B:REM..SET DATA REGISTER TO VALUE OF B
90 POKE59468,204:REM CAUSE CB2 TO "TRIGGER" SWITCH
100 FORK=1TO3000:NEXTK:REMWAIT UNTIL MECHANISM SETTLES
110 POKE59468,236:REM STOP PULSE
120 GOTO10 :REM WAIT FOR NEXT FUNCTION
```

Figure 11. *A program to test the interface between the computer and the VTR*

The program illustrated above indicates how a computer program can be used to test the equipment before attempting any 'interactive' programming. It will also show how the 'program' controls the learning material.

The following table, used in conjunction with Figure 11, should be useful.

If $A = 0$ → $B = 1$ →	59471 contains 00000001 →	PA0 and hence FA is 'triggered'.
If $A = 1$ → $B = 2$ →	59471 contains 00000010 →	PA1 and hence PS is 'triggered'.
If $A = 2$ → $B = 4$ →	.. ..	00000100 →	PAZ	R .. ..
.. .. ..	.. ..	.. ..	..	.. .. ..	.. .. ..
.. .. ..	.. ..	..	..	.. .. ..	.. .. ..
If $A = 6$ → $B = 64$ →	..	..	PA	P .. ..

Table to be used in conjunction with Figure 11

The control of the appropriate video functions have now been transferred to the micro and, by writing suitably structured computer programs, the writer can present pre-recorded learning material on video, test the trainee's understanding and then direct appropriate action (depending on his responses) and record his responses on floppy disk.

Let us look at an early example. A program has been loaded and run on the microcomputer, presenting the trainee with the following choice.

Select the appropriate lesson:

1. Soldering exercises
2. Simple amplifier construction
3. Multi-stage amplifier construction
Number?

Assume the trainee selects 1. When the micro accepts the trainee's response from the keyboard it will cause the VTR to either start playing or wind forward to a predetermined part of the tape. The program extract in Figure 4 illustrates this.

As indicated in line 5000, if the trainee selects 1. the VTR starts playing the first lesson on the tape. Line 6000 is executed if the second lesson is chosen and, as shown in line 6010, the tape will first wind on to a predetermined point determined by the value of Z which is controlled by the programmer. (A more efficient way to allow for this delay may well be to use the built-in clock.)

Having watched the selected material for a given time, the trainee is faced with a number of multiple-choice questions on the subject matter just viewed, as suggested in line 6070, Figure 12. His answers are stored on the disk for immediate or future analysis and the program (initially the programmer) then decides the next course of action, depending on the trainee's responses. Possibilities are to rewind the tape back to the beginning or to some point on the tape that illustrates some topic, about which the questions were not particularly well answered, and even single-stepping through the relevant frames. The trainee would again be asked to answer selected questions and his progress would be continually monitored. At any time he can access information about his progress.

Example B

The second example investigates to what extent the combination of technologies used previously could be used in the training of electronic assembly. Assume the trainee, given the original choice from the menu, selects option 2. (simple amplifier construction). Using the technique of software control over the visual presentation, the trainee views a pre-recorded tape explaining the design and construction of the simple amplifier as shown in Figure 13.

```
1000 INPUTX: REM WAIT FOR TRAINEE RESPONSE
1010 ON X GOTO500,6000,7000,10
5000 REM 1ST LESSON CHOSEN
5010 POKE59471,64:REM CAUSE VTR TO START
6000 REM 2ND LESSON CHOSEN
6010 POKE59471,16:FORK=1TOZ:NEXTK:REM WIND ON UNTIL Z
6020 POKE59471,8           :REM STOP
6030 PRINT"WHEN READY TO START PRESS ANY KEY"
6040 GET A$:IFA$=" "THEN6040:REM WAIT FOR KEY
6050 POKE59471,64:FORK=1TOX:NEXTK:REM VTR RUNS UNTIL X
6060 POKE59471,8:      REM STOP
6070 REM CALL UP QUESTION FROM DISK
6080 REM CHECK AND RECORD ANSWERS
6100 REM CONTINUE
6500 REM UNSATISFACTORY PERFORMANCE
6510 PRINT"
```

Figure 12. *A program using the interface between the computer and VTR*

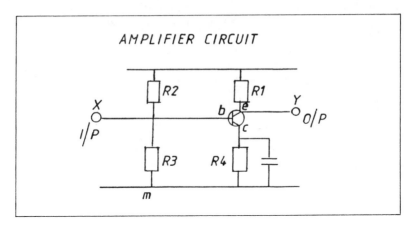

Figure 13. *Using the microcomputer/VTR link to evaluate construction ability*

The methods of evaluating the trainee's understanding of the principles involved are used as before, but a technique for evaluating his construction ability requires a more practical approach. Can our microcomputer help? Two pairs of leads are taken from the micro user port, one designated on output, the other on input (see Figure 14).

Using this arrangement, the micro can be programmed to provide via a digital to analogue converter (DAC) an output signal, which, if connected to point X in Figure 14, and with suitably designed components, should cause a signal to appear at point Y, the value of which might be, say, $Y = 10x$ (ie a gain of 10). This condition would prevail, provided the amplifier was not only properly designed but properly constructed. Can the power of the microcomputer be used in this case not only to test the output of the amplifier but also to diagnose faults?

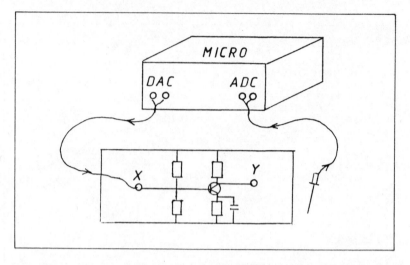

Figure 14. *A suggested arrangement for a practical demonstration
of the microcomputer/VTR link up*

If the input lead (to the micro) with suitable probe is connected via an analogue
to digital converter (ADC) to the user port, then the micro (or its programmer)
can test the values of signal and voltage at various parts of the circuit and output
(via the screen) relevant comments. Some possibilities are:

Condition	Message
B $\triangleq$ 6.7v	Check transistor polarity
B = 0v	Check R2 for high value
B $\triangleq$ 2.5v	Check node m for open circuit
B = 1.6	Check node c

If corrective messages are given and acted upon, the whole process can be
repeated until the amplifier gives the micro the correct response.

These are two activities under development. It should be stressed that the
equipment used does not reflect 'stage of the *art*' technology, and that much
more sophistication and control could be achieved using, say, videodisc etc.
They do, however, explore possibilities for harnessing new technologies
in learning.

These are a few of the uses and abuses of CAL.

Six Programming Techniques

Let us return to our CAL producing team of the subject expert, the educational
technologist, and the programmer. In many real situations, of course, two or even
all of these are embodied in one person. Usually that one person is the subject
expert at the chalk face, working, as we have said earlier, in his 'spare' time.

At the beginning of the paper we said that some programming techniques
would be described which the lone subject teacher can use to tighten up his CAL
programs. Six such techniques are described below. (These are specifically for
COMMODORE PET, but can be adapted for most other popular microcomputers.)

Figure 15 shows how you can clear the screen and present the new information
starting at the top of the screen. It avoids 'scrolling' where the new information at
the bottom of the screen pushes the old off the top. It is equivalent, perhaps, to
turning the page of a book.

```
10 REM: CLEAR SCREEN BETWEEN FRAMES
20 REM: TO AVOID SCROLLING
150 PRINT
200 PRINT""
210 REM: NEXT FRAME HERE
```

Figure 15. *A program for 'turning' the computer's page*

Figure 16 shows how you can hold the screen with information until a key is pressed. When GET is used, unlike INPUT, pressing RETURN is not needed. (Normally combined with the 'clear screen' command.)

```
500 PRINT"PRESS ANY KEY TO CONTINUE"
510 GET A$: IF A$=""THEN510
520 REM: REST OF PROGRAM FOLLOWS
```

Figure 16. *Holding the page*

```
90 PRINT"                    MENU"
95 PRINT"                   ----"
98 PRINT
100 PRINT"FOR ENGLISH TO LATIN ....PRESS 1
105 PRINT
110 PRINT"FOR LATIN TO ENGLISH ....PRESS 2
115 PRINT
120 PRINT"FOR MIXTURE OF LATIN TO ENGLISH
125 PRINT
130 PRINT"AND ENGLISH TO LATIN ....PRESS 3
140 PRINT
150 GET X
160 IF X>3 ORX<1 THEN150
170 ON X GOTO 400,500,600
400 REM: ENGLISH TO LATIN HERE
500 REM: LATIN TO ENGLISH HERE
600 REM: MIXTURE HERE
```

Figure 17. *The 'contents' page*

```
10 REM:ROUTINE TO TEST FOR 'Y' OR 'YES'
20 REM:AND FOR 'N' OR 'NO'
30 INPUT A$
40 IF LEFT$(A$,1)="Y" THEN 100
50 IF LEFT$(A$,1)="N" THEN 200
60 GOTO 20
100 PRINT "YES":REM:LINE EXECUTED IF Y OR YES
110 REM: 'YES' PROGRAM HERE
200 PRINT "NO":REM:LINE EXECUTED IF N OR NO
210 REM: 'NO' PROGRAM HERE
```

Figure 18. *Accepting and rejecting*

Figure 17 contains information which is comparable with the contents page of a book. On pressing the 'chapter number' the program jumps to the appropriate section.

In lines 150/160 any number other than 1, 2 or 3 is not accepted. Nothing happens until an acceptable number is pressed.

Line 170 ON . . . . GOTO is a convenient way of branching according to the chapter chosen. There is no limit to the number of choices offered. If X = 1, program jumps to line 400. If X = 2, program jumps to line 500, etc.

Often the user has to accept or reject something by typing YES or NO. This routine will accept any word beginning with Y (even Y itself) as YES. Similarly N with NO (see Figure 18).

```
10 REM TO DISABLE THE RUN STOP KEY (BASIC<3.0)
20 POKE 144,49
30 REM TO ENABLE THE RUN STOP KEY (BASIC<3.0)
40 POKE 144,46
READY.
```

```
10 REM TO DISABLE THE RUN STOP KEY (BASIC 4.0)
20 POKE 144,88
30 REM TO ENABLE THE RUN STOP KEY (BASIC 4.0)
40 POKE 144,85
READY.
```

Figures 19a and 19b. *Commands for putting the RUN stop key in operation once more*

Pressing RUN STOP at any INPUT or GET command will cause the user to come out of the program. This command prevents the operation of the RUN STOP key. *NB:* This will, unfortunately, also stop the clock.

It is, of course, important to know how to put the RUN STOP key in operation once more (see Figures 19a and 19b; 20a and 20b). The commands differ according to the dialect of BASIC. Commands for BASIC 3 and BASIC 4 are shown.

If the user presses RETURN at an INPUT command without first pressing any other key he will drop out of the program. Either of these routines will prevent this.

```
10 PRINT "TYPE IN YOUR NAME";
20 INPUT "    *IHMI";A$
30 IF A$="*" THEN 10
40 PRINT A$
```

```
5 REM:TO PREVENT THE USER DROPPING OUT
6 REM:OF THE PROGRAM ON PRESSING RETURN
10 PRINT "TYPE IN YOUR NAME ";:GOSUB 1000
20 IF R$="" THEN 10
30 PRINT R
40 REM:REST OF
50 REM:PROGRAM
60 REM:HERE
1000 OPEN7,0:INPUT#7,R$:CLOSE7
1010 R=VAL(R$):PRINT
1020 RETURN
```

Figures 20a and 20b. *Routines for preventing the user from dropping out of the program*

Acknowledgements

We would like to acknowledge the help given by Alan Lord, Senior Technician and John Robertson, Lecturer for their assistance with the electronics and programming aspects.

References

CEDAR Project (1980). Imperial College, London.
Nichols, C A (1980) *CET News*, 10, June.
Notre Dame College of Education (1979). From a CAL consortium at the annual conference of the Association for Science Education.
Wright, D (1981) Computer-assisted training in practice. In Percival, F and Ellington, H (eds) *Aspects of Educational Technology* XV. Kogan Page, London.

4.3 The Structure of an Intelligent Computer-Aided Instruction System

P Farrell-Viney
SPL International, London

Abstract: This paper is an attempt to link two different but converging disciplines, computer-aided instruction (CAI), and artificial intelligence (AI) (also known as 'expert systems', 'intelligent systems', and 'knowledge engineering') with a view to laying the theoretical groundwork for an 'intelligent' computer-based instructional system.

The paper examines the two disciplines, their background, areas of overlap and limitations, and then considers the area of knowledge representation and manipulation. It goes on to present an overview of the solution in terms of its components, their interactions and functions which are analysed in some detail.

The Converging Disciplines of CAI and AI

Both CAI and AI systems are concerned with the processing of knowledge, its acquisition, representation and transfer, using computers as a medium.

Both employ a controlled input/output model, and knowledge database. The difference is that in CAI the model and the database are in the teacher's mind, and in AI they are in the system. CAI systems have only a limited ability to acquire student-related data (test scores, branching choices, response times), and both the subject matter and the presentation logic remain in the teacher's mind. Thus presentation-strategy and subject-matter changes depend on the teacher's ability to interpret the student's use of the system, and any non-system-dependent output the student may provide.

However, recent attempts by Sleeman (1981) and others have indicated the possibility of constructing a model of the student from data captured while the student is learning from an Intelligent CAI system. Landa (1979) and Lawless (1979) have suggested some theoretical bases on which such a model could be constructed.

From this brief overview we can see that, while both disciplines are concerned with knowledge, their purposes and relationships to knowledge differ.

Background of CAI and its Limitations

Current CAI has five inherent defects:

1. *Cost.* This is principally a software/courseware labour cost, common to all professional computer programming. It is caused partly by a lack of standardization, and partly by the very limited software tools available for programmers in general and teachers in particular.

2. *Limited string-handling facilities.* This has two important consequences: since current student responses must consist of either numbers, algorithms expressed in a computer language, or character strings which must be matched on a structured AND/NAND/OR/NOR basis, the possible objectives, cognitive or otherwise, available to teachers must be correspondingly limited

(Bird, 1980). Unsurprisingly, therefore, the most successful CAI programs generally have a numerate, behavioural basis.

Attempts by teachers to overcome the character-string limitation, by providing multiple-choice answers, provide the students with clues to the answer structure, possible clues to succeeding answers, the 'correct' response domain area, and an incentive to guess.

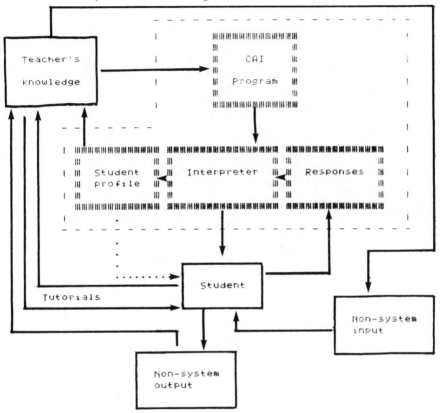

A command-based Interpreter (such as PILOT or TUTOR) is driven both by a teacher-written program and the student's responses. Solid lines show the transfer of information. Dotted lines show optional feedback to the student. Broken lines show the boundary of the system. The knowledge is effectively external to the system.

Figure 1. *The typical CAI system within a teaching system*

3. *Effective separation by the teacher.* This concerns the effective separation of subject matter and pedagogic expertise in the teacher's mind from the CAI system, and the consequent diagnostic limitations.

4. *Effective separation — data from instructions.* The fourth aspect concerns the separation of data from instructions. This has been so inherent in computer practice, from the second to the fourth generation, that it is still difficult to see it as a limitation, but it is the principal reason for the non-auto-adaptability of systems. If you want to change a program you must stop it, go into EDIT mode, modify, debug, and then re-run it. Thus all possible fatal user errors must be foreseen and rendered harmless to the system. All possible student responses must be anticipated and built into the system.

5. *The lack of suitable 'didactic debugging' tools.* One theoretic exception to this is Merrill's Resynthesis system based on Component Display theory (1981); even so this currently (1982) operates only on frames, and does little to improve sequencing. Additionally, no help is available for those non-programming or simply busy teachers who want to develop simulation, drill or gaming routines.

These limitations may be seen as the top or most visible layer of two areas of knowledge: pedagogical, and technological. Artificial Intelligence is a multi-disciplinary study using computers which started 20 years ago. It is concerned with vision, manipulation, speech and the replication of knowledge.

Central to much of Artificial Intelligence is the concept of the frame defined by Minsky (1975). This is quite different from the 'frame' concept in CAI. In AI, a 'frame' is a data structure (consisting of numbers, words, or instructions) which can be used to represent an archetypal situation (sitting down, the act of 'finding', defining an arch). This database contains information about how to use the frame, what we should expect to happen next, and what to do if such expectations are not confirmed.

This information is structured as a network of nodes and relations, some of which are fixed and essential, and each of which is filled with a default value. The fixed nodes are the *sine qua nons* of a frame. Thus if the 'base area' node of a 'street' frame is not filled with a 'road' value, then it is not a street. These nodes themselves may be the name of a frame.

This parallels what happens in our minds, in that we recognize a 'street' as such, by mapping our archetypal ideas of a 'street' on to the 'street' image we might have in our brain on walking up Oxford Street. As soon as we register that we are 'in a street', as opposed to being 'in a taxi', our mind checks its database of remembered streets, trying to find a match. At some point, it either gives up and tells us we are lost or that we are in Oxford Street: that is, all the essential nodes of both 'street' and 'Oxford Street' have been matched.

The non-essential, or 'terminal' nodes of a frame can be likened to Selfridges store. Oxford Street will still be Oxford Street without it, but if the value of the 'road' node changes from 'hard tarmacked surface' to 'water' then you are no longer in a 'street'. You are either in Venice, or Oxford Street has been flooded. Check for gondolas!

Related frames can be linked to form frame systems, and the effects of actions can be represented by transformations between the frames of a system. Thus, if the 'base area' node of the 'Oxford Street' frame is filled with 'water', when all the other nodes retain the same values, and there are no gondolas, one can infer that Oxford Street has been flooded. Such a deduction can be effected by an information retrieval system. In the event that no currently-held frame fits reality, such a system can supply a new frame.

Minsky's theory is now supported by a number of AI languages, notably LISP, FRL (frame representation language), PLANNER, CONNIVER and SMALL TALK. These enable the intellectual constructs developed through frame theory to be computerized, by providing ways of defining facts and the relationships between them.

Thus, to use an example of Winston (1980), the sentence: 'Prince Charming found Cinderella with her glass shoe' can be defined thus:

Action:	find
Agent:	Charming
Object:	Cinderella
Instrument:	shoe 1

This describes a FIND relationship between Prince Charming and Cinderella, and can be seen as a frame. The computer now knows that Prince Charming and

Cinderella enjoy a FIND relationship. To widen its knowledge of Prince Charming for example, it would be necessary to create a Prince Charming frame and flesh it out using two constructs:

HAS—PROPERTY
A—KIND—OF

which can be seen as upward and downward links in a knowledge data-base. Thus, Prince Charming could have upward links to such frames as:

MAN (A—KIND—OF MAN)
SON OF KING (A—KIND—OF SON OF KING)
FICTIONAL CHARACTER (A—KIND—OF FICTIONAL CHARACTER)

and downward links to:

LOVES (CINDERELLA) (HAS—PROPERTY LOVES (CINDERELLA))
TALL (HAS—PROPERTY TALL)

Thus, it would be possible to ask such a system:

HOW DOES PRINCE CHARMING FIND CINDERELLA?
> USING HER SHOE
WHAT IS HER SHOE MADE OF?
> GLASS
WHAT IS GLASS?
> A CHEMICAL COMPOUND, MOSTLY SILICA

and even

CAN PRINCE CHARMING BE WIRED FOR SOUND?

In this last case the system, having interrogated the Prince Charming frame and not finding, even using a Thesaurus, anything resembling: WIRED FOR SOUND, executes a Tree-search, moving up the various hierarchies attached to the Prince Charming frame. Bionic research being what it is, it regretfully answers: NO.

Representation of Knowledge

Mitchell (1981) suggested that knowledge could be represented as a net, observing that while you could grab any node and shake it to form the appearance of a hierarchy, any other node would have done just as well. In everyday terms this is true; we commonly use such terms as BUS, CAR, or CHEST-OF-DRAWERS. But when we descend to MINI-METRO and CHIPPENDALE, or ascend to TRANSPORTATION or FURNITURE, we go from the specific to the general, using the tool of the collective noun where necessary. This is very important for knowledge data-base designers for three reasons:

1. Class attributes can be assigned by class rather than by examples. Thus MALE contains all the attributes of the human class plus a few others. Similarly, PRINCE contains all the MALE attributes plus a few others. Thus, the storage space required for PRINCE attributes needs to be only as large as those attributes that distinguish him from MALE.
2. As we know, any fact or relationship can exist in a number of contexts. Prince Charming, for example, could exist in ANIMAL, MONARCHICAL, LITERARY and THEATRICAL contexts — as many as we can define for him. Some might tend to map on to one another, such as the LITERARY and THEATRICAL contexts. Such contexts can usefully be represented as 'tangled' hierarchies, and accessed by means of the attribute name, thus reducing the access time.
3. Access time can also be reduced by recalling that when we think about

a subject our thinking tends to revolve around it. (*Pace* de Bono). Having thought about Ohm's law, we then tend to ask questions about: the nature of Mr Ohm; his law; the nature of laws.

If the knowledge data-base is logically ordered, all of these topics will be known to the OHM'S LAW frame in the same way that we employ 'advance organizers'.

Inference

Changes between frames can be used to infer an event, such as the example of the transition of OXFORD STREET from a dry to a flooded state.

The ability to draw inferences is one of AI's great strengths. Another is to make one frame depend on the other:

JULIUS CAESAR IS KILLED BY CASCA

defines a KILL relationship between CAESAR and CASCA. In order to ensure that CAESAR has the DEAD property attached to his frame, we can specify an IF-ADDED demon to lurk in the system waiting for events like DEATH to be defined/occur so that they can leap out, add their attribute to the appropriate frame, and return to wait for more incoming data. Such data could be drawn by inference from other frame transformations.

This discussion of knowledge, and the inferences it provides, may seem distant from the problems of imparting it. However, Winston (1980) has shown how to use the example of water flow along a pipe as an example of Ohm's law of electrical resistance. Both the water flow and the law can be represented, and the student may ask questions about either. Ohm's law may then be analogously mapped on to the water flow example.

To represent knowledge, however, is not to impart it. A knowledge data-base is at least as useful as a book. The possession of books does not, however, imply the ability to use the information therein. This is discussed in the next section.

Proposals for a System

The system would be divided into the main parts of housekeeping and teaching.

Housekeeping

This would look after the standard CMI functions:

- ☐ Administration of students (test results, allocation on courses).
- ☐ Resource allocation (human and other).
- ☐ Information provision (memos, mailbox, bulletins).
- ☐ Staff/system interface.
- ☐ System monitoring and tuning.

Teaching

The core of the teaching facility would be three inter-related sub-systems called (i) BRIT(named after the Encyclopaedia), an AI structured subject-matter data-base; (ii) MR CHIPS, a didactic expert system which assumes the role of 'teacher'; (iii) TOM, the student details data-base containing the following details about each user:

- ☐ Administrative information and test scores.
- ☐ A representation of acquired knowledge.
- ☐ A representation of the student's cognitive skills.

These systems relate thus:

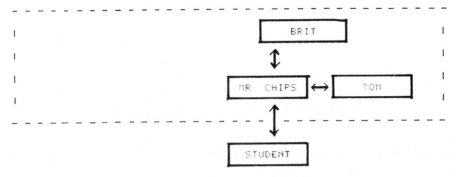

Figure 2. *The teaching sub-systems*

The student asks questions of MR CHIPS. MR CHIPS interrogates BRIT to find the answer, and then uses TOM as a guide to determine how much material should be taught and in what way. At intervals, MR CHIPS tests the student and stores the results in TOM.

The teaching system relates to the housekeeping system thus:

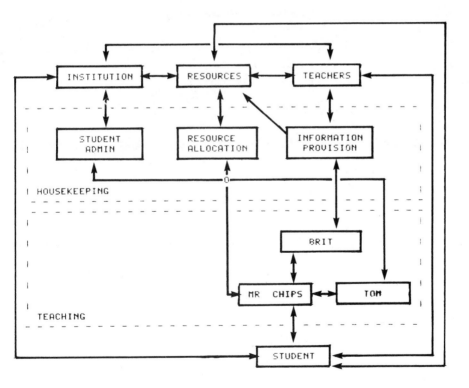

Figure 3. *The complete system*

This system would be expert in at least three ways:

1. Through a series of teaching rules governing the presentation, testing, and simulation of information, contained in MR CHIPS.
2. Through the rules inferred from the information (subject matter) itself, contained in BRIT.
3. Through an analysis, both of the knowledge gained by the student and the order in which it is gained, made by TOM.

BRIT
This would be a modified version of the literature guide system described by Nishida and Doshita (1980) which employed a three-level structure for knowledge representation.

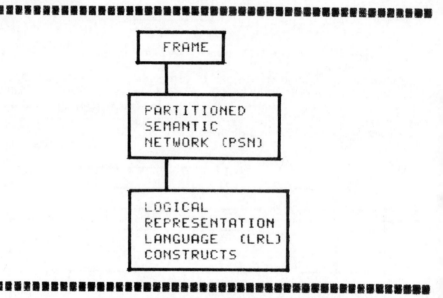

Figure 4. *Knowledge representation structure*

This contains the knowledge of any document. The document is first parsed, and the logical core is translated into an LRL construct (eg FRED, TAKE). These constructs are then combined to form 'real-world' relationships (eg FRED TAKES THE DOG FOR A WALK). These PSNs are them combined into FRAMES which can then be interrogated to discover who FRED was and where the DOG took him.

The modifications. Each LRL node, PSN and FRAME would be labelled: fact, concept, principle, and procedure. Thus, all subject matter would exist in at least two worlds:

☐ The 'real' world.
☐ A 'subject-matter' world, possibly describing the entailment structure, references and test/simulation parameters. The labelling would be automatically executed by the system.

A primitive classification algorithm is shown in Figure 5. Information is presented to BRIT by teachers or other information providers thus:

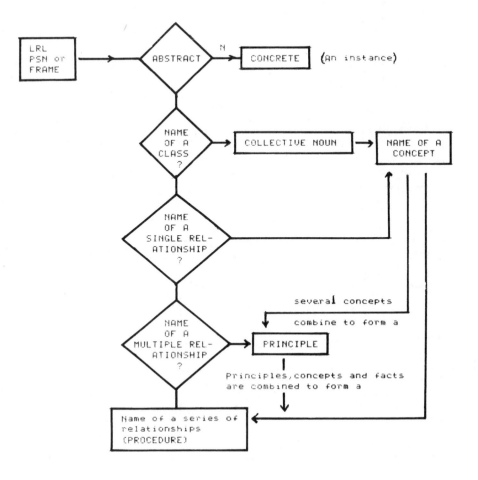

Figure 5. *A subject-matter classification algorithm*

☐ In the form of statements made in natural language, containing either information or domain-specific constraints (rules by which the items of information relate).
☐ In the form of texts, either typed or read by an optical character reader (OCR).
☐ In the form of addressable video-tape frames. These may be either sequential, to be projected 25 per second, or single, corresponding to slides.

MR CHIPS

MR CHIPS has five primary functions:

1. Student interface.
2. Information presentation.
3. Testing, both surface and deep, using problem, simulation, and game generators.

4. Administration.
5. Administering a pre-test.

MR CHIPS interfaces with the student as shown below.

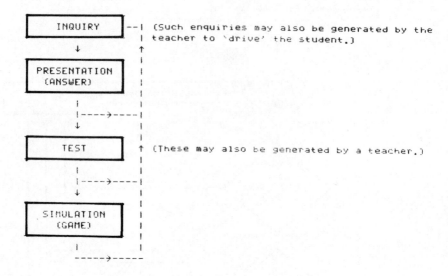

Figure 6. *A simple knowledge acquisition cycle*

This cycle makes partial use of the difference suggested by Marton (1975) between deep and surface processors on the one hand, and Romiszowski's (1980) distinction between knowledge and skills on the other. Thus, information is repeatedly elicited from BRIT, via MR CHIPS. This may only be surface processed by the student who may pass the subsequent test. However, such minimal processing would be shown up by the game or simulation which would be designed to test the student's skill.

Note that the behavioural cycles of 'presentation-test-feedback', and 'demonstrate-prompt-release', while possible on this model, are not necessarily used.

There will be four types of query:

1. Interrogative (WHAT, WHY, HOW . . .), and Interrogative plus GIVENS (WHAT IF . . .)
2. Imperative (FIND X)
3. Declarative (I WANT TO . . .)
4. Request for a pre-formed CAI sequence.

BRIT may only be queried through MR CHIPS. The queries may be in natural language. Each query is then parsed, and a key paragraph, containing a PSN structure corresponding to the query, is generated. This then generates a number of candidate paragraphs from the PSNs. MR CHIPS then consults TOM to find out:

☐ What constraints are to be imposed on the information (level of detail, user's intended use)?
☐ How much does the user know already?
☐ Will an instructional sequence need to be generated to bridge the gap between the user's current knowledge and the proposed answer? If so, a model of the entailment structure would be displayed on the video. Such a sequence would later be tested.

☐ What is the user's cognitive ability level? Will any guidance be necessary? (Merrill (1981) has classified these as Secondary Presentation Forms.)

This is then used as the criteria for the information format choice to be made by MR CHIPS.

The fact that the system would be student-query rather than courseware-based causes a change in focus at all stages. This is due to the need to define what Merrill has referred to as the three task levels:

REMEMBER
USE
FIND

Since with an inquiry-based system there is no way of determining the task level without depending on non-system inputs, a set of assumptions will have to be made:

1. Any information elicited from the system by the student must be REMEMBERed (presented and tested to at least the REMEMBER level).
2. Concepts, procedures and principles elicited from the system must also be presented at the USE level.
3. Those facts which must be learned at the USE level must be appropriately annotated by a teacher. (Such a classification may be required if part-task simulators, for example, are to be considered.)
4. Material to be presented at the FIND level must also be appropriately annotated by a teacher.

Clearly, such assumptions require considerable teacher intervention in some subject-matter areas, but this could, it is to be hoped, be simplified by providing teachers with some form of global edit tool to assign the classification *en masse*, depending on course requirements.

Information presentation. A considerable body of knowledge concerning presentation and sequencing has been developed (Hartley, 1972; Merrill, 1981), and it would not be impossible, for example, to program Merrill's prescriptions for primary and secondary presentation forms using a subject-matter-based criterion. However, as Lawless (1979) has observed, different students will need different degrees of help, depending on their own cognitive processing abilities. Landa (1979) and Sleeman (1981) have suggested approaches but this is an area still requiring much research before the definition of a student's cognitive processing ability achieves the same prescriptive elegance of Merrill's CDT, and before specific 'processing defects' can be matched by remedial prescriptions.

Help. While the system may be 'teacher-driven' by inserting a series of tests to be administered by MR CHIPS, the onus is generally on the student to make his or her own inquiries. Thus, those students unaccustomed to the rigour of self-directed study, may well feel as lost as those students 'coming up for air' during long SI sessions.

To avoid this, MR CHIPS would, like any good tutor, periodically discuss the student's short- and long-term study goals with him, aided by a battery of teacher-devised curricula. Such a discussion will, it is to be hoped, be echoed and amplified by the student's human tutor. Thus, rather than proceeding blindly, the student will be able to progress at his or her own pace through the knowledge network, using a series of intellectual stepping stones.

The acceptance of such goals by the student could greatly aid MR CHIPS in defining the testing and presentation methods, as well as helping to qualify the task level, since it would give the system a clearer view of the student's objectives.

In addition, MR CHIPS could provide DID-YOU-KNOW-THAT . . . prompts when he can see from the knowledge representations in BRIT and TOM that an important connection is in danger of being missed. This might obviate the need to decide the EGRULE-RULEG mix in subject-matter presentation.

Analogies. Apart from the secondary presentation forms it would be possible for students to ask for an analogy, or have it presented automatically (depending on their performance). Such a provision would be based on Winston's (1980) model. In limited subject-matter systems this would employ an analogy bank consisting of teacher-inserted situations which were felt to be of potential use. Other analogies could be obtained from students when testing at the FIND level. Such analogies would have to be sufficiently commonplace for them to be considered a natural part of a student's experience.

Broader subject-matter systems could additionally refer to the subject matter represented in TOM as a source of analogies.

Drill. A drill facility would be incorporated for fact and concept items using a demonstrate-prompt-release cycle. A paired-associated learning system has been described by Laubsch and Chiang (1973) and could also be incorporated.

Interface with TOM. All presented items would be echoed by TOM in the student's knowledge network, as being initially in a U (unlearned) state.

Testing. Testing would be based on:

☐ The three-level model of the subject matter contained in TOM: unlearned (U), transitional (T), and learned (L).
☐ Three task levels: REMEMBER, USE and FIND.
☐ A test production matrix with the following axes: (i) task level; (ii) subject matter; (iii) conditions; (iv) behaviour; (v) criteria.
☐ The rules of the subject matter domain.

Testing would occur in two phases:

1. *Operational,* which would include the REMEMBER and USE task levels.
2. *Mastery,* which would include the USE and FIND levels.

The operational testing phase would be triggered after the student had asked a set number of questions of MR CHIPS, probably five. This could be increased to nine for high-ability students. The choice of five to nine is based on Miller's (1956) observation that we can hold seven, plus or minus two concepts in short-term memory at any one time. This phase would test all appropriate items at the USE level, with the exception of those items requiring testing at the REMEMBER level only, such as some paired associates.

Test structure. There are two possible approaches:

1. To build a series of content/task-related test generators, using entailment and query items as input, and based on a three-dimensional matrix with the following axes: (i) material: FACT, CONCEPT, PROCEDURE, PRINCIPLE; (ii) task level: REMEMBER and USE; (iii) test environment: CONDITIONS, BEHAVIOUR and CRITERIA. An algebraic problem generator has been described by Gilkey and Koffman (1973).
2. To build specific test items into BRIT for subsequent access during the test phase.

Feedback. Failure (performance by the student at < 90 per cent) of any test requires that the item be represented, together with details of why the student's answer was wrong or insufficient.

Interface with TOM. Those items on which the student had achieved a > 90 per cent result would be forwarded to TOM to be included in the representation of the student's knowledge at the T (transitional) level if they were other than facts, or else at the L (learned) level.

The mastery testing phase would occur when the student had acquired a knowledge of a sufficient number of items to be taught at the USE and FIND levels for MR CHIPS to construct a simulation or game. This phase could, like the operational phase, use either system-based simulator/game generators, or a series of teacher-supplied simulations/games.

A generator would in effect be another expert system, depending on both simulation/game logic and the logic of the test input material. However, the instructional value of such a facility dictates that it be used in two sub-phases:

Phase 2a would allow the student to restart the game/simulation from any point and interrogate MR CHIPS to discover the source of his error(s). This phase can be repeated *ad infinitum*, and would be designed to present the material at the USE AND FIND levels, rather than as tests.

Phase 2b, while it could be called at any time by the student, would not, however, allow an exit until MR CHIPS had decided that the student had passed or failed. If the student failed, he could continue to repeat phase 2a.

Interface with TOM. The items tested and proved during phase 2b are then passed to TOM as L (learned).

Administration. This would provide a diary, memo and bulletin-board facility to the student. It would interface both with ADMIN and RESOURCE ALLOCATION (see Figure 3). An essential function would be to decide both re-test intervals and strategies, in order to qualify the demonstrate-prompt-release function. It would also have the responsibility of deciding the RULEG-EGRULE mix for item presentation.

The administration would also handle the updating of TOM for those areas where he had been assessed by a teacher rather than MR CHIPS, particularly for any items for which no simulation or game was provided.

MR CHIPS could also advise teachers which areas remained untested by phase 2b. He could also advise students of their weaknesses both in terms of subject matter and cognitive processing with respect to both upcoming tests and the psychological model contained in TOM. By consulting BRIT he could suggest non-system-based resources to use, such as books. Such knowledge could then be tested for at the REMEMBER and USE levels. MR CHIPS would also be responsible for providing DP facilities.

Pre-test administration. This would be used both to derive the basis of TOM and as an indication that the student had the ability to profit from the system. The pre-test would cover:

- ☐ System use, including some aspects of inquiry-based learning.
- ☐ All the analogies in the analogy bank, in the event that the subject matter contained in BRIT is too narrow to support an analogy generator.
- ☐ Tests for psychomotor skills, particularly keyboard skills, in order to be able to weight student response time for tests accordingly.
- ☐ The necessary pre-knowledge for undertaking the courses which the system supports.

TOM

TOM is the data-base containing details of each student. These come under three headings: administrative details, acquired knowledge representation, and psychological model. TOM is to be used by both MR CHIPS and human teachers as a model of each student.

Administrative details. These would cover:

- ☐ Personal and medical history.
- ☐ Exit qualification(s).

☐ Foreseen course(s).
☐ General objectives —acquired from conversations with both MR CHIPS and human tutors.

Acquired knowledge representation. This would be a copy of those parts of BRIT which the student had queried. Each item would be represented as unlearned, transitional, or learned. (Clearly all the items in BRIT will be technically unlearned but only those queried will be transferred to TOM as unlearned.) Note that no test scores are involved, since scores on any test of less than 90 per cent are considered as fails.

Psychological model. This would probably consist of several models covering the cognitive, affective and psychomotor domains. These would be derived from a constant analysis of the acquired knowledge representation, possibly using a Petri-net, to determine:

☐ Speed of response.
☐ The order in which the knowledge is acquired.
☐ The relationship between knowledge acquisition patterns.
☐ Grammatical and logical errors.

A very simple example shows how such an analysis might work:

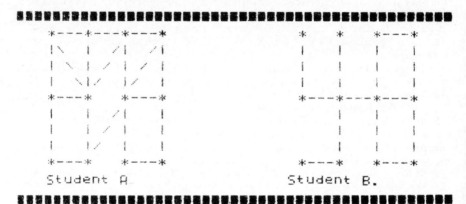

Figure 7. *Student knowledge representations*

Here we are assuming that the underlying knowledge is the same. Student A clearly has more connections between items than student B. If, as Lawless (1979) observes, knowledge is about making connections, then, clearly, A knows more than B.

This psychological model might be weighted by the incorporation of an 'ideal student' model with which MR CHIPS could make comparisons.

Warnings

This is not an attempt to re-invent the wheel, but rather to assemble existing wheels, chassis, motor and controls. In doing so it is believed that four kinds of problems will be encountered:

1. *Already-solved problems,* such as the design of the operating system, compilers, debuggers, and utilities, where sufficient experience is already available to remove the problem from the theoretical to the implementational plane.
2. *Partially-solved problems,* such as the design of the operator interface,

internal languages, data-base structure and teaching strategy rule acquisition, where several experiments have already been sufficiently successful to render the problem malleable.

3. *Foreseen problems*, such as the design of the psychological model of both the real and ideal student, on which some work has already been done but which remains a major theoretical area.

4. *Unforeseen problems*, which may not be appreciated until the design or implementation stages.

Some foreseen problems are:

1. This system to a large extent replicates current teaching practice, but on a one-to-one basis. Maybe we need to think past that in the same way that office automation workers needed to think past a mere automation of traditional office practices.

2. Reflective learning seems to have no place in this system.

3. Maybe TOM should have a personal construct facility added to amplify the WHAT IF . . . ? requirements.

4. MR CHIPS should also be able to analyse a student's essay for logic and construction. But how can he distinguish between 'creative reasoning' and a mere regurgitation of existing facts? (Possible answer: creative reasoning will require the generation of new PSNs for logical analysis; regurgitation should not.)

5. Congruence between the system and the student's objectives is assumed because the student decides what subject matter to inquire about, and MR CHIPS adjusts the secondary presentation forms to allow for differing cognitive abilities. However, this is only an assumption.

6. The subject-matter classification seems limited. It does not, for example, distinguish between teleological and causative relationships. This does not, however, invalidate the classification as a starting point.

By-Products

The system could be used to model learning theories. It could also be adapted to such uses as modelling and gaming, and systems definition methodology.

References

Bird, C (1980) The structure of educational technology courses for student teachers. In Winterburn, R and Evans, L F (eds) *Aspects of Educational Technology* **XIV**. Kogan Page, London.

Gilkey, T J and Koffman, E B (1973) Generative CAI in high school algebra. In Guenther *et al* (eds) *International Computing Symposium*. North Holland.

Hartley, J (1972) *Strategies for Programmed Instruction: An Educational Technology*. Butterworths, London.

Landa, L (1979) Psychological troubleshooting diagnostics as a basis for deeper adaptive instruction. In Page, G T and Whitlock, Q (eds) *Aspects of Educational Technology* **XIII** Kogan Page, London.

Laubsch, J H and Chiang, A (1973) The application of mathematical models of learning in the decision structures of adaptive computer-aided instructional systems. In Guenther *et al* (eds) *International Computing Symposium*. North Holland.

Lawless, C J (1979) Information processing. A model for educational technology. In Page, G T and Whitlock, Q (eds) *Aspects of Educational Technology* **XIII**. Kogan Page, London.

Marton, F (1975) What does it take to learn? In Entwistle, N and Hounsell, D (eds) *How Do Students Learn?* Institute for Research and Development in Post-Compulsory Education. University of Lancaster.

Merrill, M D (1981) Component display theory. In Reigeluth, C M (ed) *Instructional Design Theory*.

Miller, G A (1956) The magical number 7 plus or minus 2: some limits to our capacity for processing information. *Psychological Review*, 63.

Minsky, M (1975) A framework for representing knowledge. In Winston, P H (ed) *The Psychology of Computer Vision*. McGraw-Hill, Maidenhead.

Mitchell, P D (1981) The representation of knowledge in CAL courseware. In Smith, P R *Computer Assisted Learning*. Pergamon, London.

Romiszowski, A J (1980) A new look at the analysis of knowledge and skills. In Winterburn, R and Evans, L F (eds) *Aspects of Educational Technology* **XIV**. Kogan Page, London.

Sleeman, D H (1981) Assessing aspects of competence in basic algebra. In Sleeman, D H and Brown, J S *Intelligent Teaching Systems*. Academic Press, London.

Winston, P H (1980) Learning and reasoning by analogy *Journal of the Association for Computing Machinery*.

4.4 A Workplan to Test the Educational Opportunities for Using Small Computers in Secondary Schools

R M Bottino, P Forcheri and M T Molfino
Instituto per la Matematica Applicata del CNR. Genova, Italy

Abstract: The article describes the main features of a project, the aim of which is essentially to test the educational opportunities suggested by the use of computers in upper secondary schools in Italy.

The project is one of the activities of a group (supported by the National Council for Research) of university and secondary school mathematics teachers of Genova.

The curricula and the organization of upper secondary schools in Italy do not answer to our present cultural and professional needs. Therefore, the aim of the group is to project and to experiment with new topics and educational technologies more closely linked to our social context. In particular, we think that it is important to develop, at an elementary school level, the essential concepts of the use of computers. Our purpose is to teach using these new technologies. In this paper the reasons for this choice, as well as the specified aims of our work, are discussed.

Methodologically, the work is organized in the following way: (i) the production of outlines for teachers, about specific topics we wanted to introduce in the classes (with technical, didactic and bibliographical indication); (ii) the discussion and correction, in collaboration with the teachers, of these proposals; (iii) the drawing up of exercises for students, centred on topics on which future professional subjects will be based (for example, financial mathematics, economics, statistics, etc) — our idea is to avoid formal exercises with no real content; (iv) the testing of the material in the classes; and (v) the collection and dissemination of the results.

In this article we will show, as an example, an outline of one of the first subjects we have dealt with: the introduction and use of pocket calculators. After having discussed the general concepts relating to the structure of a computer and the composition of a program, and using pocket calculators to solve simple problems, more sophisticated technologies and high-level languages are considered.

Introduction

This article describes the main features of a project aimed at testing the educational opportunities suggested by the use of computers in upper secondary schools.

The project is one of the activities of a group of university and secondary school teachers working in Genova, Italy, supported by the National Council for Research. The curricula and organization of upper secondary schools in Italy do not answer very well to our present cultural and professional needs. The group's aim is to plan and experiment with more 'relevant' topics and educational technologies. We think that it is extremely important to introduce the essential concepts of the use of computers early on to students. Most people still do not consider it necessary to incorporate computer studies in secondary school curricula. The issue is, however, attracting a great deal of attention. Almost every student now owns a pocket calculator, and undoubtedly micro and personal computers will gain increasing importance in the scholastic world.

The problem is to use this new technology in the most efficient and didactic way possible. First, the fundamentals must be learned. It is precisely in terms of these fundamentals, regardless of the type of language or machine used, that we have developed our experiments which were conducted in the first two-year courses (ages 14 to 16) of some of the professional and commercial secondary schools in Genova.

The experiments have been developed for mathematics courses, but our intention has been to deal with various issues, using examples and applications closely connected to the professional curricula which the students will confront later in their studies (ie business mathematics, economics, statistics, etc). Our purpose is to teach with the aid of this new technology.

Initial Aims

We have chosen to start by using pocket calculators. First the non-programmable types since these are what most of the students own, and then the programmable types, thereby using simple instruments with which the students are already relatively familiar. Although the low cost of these instruments makes it possible for almost any school to acquire them, our group bought a number of HP-33E pocket programmable calculators so that they would be available for use in the event of bureaucratic or school budget problems.

Before starting work with the students, we organized a series of seminars devoted to familiarizing teachers with these instruments, indicating both possibilities and limits. The problem of the teacher's own background is undoubtedly one of the basic difficulties in any attempt to revise teaching procedures.

The pocket programmable calculators can be introduced with relatively little difficulty, especially when one considers the problems, both physical and psychological, of using a big machine.

Motivations and Aims of Classroom Work

This year, the experiment will last for four months after the students' pocket calculators have been used. Reverse Polish Notation and eventually basic programming procedures will be introduced.

Many teachers have observed that students do not know how to use their own pocket calculators correctly. They often do not understand the use of memories, particularly arithmetical ones, and often, even when performing long computations, usually for studying business problems, they have noted the intermediary results but have not checked their answers. The idea, therefore, was to teach them to understand their own machines, which, even if elementary, would be useful in introducing some problems connected to the use of calculating instruments, for example approximate calculations, significant figures, evaluating results, use of memory, etc.

The pocket calculator provides a starting point for reflections on the connections between operations and the use of parenthesis, subjects which are included in the first two-year curriculum which is almost the same in any school in Italy, which are treated very formally and are therefore usually not assimilated very well by students. The later use of Reverse Polish Notation constitutes an excellent review of previous subjects studied.

The intention is to avoid formal exercises as much as possible, attempting instead to give an idea of methods and problems which are common to computer science, for example algorithms, the top-down approach, etc. We have used the search for the root of a positive number to introduce the concept of algorithms, and therefore programming. Later, this algorithm will be improved with the use of conditional tests and considerations of numerical characters.

Some of the problems which are specifically mathematical are: the tabulating of a function (at a fixed and later variable rate), equation solving, the search for the greatest common divisor of two integers, Euclidean algorithm division, etc. Other problems are based on more 'relevant' issues: taking care of a statement of account, computing income tax, etc. The pocket calculator was always used in connection with other material, such as graph paper, tables, etc.

Understanding how to program a pocket calculator can help the understanding of larger machines, when more involved languages are introduced. In some technical institutes, computer science courses are offered. However, the subject is usually treated theoretically because of the lack of competent personnel and hardware. Using the pocket programmable calculators from the beginning of the two-year courses may make it easier to approach this material, since it clarifies the general concepts of computer science such as keyboard, display and memory, programming (sequential elaborations, jumps, cycles, etc).

Work Methods

Our group has been experimenting in various upper secondary school mathematics courses since 1975. Until now our method consisted of designing work sheets for the students in which new subjects were broken down into exercises, descriptive illustrations, etc. The students completed each sheet, consulting the teacher when they ran into difficulty. Even though this method offers the advantages of homogeneous experiences in the classroom, detailed instruction for the teachers, and the possibility to control what is learned, it did not give good results. The work sheets were considered too rigid, the teachers had trouble adapting them to the students' individual needs, and, above all, it was difficult to design them for use in different types of schools with different curriculum needs. This year, we have tried to modify our experiments bearing these problems in mind. The very nature of the pocket calculators makes it impossible to produce standard material for all students. Implementing and checking a program is an activity which stimulates autonomous work.

Therefore we have designed work outlines, which the teacher can adapt to the specific needs of each class. In every outline, the subject is explained indicating the minimum contents which should be discussed. A series of collateral themes is also presented which the teacher can go into more or less in depth, depending on student interest and time. We have provided exercises and have summarized sheets for the students, complementary readings, questionnaires and bibliographical information (see Table 1). The teacher can choose from among this material, or use something similar.

These work outlines are always thoroughly discussed and modified by the teachers before they present them in the classroom. All the results of these experiments are collected, so they can be distributed to a wider number of teachers.

Conclusion

Our method has yielded encouraging results. The teachers feel freer to organize the work, and are helped by the ample support material. Furthermore, the pocket calculator has proved to be of great interest to most teachers because of its wide diffusion and subsequent student interest.

There are still many questions regarding the teaching of computer science, even at the pocket calculator level, in the Italian school system. Some people think that these machines encourage mental laziness and prevent students learning basic arithmetical concepts.

Our experiments have indicated the contrary. We have found that the pocket calculator stimulates activity, creativity and the overall capacity of students to learn mathematical concepts. A single example will clarify this: how many students (or teachers) remember the Euclidean division algorithm usually learned in primary school? By writing a simple program, students are able to understand every single

---

OUTLINE FOR POCKET CALCULATOR

A —   Work Outline

Minimum contents	Additional contents
Operational hierarchy	Comparing the displayed figures to introduce approximation theory
Formula manipulation	
	Usual and exponential notations
Use and knowledge of memory formulas	Different numbering system
SOA and RPN notations	

B —   Materials

B1 — To be used directly with the students

Informative questionnaire, concerning students' knowledge of the pocket calculators.

Guided exercises, enabling students to understand the different characteristics of the most commonly-found pocket calculators, including their formalizing and computation exercises, which are devoted to economics or business study, and summarized sheets concerning algebraic and RPN notation systems and work sheets introducing the approximation theory.

B2 — Autonomous work to be guided by the teacher

Students should write a manual for using their own machines. This means that students learn to express themselves correctly and concisely, and learn to explain different computing procedures in detail. Furthermore, the teacher does not have to give general, usually uninteresting, initial explanations to the students.

Finally, once the student's (or group of students') work has been completed and corrected, a technical summary can be distributed.

Table 1. *The use of the students' calculators*

step, and realize the need for all the conditions of the equation. They move from abstract formulation to concrete procedure.

If the pocket calculator is used with attention, to stimulate not only the curiosity of the student but also his or her capacity to investigate, ask questions and look for answers, it can contribute to the development of important qualities such as autonomy and critical judgement.

References

Bottino, R M (1981) Didattica della matematica supportata da calcolatori tascabili programmabili: un esempio tratto da un ciclo di seminari per insegnanti della scuola secondaria superiore. In *Proceedings of AICA Annual Conference,* 3, p 1241.

Cortini, G and Fasano Petroni, M (1980) *Fisica e matematica con il calcolatore tascabile.* Loescher, Torino.

Erschov, A P (1981) Programming, the second literacy. In Lewis, R and Tagg, E D (eds) *Computers in Education, preprints of WCCE 81.* North-Holland, Lausanne.

Geymonat, G (1981) Possibilità d'uso dell'elaboratore nell'insegnamento delle scienze. In *Proceedings of AICA Annual Conference*, 3, p 1213.

Green, D R and Lewis, J (1978) *Science with Pocket Calculators.* Wykeham Publications Ltd, London.

Henrici, P (1977) *Computational Analysis with the HP-25 Pocket Calculator.* Wiley and Sons, New York.

4.5 The Efficiency of COMAL-Structured BASIC

R Atherton
Bulmershe College of Higher Education

Abstract: This paper discusses the effects of introducing COMAL-structured BASIC into secondary schools, and instances developments and evaluation comments from a user group.

'The most effective way to ensure the value of the future is to confront the present courageously and constructively.'   *Rollo May*

Background

There is a display, in the foyer of a Berkshire school, which shows the four generations of computers symbolized by four hardware items. But the other half of a computer system is its software and this has evolved too. We can show the same kind of progress with rough dates.

Period	*Hardware*	*Software examples*
1950-1960	Glass valves	Machine codes, assemblers
1960-1970	Transistors	COBOL, FORTRAN, BASIC, ALGOL
Early 1970s	Primitive chips	PASCAL
Late 1970s	Microprocessors	COMAL, structured BASIC, user-friendly operating systems

Many of the early UK users of BASIC appreciated its virtues: easy syntax, short vocabulary, clear notation, easy operating environment. It was a revolution in software as important as the parallel move to transistors. Computer education could not get far with ALGOL or FORTRAN, which were too difficult. Only when BASIC appeared did the possibility of a big development occur. But something was wrong. Here are some quotes:

'The desire for a new language for the purpose of teaching programming is due to my dissatisfaction with the presently used major languages whose features and constructs too often cannot be explained logically and convincingly and which too often defy systematic reasoning. Along with this dissatisfaction goes my conviction that the language in which the student is taught to express his ideas, profoundly influences his habits of thought and invention, and that the disorder governing these languages directly imposes itself onto the programming style of the students.'

Niklaus Wirth, 1973 Pascal Manual

'Modern languages like PASCAL and COMAL are like good English prose beside which BASIC is like a series of primitive grunts.'

Views of Hull University Lecturers, 1981, reported in New Scientist, *October*

'BASIC is an educational and intellectual disaster.'

John Laski, 1981, Times Educational Supplement, *November*

'In view of the future importance of computer literacy to the UK it would be nothing less than a national tragedy if thousands upon thousands of eager minds were introduced to the technology of the 1980s through the modes of thought of the 1960s. It is not too late to reconsider: we urge you to reassess your software policy.'

Letter to BBC, 1981, from 11 lecturers at the Polytechnic of North London, November

'It is practically impossible to teach good programming to students that had a prior exposure to BASIC . . . they are mentally mutilated beyond hope of regeneration.'
Edsger Dijkstra, 1981, Computer World, *November*

Despite comments like these, from intelligent, well-informed people, BASIC has become one of the most widely used languages in the world. Data are hard to gather but UK school examination statistics are one source. The statistics for computer studies took a big jump in 1981. A rough table shows how O level is moving on very quickly.

Computer studies			
Year	CSE	GCE(O)	GCE(A)	Total including CEE and GCE(AO)
1976	13,000	3,000	1,500	18,000
1977	15,000	6,000	1,750	23,000
1978	15,500	8,500	1,750	26,500
1979	16,000	11,500	2,300	31,500
1980	18,000	15,000	2,800	37,500
1981	23,500	22,500	4,000	52,500

It is very difficult to assess how much there is in the way of computer-assisted learning, computer-managed learning, computer awareness and school administration, but in the field of computer studies alone, 52,000 children have learned BASIC, and that implies a four-figure number of teachers.

Can it be that thousands of children and teachers have been 'mentally mutilated beyond hope of regeneration'? I picture a 19-year-old woman, now a first-year student. She will probably become a conscientious and competent teacher, but just now she is slightly bewildered — like someone whose two-finger typewriting experience is getting in the way of learning correct touch-typing, or somebody who has become expert at Roman numerical arithmetic wondering why she should learn the new-fangled Hindu-arabic system. Redemption is possible but it is not easy.

BASIC is a quite extraordinary mixture of the very good and the very bad. Its virtues, simplicity and ease of use are tremendous for teaching non-specialists or beginners, but its deficiencies, exposed by the hard-won progress of the 1970s, are very serious indeed, like the girl in the rhyme who was,

'. . . very, very good,
But when she was bad she was horrid.'

The virtues of BASIC were and are recognized by Christensen, the inventor of COMAL. He decided not to abandon BASIC but to improve it. He specified the additional structures and called the result COMAL (Christensen, 1975). It is no coincidence that the American National Standards Institute has come to exactly the same conclusions. Their new standard for BASIC has all the COMAL structures, though, inevitably, the notation is a little different. The British Computer Society Schools Committee, the Open University and Dartmouth College, USA (where BASIC was invented in 1965) have all come to similar conclusions.

Staff and students at Bulmershe College have been testing and evaluating COMAL for six years, but it has only been available on their computers for two

years. In that time they have learned that COMAL is more than just a theoretically-
and educationally-sound language. It is very efficient in practice. It is also fun.

In Denmark teachers across the curriculum and across the age-range are in
control of computers. Because COMAL is, after initial familiarization, both easier
and more powerful than BASIC, the non-specialist teachers are able to control the
new learning medium. Their computer-assisted learning materials bear the stamp of
the subject teacher who can write good programs — not the computer specialist
who writes materials for others without a full understanding of their needs.

The clarity and control of COMAL, together with the very good direct access
files that go with it, take data processing and school administration from a
borderline possibility into a clear reality.

Control is perhaps the key word. Teachers should be in control of the computer
as they are in control of other learning resources. The best example, Denmark,
seems to indicate three factors which contribute to this. Their systems are: easy to
use; versatile and powerful; and easy to program. By comparison, most of the
machines in the UK fail to match these criteria in varying degrees. Enormous
energy, money and time is spent on technical problems to do with operating and
transferring software.

It is not difficult to pinpoint the causes of the trouble, nor is it difficult to
propose solutions, though, of course, actual progress in classrooms is not so easy.

Public enemy number one is the GOTO statement. Computers do useful work by
executing stored instructions in sequential memory locations in the machine.

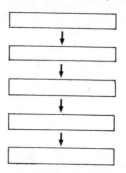

But it turns out that programmers need to interface with this natural sequential
operation in three main ways.

1. *Repetition* (repeat certain instructions)

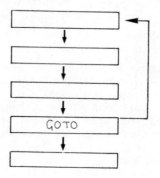

2. *Decisions* (omit certain instructions)

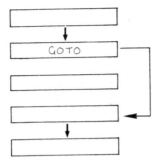

3. *Modularity* (execute a specific block of code and then continue)

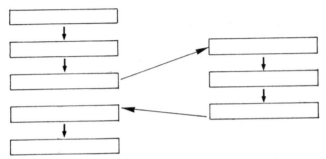

At the level of the machine these processes are achieved by writing something like:

GOTO (an instruction in a certain location)

A high-level or user-oriented computer language is an attempt to help the user to write his instructions in a more natural way and the quality of this help has improved steadily for about three decades. Further, it has been shown that these three concepts (repetition, decisions and modularity) are sufficient to enable almost all problems to be neatly analysed and coded into a program. Words have been embodied into languages so that the user may concentrate on the problem, not the internal workings of a machine. Thus he may use normal words like REPEAT, UNTIL, OR in fairly natural ways such as:

REPEAT (get a record from a file)
UNTIL (the desired record is found)
OR (end of file)

Internally this would cause the equivalent of GOTO statements but the user need not, and should not, think about that. The system will translate what he writes. Rather, he should learn about the different types of repetition, decision-making and modularity so that he can learn to break any problem down into such elements, establish the right relationships between them and to produce neat, readable program designs and similar programs.

Good software like COMAL, with reasonable file-handling capability and a high standard of user-friendliness, implies a disc-based system with about 48K-64K of main memory. Smaller systems can only support the more primitive types of software but manufacturers and, regrettably, many educationists seem to work down to a price rather than up to a standard. For this reason there has been a flood of machines with marginally viable hardware, and software which owes more to the 1960s than to the last quarter of the twentieth century. But there is another reason why the computer education spending spree of the late 1970s gives some cause for concern.

In economics there is a saying that bad money drives out good. It would certainly be true to say that bad computers can force good ones, not only out of the classrooms, but even out of the market. The mere existence of a computer at £60 or £600 will make it difficult for a school to get at a price which might imply a reasonable specification. And if an area (or a nation) standardizes by political or financial pressure on one machine, it becomes difficult for a school to acquire anything different, whether it is better or not.

Despite these problems a small group of schools in Berkshire managed to acquire machines at the beginning of the academic year 1981/82, with the following specification.

    64K main memory
    Single mini-disc drive
    Keyboard
    25 line x 80-column screen
    Built-in interfaces for printers, etc
    COMAL with direct access files

After one term a report was prepared for the Berkshire Computer Education Working Party, and relevant details are given in Part 2 of this paper.

Evaluation of the RC Piccolo with COMAL

These notes have been agreed by the Piccolo Users' Group. The appendices give some details of activities or comments from individual schools.

Unified System

These notes do not emphasize the distinction between hardware and software. The Piccolo is a well-integrated system in which hardware and software have been designed to complement each other.

General Use

The system is very easy to use by all kinds of users because it starts itself and requires only three words initially (LOOKUP, LOAD, RUN). It accepts upper or lower case commands, only distinguishing where necessary, for example when accepting a program name or listing a program. There is no setting up to do. Discs or the printer may be used immediately.

Computer-Assisted Learning

There are about ten items ready for use in the fields of spelling, arithmetic, geography and physics. A start has been made in geography and the signs are hopeful. Non-specialists who have not reacted well to the 380Z are showing more interest.

The programs which come from Denmark are fairly easy to translate. Only the text needs to be changed. Standards are high because the material is written by non-specialists who can control the medium themselves. There should be a steady flow of material from Denmark and, later, from Holland, Ireland and the USA. Some material will be written in Berkshire and other UK areas, but it will take time (see Appendix II).

Computer Awareness

The simplicity of use makes the machine suitable for those wishing to use it as a medium for acquiring general familiarity.

Other Software

A CESIL system has been written by Kenneth Payne (Garth Hill School), following the general principles established by Microcesil and followed by Epcesil.

UCSD Pascal with assemblers, editors, utilities, etc is available at extra cost. This, along with UNIX, is rated by experts as one of the best small operating systems in the world. It is very suitable for advanced students.

CP/M is available and so far has been used with Wordstar, Datastar and Mailmerge word-processing programs.

Educational Advantages

The Student

(a) *Problem analysis and programming.* Students acquire a 'tool-kit' of about half-a-dozen constructs (three in the early stages). These are sufficient for the analysis and programming of virtually all problems. The acquisition of these concepts takes a little time, but thereafter the analysis, program design and coding take about half the time of the equivalent program in BASIC.

(b) *Debugging.* The emphasis moves from debugging to writing correct programs, but bugs which do occur are easy to spot because the programs are easy to read. Debugging takes a very small fraction of the time compared with BASIC.

Amendment or development of programs is easier for the same reasons as apply to debugging.

(c) *Entry of programs.* The entry of programs would take a little longer because long variable names are used, but the automatic provision of line numbers, automatic indenting and other seemingly small details more than compensate for this.

The line editor is very simple. The four 'arrow' keys enable instant use. One does not have to learn how to edit.

Syntax is checked as a line is entered and incorrect syntax is not accepted. This is particularly helpful for the less able.

The Teacher

(a) *All the above.* Teachers are also students and programmers and therefore all the above advantages apply.

(b) *Teaching schemes.* Because the principles of problem analysis and programming are clearly identified, teaching schemes can be better planned.

(c) *Discussion of algorithms.* Because COMAL is the simplest embodiment of the necessary concepts, it can be used as a framework for discussing problems and algorithms. It is, in fact, a very good program design language.

(d) *Classification of problems.* Problems can be classified according to: types of structure (repetition, decisions, procedures); depth of nesting; length of program. A points system is being tested.

(e) *Estimating attainment.* Attainment can be estimated on a more systematic basis. Weaknesses can be pinpointed more easily. There are fewer possible ways of solving a given problem, and wrong solutions are both less likely and more obvious when they occur.

(f) *Examination designs.* Examinations can be designed to test exactly what one wishes to test, and fundamental ideas can be emphasized because they are more explicitly recognized.

The School

(a) *Administration.* Administration packages can become a clear reality instead of a borderline possibility. This is because of the clarity and control of a COMAL program, the very good direct access files and the 80-column screen.

(b) *Transfer of software.* Software is easily portable between Piccolos because of the 'complete machine' concept. There is currently only one configuration and there need never be more than two or three.

   Packages or program designs are portable from a COMAL system to any other at the cost of coding and re-typing. A good program design is more easily portable than a bad program.

(c) *Non-specialized use.* An easy system encourages the spread across the curriculum and across the age-range. The Piccolo can be used by almost anybody.

Graeme Horton	Bulmershe School
Kenneth Payne	Garth Hill School
Helen Rixon	Kendrick School
Roy Atherton	Bulmershe College
Steve Hitchman	Little Heath School
Roger Loveys	Highdown School
Pat Dodds	Highdown School

Appendix 1

Piccolo Comments — Little Heath School

Uses: school files for form and set lists, computer studies teaching, teaching teachers programming. CAL is still based on the 38OZ machine.

Organization: small room off a main teaching classroom. Moved from one room to the other on a trolley. Pupils are rationed and have to sign a booking sheet.

Teaching programming: much easier than the 38OZ — a more user-friendly system. Need for a CESIL type of language.

CAL production: nothing as yet but will emerge in time. No one has the time to create the programs and there is still a lot of resistance on the part of teachers.

Data processing: school files system. The files system on disc is very easy to use and explain, and this is one of the strong points of the machine. For less able pupils the ideas of updating files, deletion, etc can be introduced through using procedures.

Use by non-specialists: everyone who meets the machine likes it — it is very attractive. This has increased the use by, and interest in, the computer throughout the school. Teachers have asked for a programming course.

Intensity of use: used throughout the day from 8.50 am to 6.00 pm.

These notes were prepared on the WORDPRO programme from Highdown School. The user found no problems with the program and it actually saved time.

Appendix 2

Programs written at Highdown School in First Term 1981/82

WORDPRO: very simple word-processor. Uses screen as sketch pad. Graphics/ non graphics and printer OP.

MARKSRT: cumulative large-scale mark grading and sorting.

EXENT: lists and sorts up to 300 exam entries. All entries held for each candidate in abbreviated form. PAPENT decodes and assigns exam numbers.

GRADE: uses data from EXENT plus results to tabulate and analyse exam results ($<$ 200 pupils).

CAVES: adventure game.

SIXTH: data manipulation — set lists, tutor lists, etc.

ADD: random remedial arithmetic testing competition.

GEOGRL: population changes — birth/death rates.

GEOGRLI: population pyramids forecasting (ref S C DEMOG).

GRIDPD2: produces random word-search from given words (and solutions).

TIMETAB: parents' evening timetabling.

References
Atherton, R (1982) *Structured Programming with COMAL*. Ellis Horwood.
Christensen, B R (1975) The programming language COMOL (Denmark). *International World of Computer Education.*

Section 5:
Methodologies

5.1 A Methodology for Identification of Generic Leadership Skills

Jeanne M Hebein
Human Resources Research Organization

Abstract: The present study outlines a methodology for the identification of skills required in the performance of four levels of leadership and supervisory functions. The objective of the research is to identify those non-technical skills common to the four leadership positions, and those skills that differ between levels. As a result, the set of generic skills underlying supervision/leadership performance can be identified.

Identification of such a set of generic leadership skills would be invaluable in the development of evaluation instruments to determine the effectiveness of existing leadership training, to identify individual skill areas requiring further training, and to evaluate leader effectiveness and leadership potential.

Introduction

It is difficult to describe any job and to discover what behaviours or skills are required for job performance. This is especially true for supervisory or leadership positions since performance requirements vary greatly from one setting to another based on the types of actions involved, the individuals initiating the actions, and the specific situations in which the actions occur.

Traditional analysis procedures are useful in identifying and describing technical job-related tasks and skills. However, these methods are not adequate when identifying the non-technical skills associated with leadership and supervision. Too frequently these skills have been avoided because of the difficulty encountered in analysing them, and only the technical tasks and skills performed by supervisors have been identified (Hebein, 1982).

This paper focuses on the development of a methodology for identifying the set of generic skills that underlie successful supervision/leadership performance of non-commissioned officers (NCOs) in the United States Army. The objective of the research conducted was to identify those non-technical skills required by personnel at four different supervisory levels within the NCO Corps. It was then determined which skills are common across the four levels of NCOs and which skills differ between levels.

Identification of Non-Technical Skills

The steps involved in the identification of these non-technical skills included:

1. The derivation of lists of non-technical tasks performed at each of the four supervisory levels.
2. The clustering of these tasks into a relatively small number of measures or job dimensions.
3. The identification of the specific skills required for performance of each of the job dimensions.
4. Determination of the generic skills required for performing all levels of leadership.

Generation of Task Lists

The initial step in the identification of the non-teaching skills required of NCOs in successfully performing their leadership duties was the generation of lists of the specific leadership tasks of non-commissioned officers occupying the positions of First Sergeant, Platoon Sergeant, Section Chief, and Squad Leader.

The lists for the four leadership positions were based on a First Sergeants' task list prepared by the Sergeants Major Academy, Fort Bliss, Texas, in an effort to identify the common tasks associated with the duty position of First Sergeant (US Sergeants Major Academy, 1979). The tasks associated with the other duty positions were derived from the First Sergeants' task list by revising the task statements to fit the appropriate duty positions, by deleting those tasks that did not apply, and by adding tasks specific to a given position.

The process of translating the First Sergeants' tasks into work statements describing the tasks of the other duty positions was accomplished in three phases (Sharon and Kaplan, 1982).

(a) The original translation of the First Sergeant's task list was accomplished with the assistance of experts on the NCO duty positions being studied. As a result, three additional task lists were developed, one for each of the duty positions of Platoon Sergeant, Section Chief, and Squad Leader.

(b) The tentative lists were then given to eight job incumbents (two subjects per duty position) to identify those tasks which were, in fact, the non-technical tasks performed by them in their jobs. All proposed changes were discussed with the subjects at great length to clarify the meaning and phrasing of the task statements. The lists were then revised and prepared for the final step in the process.

(c) Two groups of NCOs familiar with the specified duty positions and the task requirements of those positions were asked to review the tentative lists and make any additional changes. The two groups consisted of 16 instructors from the NCO academies located in West Germany and six members of the Sergeant Morales Club, an honorary club of individuals who are recognized for their superior performance as NCOs. An equal number of subjects per duty position was maintained. Members of the research staff met with the two groups and in extensive interviews discussed suggested revisions with them in an effort to reach agreement on the task statements, their accuracy, and their applicability to the duty positions being studied.

As a result of the information gathered in these three steps, task lists were developed for the four leadership positions. An example of the types of task statements derived for each of the duty positions appears in Figure 1. The four lists of tasks are presented in a format which allows for comparison of the lists and for identification of the changes that were made from the First Sergeant's list for each of the other positions.

Validation of Task Lists

Following development of the task lists, a survey was developed for each leadership position containing the specific tasks performed by personnel in that position. The surveys were administered to a minimum of 100 subjects per duty position or a minimum of 400 total subjects. The survey required the respondents to indicate the frequency of performance for each task; the importance of each task to overall job performance; the difficulty of the task for job incumbents and for those new to the job; and the consequences of not performing a task or of performing it inadequately (see Figure 2).

DUTY POSITIONS

LEADER TASKS

FIRST SERGEANT	PLATOON SERGEANT	SECTION CHIEF	SQUAD LEADER
PREPARE AND MAINTAIN DUTY ROSTER	MONITOR UNIT DUTY ROSTER FOR PLATOON	MONITOR UNIT DUTY ROSTER FOR SECTION	MONITOR UNIT DUTY ROSTER FOR SQUAD
INITIATE ADMINISTRATIVE ACTION ON AWOL SOLDIERS	REPORT AWOL SOLDIERS	REPORT AWOL SOLDIERS	REPORT AWOL SOLDIERS
MONITOR RATION RECORDS AND REPORTS	NA	NA	NA
IMPLEMENT TRAINING TO CORRECT INDIVIDUAL/UNIT DEFICIENCIES	IMPLEMENT/CONDUCT TRAINING TO CORRECT INDIVIDUAL DEFICIENCIES IN PLATOON	IMPLEMENT/CONDUCT TRAINING TO CORRECT INDIVIDUAL DEFICIENCIES IN SECTION	IMPLEMENT/CONDUCT TRAINING TO CORRECT INDIVIDUAL/SQUAD DEFICIENCIES

Figure 1. *Example from NCO leader task lists*

FIRST SERGEANT TASKS

TASK STATEMENT	How often do you perform the task? 7—Several times a day 6—Almost every day 5—1 or 2 times a week 4—1 or 2 times a month 3—1 or 2 times every mos. 2—1 or 2 times a year 1—Do not perform	How important is the task to your over-all job performance? 7—Extremely important 6—Very important 5—Fairly important 4—Somewhat important 3—Not very important 2—Fairly unimportant 1—Not important at all	How difficult is the task for you? 7—Extremely difficult 6—Very difficult 5—Fairly difficult 4—Somewhat difficult 3—Not difficult 2—Fairly easy 1—Very easy	How difficult is the task for new 1SGs? 7—Extremely difficult 6—Very difficult 5—Fairly difficult 4—Somewhat difficult 3—Not difficult 2—Fairly easy 1—Very easy	How serious would it be to your unit if a task was not performed or was performed inadequately? 5—Very serious 4—Not very serious 3—Somewhat serious 2—Fairly serious 1—Very serious
1. Receive and route correspondence					
2. Provide training guidance to sub-ordinates					
3. Conduct physical security inspection					
4. Establish operat-ing posts					
5. Prepare enlisted personnel rating scheme					

Figure 2. *Example of a leadership task survey*

The results of the survey provided validation of the original task lists for each position with a larger population. The analysis also provided priority of the tasks according to importance, difficulty and criticality within each position. Comparisons could then be made between positions and the common and unique tasks determined.

Task Categorization

Once the tasks performed by NCOs in the four leadership positions were identified and validated, they were then organized into a limited number of categories or job dimensions. This categorization was required for the structuring of the interviews conducted in the third phase of the research project.

The breakdown of task lists into job dimensions involved both the research team and a panel of experts from the NCO academies and was conducted in four consecutive steps.

Initially, task lists were divided by the researchers into general categories such as administration, personnel management and general military. The list of tasks divided into these broad categories were then given to the panel of experts and each member independently sorted the tasks into more specific sub-categories. A forced choice sorting method was used requiring the experts to break down the general categories into two or, at the most, three sub-categories in order to control the level of specificity of the job dimensions.

Following independent sorting of the tasks into sub-categories, the individual decisions of panel members were analysed. Agreements among panel members on sorting of the tasks were tabulated. The disagreements or differences in categorizations of the tasks were negotiated, which resulted in the assignment of all leadership tasks to categories agreed upon by panel members and researchers. A designation of the title for each category or job dimension was then made by the research team with suggestions from the panel of experts. Examples of the job dimensions selected and the types of tasks categorized in the job dimension are shown in Figure 3.

Generic Skill Derivation

In the final phases of the research effort, job incumbents within the four leadership positions were interviewed to obtain descriptions of prototypical performance on the job dimensions identified in phase (b) (see p 133). Since the purpose of the interviews was to obtain descriptions of performance illustrating the full range of skills required for a given job dimension, the non-commissioned officers selected for the interviews were those most likely to have such skills and be capable of describing the actions involved. For each job dimension, two NCOs in each leadership position were interviewed.

At the beginning of each interview, the NCO was given a brief description of a job dimension. The NCO was then asked to describe an example or incident he or she participated in or knew about which illustrated the kind of problems encountered in performance of the tasks within that job dimension and the manner in which these problems were successfully overcome. During the course of the interview, the interviewer probed to insure that a full description of the prototypical incident was obtained. In particular, interviewers were required to obtain information about the following:

1. Sources of information used.
2. All actions taken.
3. Co-workers or subordinates involved.
4. Products or outcomes.

JOB DIMENSIONS

	TRAINING	MAINTENANCE	SECURITY	ARTEP* AND PERIODS OF HOSTILITY
T A S K S	1. Conduct NCO calls	1. Inspect unit buildings and grounds	1. Safeguard "For Official Use Only" material	1. Evaluate/supervise evacuation of sick and injured to aid station
	2. Recommend personnel to attend service schools/additional or specialized training	2. Inspect organizational equipment (TASC, NBC, tents, field mess, etc.)	2. Conduct physical security inspection	2. Conduct tactical road march
	3. Provide input to training schedules	3. Inspect weapons	3. Determine unit physical security requirements	3. Establish a tactical bivouac
	4. Plan unit NCO training	4. Spot-check vehicles for preventive maintenance indicators	4. Maintain a safe or cabinet security record (DA Form 672)	4. Employ/supervise employment of camouflage techniques
	5. Provide training guidance to subordinates	5. Monitor vehicle safety program	5. Review security access roster	5. Conduct rear area protection operations

*ARTEP - Army Training & Evaluation Program

Figure 3. *Example of job dimensions and related tasks*

The interviews were then scored according to an *a priori* scoring system which contained a list and description of skills with criteria for assessing presence or absence of the mention of each skill in the interview protocols. Using the scoring guide, each portion of the interview was evaluated for presence of the skills appearing in the scoring guides. Where mention of a skill occurred, its presence was noted on a score sheet. This resulted in a tally for each skill of the number of times that actions reflecting that skill were mentioned.

The number and pattern of skill requirements determined from the interviews provided the basis for determination of those skills unique to a leadership position and for the derivation of generic skills, which are the common skills across positions that underlie more specific task-related performance. The final outcome of this task was a set of statements of generic skills underlying leadership performance with supporting descriptions and documentation.

Summary

A methodology has been suggested for the development of a comprehensive, descriptive model of generic skill requirements across several leadership positions. This methodology calls for the identification of all the non-technical tasks actually performed by job incumbents in leadership positions, followed by a determination of the frequency, importance and difficulty of each of the identified tasks. These data then serve as the basis for the derivation of job dimensions common to a range of leadership positions. These empirically derived job dimensions provide the structure and direction for in-depth performance interviews with job incumbents. Incidents of effective prototypical leadership performance within the limits of the identified job dimensions are related by the interviewee and used in the determination of the critical dimensions or functions of the managerial job. Analysis of the interviews results in a list of all the skills and behaviours required for effective performance of the specified job dimension. Based on the job dimensions identified, leadership positions are then described according to non-technical task and important skill requirements that are both common to various positions and unique to a given position. In addition, a limited number of generic leadership skills that are common to all levels are identified and described.

Such a methodology yields a comprehensive, behaviour-based description of a range of leader behaviours for different leadership positions. This information is of value in determining the training needs and leadership potential of job incumbents, and in establishing criteria for selection and promotion to the leadership position described. In providing an empirical basis for these types of decisions, such research is a step toward a thorough mapping of the differential characteristics and requirements of a range of leadership positions and functions in a variety of settings.

Acknowledgements

The work reported here was performed at the Heidelberg Office of the Human Resources Research Organization (HumRRO), under contract with the US Army Research Institute for the Behavioral and Social Sciences (ARI). The research was conducted with the assistance of Dr Joseph Olmstead, Dr Batia Sharon, and Mr Albert Kaplan.

The opinions and statements contained herein are the author's and should not be construed as official or as necessarily reflecting the views of the US Army.

References

Hebein, H M (1982) *Leadership Skills: A Methodological Perspective* (HumRRO Interim Report). Human Resources Research Organization, Alexandria, VA.

Sharon, B and Kaplan, A (1982) *NCO Non-MOS Specific Leader Tasks* (HumRRO Research Product RP-PO-81-2). Human Resources Research Organization, Alexandria, VA.

US Army Sergeants Major Academy (1979) *Final Report of Front-End Analysis of First Sergeant's Project.* Ft Bliss, Texas.

5.2 Education and Training Methods: How Many?

A A Huczynski
University of Glasgow

Abstract: The subject of the paper can be considered as a 'scene setter' for a conference which considers the benefits of educational technology media and methods. The focus of the paper is on the findings of the Learning Methods Project (to be published in the *Directory of Management Learning Methods*, Gower Press in Autumn 1982). The project aimed to document all known teaching and learning methods, and the book describes 303 such methods.

The presentation began by participants completing a brief questionnaire indicating which teaching/training methods they use in their work and/or have heard of (five minutes). A 20-minute presentation then followed in which the author outlined the main findings of the project, described how one can analyse different methods and concluded with a consideration of what criteria are used to select different methods. A discussion period followed.

Introduction

Ask a trainer or teacher how many different methods he uses regularly with his trainees or students and the answer is likely to be four or five. An additional two or three might also be used but much less frequently. Ask him where these are used, and in most cases his reply will be, in the classroom. Broadwell (1976) has commented that, 'Informal studies show that 95 per cent of adult training is done in the classroom and in many organizations the figure is 100 per cent'. All of this is in the face of such advances as computer-assisted instruction, closed circuit television, teaching machines, self-instructional devices and the newer, learner-controlled instruction. A survey by The Conference Board (1963) in the United States revealed that group discussion was the most commonly-used teaching method. Two hunded and twenty eight (228) participants in different companies were questioned, and it was found that 95 per cent of these organizations gave initial classroom training to supervisors and managers using the discussion method. The lecture was found to be the next most popular method (used by 92 per cent of companies), followed by the case study (83 per cent) and role playing (71 per cent). Research by Martin and Kerney (1973), based on 225 respondents, revealed that in terms of effectiveness, organizations rated the following management development techniques as best: on-the-job experience and job training (158 companies), seminars (39), conferences (23), role playing (11) and in-basket exercise (10).

The Learning Methods Project

Project Aims

It appears that many of the same teaching methods favoured over 20 years ago are still in wide use today. Why is this? Are people involved in training and staff development innately conservative in their teaching approaches? Or is is merely that these dozen or so training methods referred to earlier are all that are available? To answer these questions, the Learning Methods Project was undertaken by the author. This project is the second in a programme of related research concerned with increasing the effectives of training and development. The first project investigated the factors in the organization which influenced the transfer of training from a course into the trainee's work situation (Huczynski, 1978). The Learning Methods Project attempts in the first instance to document and describe the different ways in which supervisors and managers can be instructed or helped to learn, either on the job or in the classroom setting.

The choice of training method by an instructor is influenced by many factors such as the kind of person he is, the type and number of trainees, the time available for planning, the amount of teaching to be done, the topic taught and the resources of the institution worked in. Most readers will be able to identify numerous other variables which influence their choice of approach. Whatever the merits or demerits of using either a few or many different instructional methods, it is somewhat strange that there has been no attempt to systematically document and classify the different teaching and learning methods which exist and which constitute the trainer's 'tools of the trade'. If we were patients in a hospital we would be most annoyed if we discovered that the surgeon who was about to operate on us did not know about the range of surgical instruments now available to him but decided to use the same ones that he had always used. It was to remedy this lack of information about teaching and learning methods that the Learning Methods Project was begun in Glasgow University's Department of Management Studies. The project has two main aims. The first is to review all the relevant literature relating to methods of training, learning and development, and to extract from it what appear to be clearly distinguishable teaching and learning approaches. Each method was identified by its most commonly-used title and its key elements were described, together with follow-up reading references. Finally, a reference was made to similar or related approaches. This part of the project took two years to complete, and its findings are to be published in a forthcoming reference text (Huczynski, 1982a). The second objective of the project was to help trainers and teachers to try out new methods and approaches in their own work situations.

The study unearthed a total of 303 teaching and learning methods. Some of these are well-known and well-used, such as those mentioned at the start of the paper, eg lecture, seminar, role play. Others will be known by name to many training staff, even though they may not have used them themselves, eg action maze, critical incident analysis, outward bound training, tape stop exercise. There are others which tutors will not have heard of before, and therefore have never used, eg Buberian dialogue, community of inquiry, talking well, construct lesson plan, surrogate clients and directed conversation method. Education and training of all kinds are greatly influenced by new ideas in course design and technology. For the trainer with a job to do and with limited resources with which to do it, it may not always be possible or practicable to use some new technique. At the same time, many training methods are being used in one institution which are equally relevant and usable in others. The aim of the study was to discover what these different practices and approaches were, and to make them available in a single reference text.

The Overlap of Teaching Methods and Techniques

The original focus of the study was on the methods that could be used with managers and supervisors. The title of the book still reflects this original intention. However, shortly after the study began, it became clear that it was not possible to make a distinction between managers and other groups of learners. Thus, with a minimum of modification and inventiveness, the methods described in the study can be equally well applied to college students, apprentices, nurses, industrial workers, supervisory staff, executives and school children. In the same way it was found that many teaching and learning methods, used outside the managerial and oganizational context, had an equal relevance within it. The study identified teaching techniques used in the study of science subjects in colleges, foreign language teaching and religious education. Medical training, in particular, was found to contain a rich source of innovative approaches. It was clear that there was a great deal of opportunity for cross-fertilization of ideas with regard to methods of instruction between subject areas and disciplines.

One of the difficulties in the study was deciding which methods should be included and which should be excluded. Within management education and training there is a large overlap with what have been called organizational development (OD) techniques on the one hand and psychotherapies on the other. The importation of OD techniques from the United States during the last 20 years has had a significant influence on management development and training methods, both directly and indirectly. Organizational development approaches emphasize company-wide change programmes and the methods and techniques they use are not necessarily either appropriate, or relevant, to the trainer dealing with the specific training needs of an individual or group. In the same way, psychotherapeutic approaches in the form of bio-energetic analysis, Alexander technique, encounter therapy and similar methods have all had an influence on management training. Perhaps the best known and most widely used psychotherapeutic technique is Transactional Analysis (TA), which has been embraced by tutors in a great many organizations. To deal with the problem of what to include in the study, it was decided to document only those specific OD techniques which can be separated from their organization-wide content. For example, team development in the form of group training is clearly relevant to the training officer. As far as the psychotherapies are concerned, those which have established themselves in management training are described. Thus, in addition to TA, there are descriptions of T-group training and other laboratory methods such as psychodrama. In fact, the psychotherapies are described in detail in another comprehensive publication (see Herick, 1980).

Which Method to Use?

Despite a wide-ranging study of the different methods of teaching and learning available, and the situations in which they seem to have been successfully used, the research project was unable to draw any conclusions as to which methods were the most appropriate under which circumstances. Perhaps this finding should not come as a surprise, given that successful learning is influenced by so many variables, for example the students' ages, their sex, past educational performance, tutor's objectives, personality, attitude to subject, and so on. All of these to some degree affect the learning process. It was therefore impossible to make any universal generalizations about which method to use when. In the study, the author chose three variables which he felt could usefully guide the decision of tutors with regard to the selection of their approach. The three variables chosen were the nature of the learning objectives, the numbers of students or trainees to be taught, and the degree of student autonomy in learning offered by the teacher or institution.

The Problems of Teaching Method Classification

In order to compare and contrast different teaching methods, an attempt was made to produce a methods classification system into which the 303 methods described could be placed. A review of the existing classification systems showed them to be inadequate theoretically and little used in practice. The research concluded that the development of a universally-valid classification system was an impossible task for two reasons. First, any method label such as 'lecture', 'role play' or 'group discussion' reveals little about the actual nature of the interaction which takes place between teachers and learners. For example, some lectures are indeed tutor-centred, and leave students passive, not allowing them any opportunities for questioning. Other lecturers, however, are very student-centred and encourage students to question them, use buzz groups and set problems for them to solve in the lecture hall. To refer to these two very different types of teacher-student interactions with the single label of 'lecture' is both inappropriate and misleading. When the phenomenon that is being classified changes its characteristics from one moment to the next, it is impossible to fit it into one single category.

The second obstacle to classification was the fact that a single teaching or learning method has many aspects to it. For example, it is to small rather than large groups, it either uses or does not use expensive equipment, and it emphasizes either practical work or theoretical ideas. Since a method has numerous facets it is difficult to incorporate it into a classification system which only uses one criterion for making distinctions between different methods. The categories thus created would be artificial. To cope with these problems, the author abandoned the idea of a classification system in favour of a teacher-styled framework (Huczynski, 1982b). The framework allows trainers and teachers to analyse any learning event which they have designed and have used with their trainees or students, and provides them with a basis for reviewing and improving it.

The Next Phase of the Project

The focus of the study was very much on the trainer in the classroom and on staff training on the job. As the research quoted earlier revealed, on-the-job training and job experience were considered to be the most effective forms of staff development. When it was not being carried out there, for whatever reasons, the training activity inevitably took place in the classroom context with a trainer present. The second objective of the Learning Methods Project was, therefore, to provide the tutor with new ideas and new approaches which he can try out for himself. As the study progressed, it became clear that the task of documenting training methods was complementary to, but nevertheless different from, that of helping trainers to experiment with new training methods in their classrooms. The reference book of the project can go a long way towards filling the need to know about what techniques are available in order to assist teachers in their work. However, to help the lecturer to apply the techniques necessitated a different type of assistance.

To achieve this transfer of learning, a series of handbooks is in the process of production. This is the next phase of the Learning Methods Project (Huzcynski, 1982c). It is intended that these handbooks should go beyond merely describing a method, and aim to set out, in a step-by-step manner, exactly what the lecturer must do and say, in order to use the method. In the author's experience, a major obstacle to trying out new methods of teaching is uncertainty about the steps involved and what to do at different stages. We tend to use the methods with which we are familiar. These are very often the ones we have ourselves experienced as learners. It is in order to break this cycle that these handbooks are being produced. It is hoped that the project can contribute to more effective education and training.

References

Broadwell, M M (1976) Classroom instruction. In Craig, R L (ed) *Training and Development Handbook*, McGraw-Hill, London.
The Conference Board Inc (1963) *Supervisory Training*. Report 612. New York.

Herick, R (1980) *The Psychotherapy Handbook.* Meridian, New York.
Huczynski, A A (1978) Practical approaches towards transferring learning into the work situation. *Journal of European Industrial Training,* 2, 1.
Huczynski, A A (1982a) *Encyclopaedia of Management Development Methods.* Gower Publishing Company, Aldershot (to be published).
Huczynski, A A (1982b) Framework for the analysis of management learning methods: 1. description of the elements; and II. applications. (Unpublished paper)
Huczynski, A A (1982c) *Handbook of Staff Teaching and Management Development Methods in Management Development.* University of Glasgow. (forthcoming)
Martin, D D and Kerney, W J (1973) The current state of management development participation and methods. *Journal of Business,* 19 (December).

Section 6: Applications of Microteaching and Microteaching Technologies

6.1 Skills Training and Self-Confrontation Applications in Different Settings

Ray McAleese
Director, University Teaching Centre, University of Aberdeen

Abstract: This article examines the problems encountered in using video self-confrontation and skills training in settings other than teacher education training.

The argument developed is that there are many instances of the use of microteaching; there are unjustified expectations that trainees can change both performance and perceptions, and there is evidence that trainees can change their perceptions with a better psychopedagogical stance.

I argue that microteaching is more appropriate when the skills can be operationalized and where there is a concrete experience for the trainee. The address draws on microteaching paradigms in training as opposed to educational settings.

Some Initial Thoughts

I would like to identify some of the general problems that exist and draw out lessons for practitioners of educational thinking. There are two positions that one can see with regard to microteaching and in particular the effectiveness of television self-confrontation. First is the *romantic* view, characterized in a recent article by Aled Rhys-William (1982)[1]. In this, Rhys-William says:

'Countless numbers of human beings through the ages have yearned like Robert Burns for the divine gift of seeing ourselves as others see us. More people than ever before, by means of the video recorder, can now have that experience.'

There is, of course, a contrasting and in some ways more acceptable view which one can call the *realist* view. The classic review by Fuller and Manning (1974) takes a more balanced and academic position:

'. . . attempts to conceptualize what actually goes on during self-confrontation are rare. Explosion without explanation seems to be the order of the day . . . Self-confrontation seems to capture the imagination of the investigators in the face of contrary evidence. It has been credited with producing the very outcomes which have been predicted and disconfirmed.'

Neither of these positions hits the truth (which probably, however, lies more with the realist view than the romantic view). However, we must be careful to see the evidence in its proper context.

In this address I am going to argue that there are many instances of inappropriate use being made of video self-confrontation and skills training. Further, many of the expectations of practitioners and administrators are unjustified. However, there are clear benefits from the analytical stance that video self-confrontation and skills training gives the trainer, in particular with regard to perceptions of a training problem shared between the trainer and the trainee.

1. In this printed version of the address the references are 'qualified' to enable the reader to identify the reason why the citation is being made. For details of this technique, the reader is asked to consult *Aspects of Educational Technology* XV, pp 299-305 for a report on a symposium at last year's conference on Information Retrieval, and the work of Duncan and McAleese on qualified citation indexing (background reading); also Duncan, E B and McAleese, R (1981) *Information Retrieval in Educational Technology*, University of Aberdeen.

A Reminder from the Past

Let me say immediately, lest the reader accuses me of being a cynic, that my last visit to Bulmershe College was in the days of the rapid dissemination of microteaching ideas. Although I was never happy with some of the general ideas relating to video self-confrontation, I was able to use and apply the ideas in both higher education and in teacher training. One of the problems lay with the over-emphasis on television. In a survey, which I carried out on all educational establishments in the UK in 1970, it was clear that the main thrust of microteaching was the *use of television in teacher education.* I have never taken this view as I am convinced that this avoids the issues regarding video self-confrontation and skills training. Microteaching is more than the use of CCTV in teacher education.

I would now like to turn to the main thrust of my address which discusses other fields in which microteaching protocols are used effectively.

The Nature and Range of the Field

Let me take an information science stance and look at the field of microteaching as a dynamic process. I am going to contrast the teaching and the training uses of skills training and video self-confrontation. If one takes, in the first instance, teacher education, the field is not characterized by the quality of its research or published results. Many of the publications are descriptive and fail to analyse the underlying forces. Most are lacking a theoretical base, but there seems to be a wide variety of types of video self-confrontation used to achieve a wide variety of ends. In training, the published research is characterized by a singularity of purpose, a clarity of objectives but very limited means to achieve the stated ends.

In general, the growth of published research has exhibited an asymptotic growth curve, with a period of slow down from about 1975. Most of the research published was in the period 1972 to 1975 (McAleese, 1980).

If one looks at the publications on microteaching, there are some 821 papers to be found, if an information source such as ERIC is used. Of the 800 or so, less than half (48 per cent) are in areas *other than* teacher education. It is on this area that I want to concentrate. The areas that emerge are listed below.

Range of Areas
alcoholics
basketball
salesmen
counselling
tennis
military
supervisory
industrial
church
police

Table 1. *Video self-confrontation and skills training in non-traditional settings*

These areas: job training, supervisory, military, etc represent the *training* areas where the ideas of self-confrontation and skills training are most clearly identified.

Video-tape, in conjunction with self-confrontation and skills training, can be used in a wide variety of contexts from 'teaching mood changing for parapsychologists' to 'the acquisition of motor skills for tennis players' (Rey, 1976). I would now like to turn to skills training, the first of the two main areas of this paper.

Skills Training

Skills training is based on the idea of *component* skills and the mastery of individual elements of a complex process in some defined order. Such component skills usually comprise the total complex, or macro skill, which is the objective of the training exercise: for example, achieving sales commitment in a client.

In using this approach we reduce complex behaviour to a series of *describable* and *repeatable* skills.

Each is learned or mastered in turn, perhaps in serial order, after a sequential algorithm has been established. In some cases, the ordering of the skills may be at random, where there is little or no lateral or hierarchical linking between the component parts. The sub-skills are combined in the global performance. Such are the ideas of skills training in the microteaching or microtraining context. One can think of these skills in many different contexts. Two should suffice to demonstrate some of the principles. I will take different settings from those with which you may be familiar. Take a social skill such as interrogating an hostile witness in a Criminal court. Such a skill would be a necessary requirement for a competent civil lawyer. Some of the component parts deal with: the use of questions, the use of answers (ie listening skills), eye contact, the use of voice projection, etc.

One can see as we begin to develop the ideas of component skills that each complex behaviour can be broken down into a fine set of component skills. This *reductionism* is the essence of the component skills approach and skills training. If one takes physical skills, which one might find in training as opposed to teaching, then there are many examples for each of us in our efforts to take part in physical sporting activities. Such are the pressures of western living that more of us are turning to physical activities to complement intellectual activities. Take, for example, golf — the game that most typifies the component skill approach and the game that has best developed the use of video self-confrontation with skills training. At a macro level, consider the selection and use of different clubs; then at a finer level the different use made of specialized clubs such as the Sand Iron, and the deft use made of the Putter from ranges of 40 metres to five centimetres. So, there is the idea of components of more complex activities. In the golfer's bag there are many clubs, each symbolizing a component skill.

Now, the sporting example may seem a long way from the complexity of training military personnel to fly helicopters, or the training of shop stewards in running meetings, yet there is a connection; that is the reduction of the complex skills to simple sub-skills, and the *recombination* of these to achieve the total performance. Such dissection, followed by recombination, is not simply an analytical approach but an approach that is expected to give better performance of the total skill, after practice of the sub-skills in isolation. I make a point of saying that this reductionism is not simply an analytical approach because it is more difficult to *analyse* a complex activity by breaking it down than it is to learn individual skills in isolation before they are recombined. There is a temporal sense in skills training. In the analytical sense the whole may come before the reductionism, and the reduction may have nothing to do with practice or evaluation activity.

The practice in the training domain has been to identify a range of skills; or, more likely, to list a range of skills identified by others, and to modify them. There is an attempt to learn from others, to use similar training protocols; there is a sense in the literature of practitioners *using others' ideas*, particularly when it comes to the range of skills to be practised.

A useful way of thinking about such component skills is in terms of open and closed skills (Rey, 1976).

Closed skills are those which are habitual or static in nature; for example, starting a lesson, serving a tennis ball or driving in golf. Open skills are perceptual or dynamic in nature. Such skills are the use of probing questions by teachers or lawyers; a half-lob in tennis; bunker play with a sand wedge in golf, or driving in traffic. It is possible for each of these skills to be defined in terms of its degree of openness or closedness. I will not do that, but simply suggest to you that the categories 'open' and 'closed' can describe the skills.

Skills training is concerned with the identification of the relevant component skills, the ordering of the training experience, the establishing of the criteria for performance, and the selection of the next goal in the series of training sub-goals.

What can one say about the proper nature of skills training and the nature of such skills? First, they should be clearly definable. Second, there should be criteria for their selection. Third, they should interlock with each other in a pattern that is clear and unambiguous. Component skills used in skills training are not a rag bag of odd unrelated skills. They are a matched set of necessary skills. They are the set of golf clubs bought at the professional's shop, not picked up at jumble sales. Not all the skills will be immediately useful but they will all eventually be useful for the trainee. Fourth, there should be testable criteria for successful execution and performance.

It is obvious from a reading of the literature that teaching skills seldom approach these criteria, but training skills more often approach the rigorous conditions which I have identified. Skills in teaching contexts are less definable, and, most important, there are seldom testable criteria for successful execution of the skill. Who will dare say what is 'good' teaching, or 'good' questioning?

The Laboratory Approach

In both the teaching and the training approaches there is a laboratory approach to the concept of training. This approach, which Ayre Perlbert has described, is the approach which sees the training experience as being in some way experimental.

It suggests finding out as opposed to acquiring defined ways of operating. This laboratory or experimental approach is very important in the teaching context. where aims and practices can differ very markedly from school to school. Teaching is more experimental and there are more models of performance criteria. There are fewer assertive dogmas of descriptive skills. Take, for example, the skill of the probing question in the classroom and contrast it with the same skill in a courtoom. In the latter there is less uncertainty about performance, as instances of proper and improper practice are codified. In teaching such precision is not the case.

If one examines the diagram which Rey suggested, one can make a number of further observations about skills training and link it to video self-controntation (Rey, 1976).

	Information feedback		
	KP (performance)	KR (results)	skills
Skills	*	*** (video)	open
	*** (video)	*	closed

Figure 1. *Skills and video self confrontation*
(based on Rey, 1976)

Knowledge of performance is better for closed skills. Knowledge of results is better for open skills. Video self-confrontation is best for closed (KP) and for open (KR) instances.

Let me turn now to self-confrontation.

Self-Confrontation

It is in the area of self-confrontation that I find most inconsistency between what we expect to happen and what actually happens. There seems to be an unwarranted assumption that the act of observing a performance will *itself* change performance. Now it may seem to you that this is an overstatement, but, from a close examination of the literature and from 13 years' experience of talking with practitioners and using the techniques, the most common misconception is of the power of television to change performance.

Self-confrontation is a meeting of self with self. It is the narcissistic tendency to examine oneself, despite the physiological evidence that this causes arousal and stress (McAleese, 1976). In arousal there is a disposition to be ready for change; in stress there is an emotional state of confusion, or, as some have seen it, 'being on the horns of a dilemma'. In self-confrontation both of these states occur; however, it is the arousal state that is most useful to the trainer.

Evidence from research studies shows that arousal is not always present before the onset of stress.

But what is this self-confrontation? Before we can understand it we have to digress to examine self-concept.

Self-concept is a complex set of interrelated mental states of awareness about specific personal characteristics; such as, *self as*: a person, an employer, a golfer!, a teacher, a user of probing questions, etc.

Self-concept changes very slowly by a process of internalizing relevant and meaningful external experiences or stimuli. For example, using my golfing analogy, if I am a person who tends to hook the ball then each time I make this mistake I receive external evidence about my self-concept of 'self as a golfer'. All external stimuli can be thought of as being probably useful in reinforcing or changing elements of self-concept. Of course, not all external stimuli are used or can be used in the short term.

This digression is most important for my argument because the meeting of external self, that is, the video or audio element of the self-confrontation, with the internal self is the essence of the training experience. The trainee experiences a meeting of the external realization of his skill performance and he has to reconcile this with his known internal competence or lack of competence. Figure 2 indicates what I mean when I talk about a meeting of external and internal realizations of self.

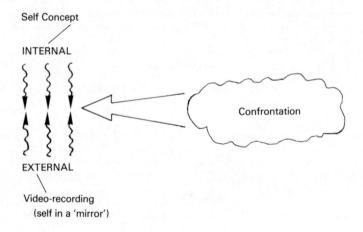

Figure 2. *Video self-confrontation*

In any meeting there can be either congruity or incongruity. It is the incongruous meeting in video self-confrontation that creates the arousal which makes the trainee more likely to change his self-concept and to accept the skills of the training experience. There is what some call *cognitive dissonance*, a term which I find more acceptable than stress. Stress has too many connotations that are inappropriate and misleading to the trainee as well as to the trainer. Cognitive dissonance is a better way of describing the process as it suggests a thinking or cognitive element in the training; not simply a reacting element as is suggested by the use of the word stress.

I would like to emphasize that the process of self-confrontation and self-concept change through external stimuli is still a little-understood process.

Such changing of perceptions and self-concept seems to me to be an example of a personal 'voyage of discovery'. The trainee is coming to terms with himself. We now reach the crux of a problem which I have been skirting around for some time. There is a danger for the trainer. It may be that self-concept change is more appropriate in teaching contexts than in training contexts. There is less emphasis on the voyage of discovery in training than in learning to become a teacher. I do not wish to over-emphasize this point; nevertheless, teaching is not always coming to terms with oneself, but with unspecific training objectives there is more scope for personal differences and 'individual voyages of discovery'. Let me turn now to the variety of contexts in training.

Contexts in Training

How is training different from teaching with regard to skills training and video self-confrontation? There are three reasons why it is different: (i) precision of skills; (ii) concreteness of experience; and (iii) socio-emotional climate of the training environment. The differences will be shown up by making comparisons of the different skills.

The Precision of the Skills

Compare the appropriate use of examples in explaining with a golf swing, achieving rotation (ie, take off) in a place, or achieving closure in a counselling situation.

The Concreteness of the Experience

Compare the selection of the appropriate question format with swimming a butterfly stroke for 100 metres, or fear felt during a simulated training exercise for infantry training.

Socio-Emotional Climate

Compare co-counselling or microteaching supervision with police superintendent training or sales executive training in achieving commitment in clients.

Training contexts have more precisely defined and operationalized skills. There is more concrete experience and there tends to be a less supportive socio-emotional climate. I am not making a value judgement about the three dimensions; I am observing differences. It is better to say in all cases that precision or concreteness is better or worse — I am observing the difference.

Implications

I would first like to argue the case that there is inappropriate use made of video self-confrontation and skills training. In the first instance audio feedback might be more appropriate. I have deliberately not discussed the various forms of feedback.

However, let me say that I am less impressed by trainers' arguments about why they use television than by their skill in setting up television recording complexes with limited resources.

Next, consider many of the training skills that use listening, auditory and language skills. Indeed, most of the well-defined skills are not visual in the sense that television makes them visual, eg questioning, explaining, closure, etc.

Often, skills that are used defy clear operationalization. Even a skill such as explaining, which has undergone a very rigorous examination in the hands of George Brown (Brown, 1978), still lacks the operational definition necessary. There are also skills that are really not skills at all: for example, in counselling or group dynamics work, where many of the variables are not within the control of the trainee. There are unjustified expectations of new training techniques. Such novel approaches are often (or always?) seen as better because of their newness. One can see this in the romantic view of self-confrontation. There is a misunderstanding of the nature of skill change and of cognitive dissonance. One can see this in the realist view. There is the ever-present bandwagon effect that bedevils all innovative work in training. I will not dwell on this now.

However, there are clear benefits arising from self-confrontation. First there is the analytical stance that is achieved by the trainee after using self-confrontation techniques. This thinking, this cognitive dissonance, gives the trainee a framework on which to hang subsequent experience. There are the shared perceptions of training. Training is not simply being better at a skill but being able to benefit from subsequent training experiences on the job. This is the multiplier effect that training must achieve. This sharpening of perceptions is one of the most important elements in training.

Under ideal circumstances, the trainee is more attentive to the possible learning experience that will occur after formal training has ceased.

Conclusions

Video self-confrontation and skills training have four lessons for me, and it is with these four lessons that I would like to conclude briefly. They can be listed simply, for I think that you will recognize them once they are listed.

First, the way new ideas are disseminated in educational technology.
Second, the difficulties of adopting training protocols with a proper understanding of the training and psychological assumptions.
Third, the bandwagon effect.
Fourth, the exploitation of new technologies, especially, in this case, television.

To round off let me remind you of something that Fuller and Manning said a few years ago (1974).

'. . . The cautions of the empiricists are certainly warranted. They see a powerful tool whose nature and effects are little understood, cutting a wide swathe and perhaps destroying the wheat with the chaff. In short, self-confrontation has potential for help and harm. It is a novel powerful source of information about those aspects of the self which are perceived by others but not by the self. Its particular value lies in its ability to communicate negative information which others could, but are loath to, communicate, and usually cannot communicate in a totally acceptable manner.'

I hope that I have suggested a few pointers for the critical evaluation of other papers on this theme at the 1982 ETIC Conference.

6.2 Evaluating a Training Programme on Lecturing

G A Brown and J Daines
Nottingham University

Abstract: This paper outlines the evaluation of a two-day training course on lecturing. Ratings by independent observers of pre- and post-training tapes indicated that there were significant changes in performance. These findings were corroborated by analyses of linguistic measures derived from the transcripts of the video recordings. New and experienced lecturers perceived the course as valuable.

Introduction

The course on lecturing is based upon a microteaching format (Brown, 1975). Each participant is asked to give two brief explanations, one at the beginning of the course and one towards the end of the course. The participants are also asked to give two brief summaries of the content and structure of two one-hour lectures which they normally give on undergraduate courses. These explanations provide a sample of the participants' verbal, extra-verbal and non-verbal behaviours, of their presentation skills and their structuring techniques. Hence the explanations provide, in microform, a sample of the lecturing skills of the participants. The summaries of lectures provide indications of the structures of underlying objectives of the participants' lectures. The explanations are viewed, discussed and analysed in groups of about six participants. An explanation guide and various techniques of analysing structures are used in the small-group sessions (Brown, 1978). The activity on summaries is also carried out in small groups but, usually, this activity is not video-recorded. The small-group sessions are interspersed with lecture/discussion classes in which the participants are introduced to relevant ideas, suggestions and research on the skills and methods of lecturing, given teaching problems to solve, and provided with well-defined brief discussion activities which are carried out in groups of three or four. Further details of the two-day programme may be found in Brown (1980; 1982).

Evaluations of the Course

Evaluating training courses for lecturers is not easy. There are a variety of problems, not least of which is that no two courses are identical, since courses are an interaction between trainers, trainees and the course materials. Also, any experimental design which is practicable within the content of training university teachers is unlikely to yield rigorous proof of the efficacy of a course. Therefore, we used a variety of techniques to evaluate the two-day course on lecturing. They included independent observers' ratings of a set of video-taped explanations, an analysis of linguistic changes as manifested in the transcripts of the explanations, an analysis of the perceived values of the course by new and experienced lecturers, and a follow-up study of a group of new lecturers.

Independent Observers' Ratings

Sixty-six video-tapes of new lecturers' courses were rated by two trained independent observers who used a simple six-item (six point) rating schedule. The correlations between the observers was higher than 0.8 in all variables, except taking account of variance (r = 0.65). This variance included such factors as use of appropriate examples, rapport and appropriate level of explanations. The tapes were presented randomly. The observers were informed that the investigators were interested in differences between the video-taped explanations. They did not know which tapes were first or second attempts at explaining. (In their second attempts at explaining, participants were able to choose whether to tackle the same or a different topic. This procedure was chosen to maintain a high level of interest in the activity.)

	First explanation		Second explanation		Residuals	
	Mn	SD	Mn	SD	Mn	SD
1. Openings	8.32	2.52	9.60	1.60	0.61**	0.43
2. Endings	7.79	2.65	9.00	2.08	0.30	1.52
3. Structure	8.30	2.30	9.90	1.73	0.90**	1.26
4. Interest	8.36	2.36	8.70	2.20	0.90**	1.61
5. Use of AVA	8.21	3.24	9.33	2.81	0.60*	1.56
6. Taking account of audience	8.60	2.33	8.90	2.19	0.40	1.59
7. Total score	49.70	12.52	55.67	9.42	1.03	3.97
8. Global impression	8.97	2.03	9.55	1.65	0.57*	1.45

* = Sig at 0.05 level
** = Sig at 0.01 level
One sample 't' at 32 df

Table 1. *Perceived behavioural changes in the explanation presentations*

The pooled scores of the observers' ratings were used to compute the predicted scores of the second explanation by means of linear regression. The actual and predicted scores were compared using a correlated 't' test. This procedure minimizes change scores and is, therefore, more stringent than an analysis of raw change scores (Linn and Slinde, 1977). Table 1 sets out the results of the analysis of the first and second attempts at explaining.

The results indicate that, for this group of lecturers, the course yielded perceptible and significant improvements in the opening moves of an explanation, its structure and interest, and in the use of audio-visual aids. The global impression of the observers indicated an overall significant improvement. The narrowing of the standard deviations provides further evidence that the training course effected changes in behaviour.

The results do not, of course, constitute a rigorous experimental proof nor do they indicate which component of the course had most effect, but it is likely that the viewing-analysis sessions, the manual and the sharing of experiences through discussion were the most influential factors.

A Study of Linguistic Changes

Transcripts of the 66 explanations of the course for new lecturers were also studied. From this study, six variables were extracted for use in a regression analysis. Three of the variables were concerned with structuring tactics and three with negative features of presentation. The results are shown in Table 2.

	First explanation		Second explanation		Residuals	
	Mn	SD	Mn	SD	Mn	SD
Signposts and frames	3.61	1.89	4.82	2.38	0.79*	2.02
Foci	2.36	2.59	2.60	2.01	1.27	2.42
Links	5.39	2.58	6.24	2.16	0.30*	1.62
Hesitations	2.30	3.53	1.55	1.91	−0.11	0.88
Stumbles	2.42	3.23	1.28	1.46	0.03	1.23
Incomplete sentences	2.27	2.74	1.58	1.94	−0.19	1.72

* = Sig at 0.05 level
One sample 't' tests used at 32 df

Table 2. *Recorded linguistic changes*

The course on explaining appeared to produce significant changes in structuring tactics, such as the use of explaining links, signposts and frames, but not in the use of foci. The frequency of hesitations, stumbles and incomplete sentences was reduced, but not significantly. It should be noted that relatively high frequencies of these presentation variables is probably associated with anxiety. Anxiety levels are likely to have been higher during the first attempt at explaining.

Perceived Values of Course

Table 3 sets out the ratings of two groups of new lecturers, and Table 4 of two groups of experienced lecturers who participated in the course. The new lecturers were in their first full-time posts in a university: they were from all faculties of the university. Approximately two-thirds were medical or applied scientists; the remainder were lecturers from arts or social science.

The participants were asked to rate each component of the course on six-point scales to give a global rating of the course, and on three dimensions: 'interest', 'usefulness', and 'thought provoking'. A global rating was taken on the grounds that 'the whole is greater than the sum of the parts'.

Viewing and analysis of the participants' own video-tapes received the highest ratings. This is a common finding on training courses which use video analysis. The low ratings of the 'lecture preparation' activities by the second group of new lecturers were due to an unexpected reaction of that group to the activities on preparing lectures. The preceding year's group had suggested that these activities in the plenary sessions should be carried out in groups of three or four, drawn from the same or closely allied disciplines. This procedure was adopted for the second group; it resulted in an aggressive debate between 'arts' and 'science' lectures, which obscured the main points of the exercise.

The activity on lecture structure is, in fact, rather difficult. First attempts at it left participants somewhat dissatisfied. The second attempt, when the participants

	1st year $n = 33$		2nd year $n = 21$	
	Mn	SD	Mn	SD
1. Activity 1 on explaining	4.8	0.68	4.81	1.25
2. Business of explaining	4.28	0.57	4.48	0.93
3. Activity 2, viewing and analysis	5.25	0.75	5.62	0.59
4. Activity 3, structure of lectures	3.65	0.99	3.95	1.16
5. Designing explanations and lectures	4.41	0.79	4.57	0.81
6. Activities on lecture preparation	4.25	1.12	3.62	0.97
7. Activity 4, explaining revisited	4.81	0.66	5.38	0.92
8. Structure of explanations	4.52	0.52	4.38	0.92
9. Activity 5, viewing and analysis	4.82	0.64	5.14	0.18
10. Activity 6, structure of lecture revisited	3.90	0.70	4.38	1.16
11. Helping students learn	3.71	0.47	4.05	0.86
Global rating	4.65	9.49	5.14	0.73
Interest	4.64	0.61	5.00	0.63
Usefulness	4.76	0.66	5.04	0.86
Thought-provoking	4.61	0.85	4.95	1.02

Notes
All items rated on six-point scales
For first 11 items:
  6 = Extremely useful, 5 = Very useful, 4 = Useful, 3 = Fairly useful,
  2 = Barely useful, 1 = Irrelevant
For remaining items:
  6 = Very high, 5 = High, 4 = Above average, 3 = Below average,
  2 = Low, 1 = Very low

Table 3. *Rating of the course in terms of values: new lecturers*

knew more about the design of lectures and explanations, yielded higher results in both years.

In addition to rating the course, all participants were invited to write any comments on the course that they wished. This procedure samples lecturers' perceptions, feelings and observations of the course which rating schedules cannot tap easily.

The comments confirmed the ratings received. The viewing and analysis were mentioned most frequently. There were also suggestions to include more video activities, four sessions on audio-visual aids, improving chalkboard work, vocal projection, the use of explaining in laboratory work, learning from lectures and lecture course design. There were no recommendations to remove any part of the existing course. Most of the suggestions have been incorporated into the current series of two-day and half-day courses for new lecturers, now spread through the academic year.

	1st year n = 16 Mn	SD	2nd year n = 18 Mn	SD
Activity 1, on explaining	4.81	1.11	5.05	0.87
Business of explaining	4.19	0.75	3.78	1.35
Activity 2, viewing and analysis	5.69	0.48	4.72	0.95
Activity 3, structure of lecture	4.75	1.27	4.38	1.36
Designing explanations and lectures	4.50	0.73	3.44	1.24
Activities on lecture preparation	3.81	0.91	*_	*_
Activity 4, explaining revisited	4.88	0.72	4.55	1.19
Structure of explanations	4.38	0.81	4.33	1.24
Activity 5, viewing and analysis	5.31	0.95	4.94	0.80
**Activity 6, structure of lecture revisited; interactive lecturing (1979)	4.31	1.35	3.40	1.24
Helping students learn	4.44	0.96	4.39	1.04
Global rating	5.19	0.54	4.33	1.02
Interest	4.88	0.72	4.40	1.09
Usefulness	5.00	0.63	4.00	1.14
Thought provoking	4.88	0.88	4.55	1.19

Notes
1. All items rated on six-point scales
   For first 11 items:
      6 = Extremely useful, 5 = Very useful, 4 = Useful,
      3 = Fairly useful, 2 = Barely useful, 1 = Irrelevant.
   For remaining items:
      6 = Very high, 5 = High, 4 = Above average,
      3 = Below average, 2 = Low, 1 = Very low.
2. * No separate evaluation of activities on lecture preparation for this group.
3. **A set of activities on interactive lecturing was used instead of lecture structure.

Table 4. *Rating of the course in terms of values: experienced lecturers*

The ratings of the experienced lecturers were similar to those of the newly-appointed lecturers. Activities concerned with video-recordings, viewing and analysis achieved the highest scores. The activities on lecture preparation received the lowest ratings by the first group of experienced lecturers and the activity on 'interactive lecturing' by the second group of experienced lecturers. The latter activity was introduced instead of a second attempt at structuring lectures — since it was thought that one attempt at lecture structure would be sufficient for experienced lecturers and that they might prefer to expand their repertoire of varying student activities during lecturing. The ratings of 'interactive lecturing' suggest that interactive lecturing was not a high priority for this group of experienced lecturers.

Both experienced and new lecturers rated the course highly on the three dimensions of usefulness, interest and thought provoking. They also gave high ratings to most of the activities and presentations. The lowest ratings were given to the final attempt at 'lecture structure' and 'helping students learn' by newly-appointed lecturers, to the activities on lecture preparation by the first group of experienced lecturers; and to designing explanations and lectures and 'interactive lecturing' by the second group of lecturers. These 'lowest' ratings were in the fairly useful to useful category. The ratings indicated that further design work is required on lecture structure and preparation.

The differences in ratings of the newly-appointed and experienced lecturers may reflect differences in experience. Newly-appointed staff may not have grasped the importance of lecture structure, or of helping students learn from lectures. This is borne out by the findings of the follow up study described in the next section of this paper. More experienced staff may have regarded the activities on lecture preparation and design as obvious. The video-taped activities and the viewing self-analysis sessions received the highest ratings by both new and experienced lecturers.

A Follow Up Study

Six months after completing the course, one group of new lecturers was asked to complete two simple rating schedules on the course and some features of lecturing. Sixteen completed the schedules. Of the remainder, three had not given any lectures because their Heads of Department wanted them to concentrate on their research and the rest did not reply.

Table 5 sets out the course evaluations of this group immediately after the course and six months later. The respondents, when rating the course six months later, were asked to consider how useful, in retrospect, the course had been to them. They were supplied with a brief outline of the course as well as the evaluation sheet.

Viewing and analysis remained the most highly-rated activities. The inputs of 'business of explaining' was rated lower, whereas the activities on lecture preparation, lecture structure and helping students learn were rated more highly. These higher ratings may partially reflect the effect of experience of lecturing upon their perceptions of the course. The overall ratings of the course six months later were in the useful to very useful domain. One may conclude, therefore, that the perceived value of this course still remained high after the experience of actual lecturing. However, we bear in mind that the sample in this follow-up study was only a single group of new lecturers.

Discussion and Conclusion

Two major types of evaluation were used in this study: the analysis of behavioural changes and the perceived value of the courses to new and experienced lecturers. The analysis of behavioural changes provides good evidence that the course improved presentation and structure of brief explanations. In so doing, the course is likely to have influenced the presentation and structure of lectures. But one should treat these results with caution. No direct observation of changes in lecturers' presentations to undergraduates was undertaken in this project. Indeed, such a procedure would have been laborious, time-consuming and difficult to control experimentally. However, the follow up study of new lecturers does indicate that the course continued to be perceived as valuable after their first six months of lecturing. The ratings of groups of new and experienced lecturers indicate that the course was considered to be useful, interesting and thought-provoking.

Whilst measures of the perceived values of courses do not provide direct measures of learning, they do provide evidence of attitudes, and favourable

	Post course		Follow up	
	Mn	SD	Mn	SD
1. Activity 1, on explaining	4.81	1.25	4.35	0.93
2. Business of explaining	4.48	0.93	3.25	0.93
3. Activity 2, viewing and analysis	5.62	0.59	5.56	0.51
4. Activity 3, structure of lectures	3.95	1.16	3.69	1.14
5. Designing explanations and lectures	4.57	0.81	4.50	1.21
6. Activities on lecture preparation	3.62	0.97	4.06	1.18
7. Activity 4, explaining revisited	5.38	0.92	4.62	1.09
8. Structure of explanations	4.38	0.92	3.56	1.03
9. Activity 5, viewing and analysis	5.14	0.18	5.06	0.89
10. Activity 6, structure of lecture revisited	4.38	1.16	4.69	0.60
11. Helping students learn	4.05	0.86	4.44	0.89
Global rating	5.14	0.73	4.75	0.77
Interest	5.00	0.63	4.44	0.89
Usefulness	5.04	0.86	4.81	0.75
Thought provoking	4.95	1.02	4.00	1.15

All items rated on a six-point scale
n = 21, 16

Table 5. *A summary of the retrospective course evaluation*

attitudes are a necessary constituent of long-term changes in behaviour. Put another way, courses which are not perceived as useful are unlikely to have any long-term effects.

The combination of the observed changes in lecturing behaviour and the favourable attitudes expressed by the participants to the two-day course strongly suggest that the course helps lecturers to improve their lecturing and to activate their interest in lecturing.

Acknowledgements

This research was funded by the Social Science Research Council under grant HF 4441.

References

Brown, G A (1975) *Microteaching: A Programme of Teaching Skills.* Methuen, London.
Brown, G A (1978) *Lecturing and Explaining.* Methuen, London.
Brown, G A (1980) *Mimeo on University Teaching Methods.* University of Nottingham.
Brown, G A (1982) *Two Days on Lecturing in Studies in Higher Education.* (to be published)
Linn, R L and Slinde, J A (1977) The determination of the significance between pre- and post-testing periods. *Review of Educational Research* 47, pp 1-52.

6.3 Microteaching and the Microcomputer

J C Rodenburg-Smit, G C Lebbink, R A M van Brunschot and M J M Verbruggen,
University of Technology, Eindhoven

Abstract: First, the role of the mini-computer in microteaching sessions is clarified and there is an explanation of the organization of teacher training for the higher levels of secondary schools at the University of Technology at Eindhoven, The Netherlands.

Second, information is given about the chosen method of microteaching and the types of feedback a student-teacher will receive on his or her teaching behaviour, including feedback of observation by means of the mini-computer.

Third, in addition to skill training, the paper gives details of other activities such as theme-centred sessions. Both are aimed at teaching students to be conscious and reflective about their own teaching behaviour. An example is given to show the connection between practical and theoretical education topics.

Finally, there is a brief description of plans for evaluating and developing microteaching and observation by means of the computer.

The Pre-Service Teacher Training at the Eindhoven University of Technology, Department of Educational Psychology

This department participates in pre-service teacher training. Its staff members give lectures about theories of learning, psychological development, personality development, educational measurement and testing. In addition, the practical training of teachers is performed by means of microteaching and theme-oriented workshops. Other members of staff at the University are responsible for the pre-service training of students in the field of teaching school subjects. Also, there is training in the school itself.

In the microteaching sessions each student gives three lessons of 15 minutes' duration. The first and second lessons are given to a group of eight colleagues (peer group). The third lesson is given to 16- and 17-year-old pupils from a secondary school. This particular training requires one morning or afternoon per week during a semester.

A questioning technique forms the basis of this training. It combines elements of lecturing (eg the teacher uses a high level of structure) with elements of free discussions (eg each participant can make his own contribution). This technique requires a teacher to elicit what pupils already know. It requires the pupils to think. An objective is that *all* pupils understand the content of the lesson.

The aim of microteaching training is to give students the opportunity to experience teaching situations, which can help them to understand their attitudes to teaching.

The interaction between a teacher and pupils affects the way he gives a lesson. This is something that can only be learned in practice, not from books. It allows a teacher to use his ability in the best possible way as it teaches him something about his own personality. For example, he is more capable of selecting the correct method of teaching, within the framework of a questioning technique that suits him, the pupils and the subject. Of course, we cannot define the question technique precisely because it involves free selection, which does not have such a formal structure as a mini-course (Borg, Kelly, Langer and Gall, 1970).

It is the opinion of McNamara (1981) that teachers need to be more conscious and reflective about current teaching practices. This is more likely to be true for in-service and pre-service training, done in schools. In our opinion, at the University of Eindhoven we can create a controlled environment (microteaching) in which a student can experiment with his method of approach to pupils. Consequently, the questioning technique helps the student to discover his own style of teaching and to develop his own attitudes towards teaching.

Feedback in the Microteaching Groups

A Microteaching Group

A microteaching group consists of 10 students and two supervisors. In each session three (different) lessons are given. The teaching material of a particular lesson is prepared by two students. One of them is a teacher and the other is an observer during the lesson.

The other eight students are 'pupils'. They learn naturally because the subject matter of the lesson is new to them. After the lesson the pupils and the teacher express their feelings and thoughts in a discussion so that the teacher can get a better understanding of his classroom presentation. One of the supervisors, a staff member of the department of educational psychology, leads this discussion.

The supervisor also organizes a 'pre-discussion' (a discussion one week or more before the lesson). The student-teacher and his companion have to describe the way they planned their lessons. They talk about the presentation of each lesson and they say what they want the discussion after the lesson to be like.

Observation with the Aid of a Microcomputer

In order to record classroom activities during a microteaching lesson, a microcomputer is used. This computer is programmed to simultaneously process codes of several different category systems. One of these systems, the headline system, enables all activities to be categorized and records verbal interaction. In addition, sub-systems can be connected to the headline system for recording teacher responses and for evaluating pupils' answers. These sub-divisions are similar to subscripted categories used in FIAC systems (Flanders, 1970). In principle, every category in the headline system can be sub-divided or evaluated with a sub-system. The configuration of hardware components used with the observation system is shown in Figure 1.

program sequence / group members	Pre-discussion	Lesson	Post-discussion	Video session
staff member A	supervisor	supervisor	leader (chairman)	supervisor
staff member B	—	observer	informant of observational data	—
student teacher 1	shows preparations	teacher	participant	participant
student teacher 2	companion	observer	reporter	participant
student teacher 3-10	—	pupils	participants	—

Table 1. *The distributions of the group members over the tasks in the microteaching sessions*

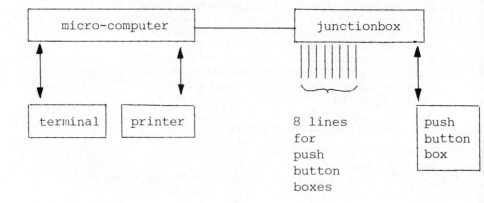

Figure 1. *Hardware configuration*

Information sources are boxes each of which has 10 manual push-button switches. These push-buttons are manipulated by operators according to the activities and responses that are observed. Each activity is given a code number corresponding with a push-button switch. A numeric display on top of the box shows the code corresponding with the button which was pushed last. The same display is used to let a sub-system observer know what the headline observer is doing, provided that the sub-system observer is in the waiting mode. The headline system is a modification of FIAC. Its 10 categories are in Table 2.

---

1. *Illustration.* Visual presentation by the teacher on the blackboard or a screen.
2. *Lecturing.* Giving facts or opinions about content or procedures.
3. *Question.* The teacher asks a question with the intent that a pupil will answer.
4. *Supplementary information.* Remarks by the teacher in order to clarify his question.
5. *Thinking pause.* The time taken by the pupils before answering a question from the teacher.
6. *Indication.* The teacher indicates verbally the pupil addressed.
7. *Teacher's response.* The reaction of the teacher to the answer received from the pupil.
8. *Answer.* A pupil replies to a question from the teacher.
9. *Pupil's initiation.* Talk by pupils which they initiate, for instance asking questions.
10. *Silence or confusion.* Silence except thinking pauses, periods of confusion in which communication cannot be understood by the observer. Also activity that cannot be classified into the above categories.

Table 2. *Headline categories*

The 10 categories of the sub-system for recording teachers' responses are in Table 3.

1. *Encouragement.* The teacher stimulates the pupil with appropriate comment.
2. *Direction.* The teacher gives some feedback that indicates to the student what was right or wrong in his answer.
3. *Echo.* The teacher repeats pupil talk word for word.
4. *Improvement.* The teacher adds information to the pupil's answer.
5. *Criticism.* The teacher makes irrelevant critical remarks to the pupil(s).
6. *Answering.* The teacher answers a question from the pupil.
7. *Co-operation.* The teacher stimulates the pupil with cues to improve a given answer.
8. *Participation.* The teacher gives another pupil the opportunity to react to the pupil's question or answer.
9. *Suggestion.* The teacher questions or stimulates the pupil to explain his answer or remark.
10. *Repetition.* The teacher repeats the original question.

Table 3. *Teacher's response categories*

Possibilities to evaluate an answer from the pupil are in Table 4.

1. Right
2. Wrong
3. Partly right
4. No way to say right or wrong
5. No answer
6. Answer given by the teacher himself

Table 4. *Evaluation of an answer*

After a lesson, a time-line (left to right) of the headline categories is printed. Additionally, the information from the sub-systems is printed underneath the corresponding headline categories. At the end, frequencies and time measures of the headline categories are printed.

Feedback Sessions

The first feedback session concerns the group discussion that follows immediately after a lesson, while the second session involves the video-tape playback of a recorded lesson.

One of the objectives of a feedback session is to make a student-teacher aware of his behaviour in the classroom so that he can reflect upon it and improve his presentation next time. Before each lesson the students receive a short instruction on the purpose of feedback and how it can be given effectively (NTL Institute, 1967).

Another objective is to confront a student-teacher with the reactions of pupils to his presentation, because they are the only people who can let the teacher know if he has been successful or not.

In the 'post-discussion' (immediately after the lesson), the student-teacher initiates the discussion by asking the pupils questions or expressing his feelings and thoughts. The student-teacher can benefit from the views expressed during the discussion and, if necessary, try to improve his presentation. The computer print-out is useful for relating the opinions expressed to observed patterns of behaviour.

Video-recordings are made of each lesson and the student-teacher sees his own presentation at the end of the microteaching session. The supervisor and the observer are with him. He can stop or replay the recording in order to get a better understanding of his behaviour or to discuss points of interest with the supervisor. Often, the video-recording confirms the teacher's own feelings, which he had already explained to the group.

Theme-Oriented Workshops

During the course, students participate in microteaching training once a week; each session takes half a day and training extends over four months. One afternoon per week the students study more theoretical topics, such as leadership, motivation, working in groups, and the objectives of education. In the first part of the workshop the students are provided with background knowledge on the topics to be presented from books, articles, or video-recordings. In the second part, the students participate in activities such as role-playing, discussions, or interviews. Their experience from giving microteaching lessons and working in learning groups, plays an important part in these activities. For example, they can reflect on the answers to questions such as:

- ☐ How do you teach children who are not motivated to do schoolwork?
- ☐ What is your opinion of the classroom as a social system?
- ☐ Which of your activities as a teacher do you think are the most important? And why?

It is valuable to connect the experiences of student-teachers with the accepted teaching theories. An example will illustrate this point. The theme of the workshop in this example was leadership.

The students were asked to read an article on different kinds of leadership in the classroom in order to help them to reflect on their own teaching experience. After a discussion, they were paired off and each member of a pair interviewed the other, using the following basic questions:

- ☐ How did you propose to lead the group when you were planning your lesson?
- ☐ How do you feel about the results and what new things did you learn?
- ☐ Are you satisfied with your presentation?
- ☐ Do you wish to change anything? And, if so, in what way?

Of such a pair of students, one student gave the following answers:

- ☐ 'I felt that I was an outsider during the lesson and not a member of the group while leading it'.
- ☐ 'I wanted to be more involved in the group learning processes'.
- ☐ 'I shall now try to work with small classes of pupils in order to learn whether I can become more involved with them'.

The other student (of the pair) remarked that:

- ☐ 'I did not respond to members of the group the way I do to other people'.
- ☐ 'I felt that I had too little contact with the pupils in the group and there was not enough interaction'.
- ☐ 'Usually, I am more receptive to people'.
- ☐ 'I would have had no idea how to respond to the pupil's reactions if I had not been prepared for them'.
- ☐ 'My presentation was not consistent although I intended it to be'.

As a result of reflecting on the views expressed in the interview, these two students are revising their approaches to teaching and both expect to benefit from attending this workshop.

Plans for Future Courses

This is the third time microteaching and theme-oriented workshops combined have been used. The course was improved by solving organizational problems, and incorporating opinions of the students from interviews and questionnaires. Additionally, the description of the questioning technique offered to the students was changed. Our former description consisted of a list of aspects, whereas lately the intention to encourage interaction and the participation of all pupils is emphasized.

We want to make the course more sophisticated by using more systematically evaluation techniques and research, and we should like to know if our design really guarantees more benefits than pure skill-training as we supposed it would. Some of the following questions need to be answered:

- ☐ Are the teaching situations in the course helping the students to understand their attitudes to teaching?
- ☐ How can information from the observation system be related to what students remember of a lesson, content and particular interactions?
- ☐ Does the questioning technique allow the students to develop their own styles of teaching?
- ☐ Are individual students encouraged to change their teaching behaviour and their attitudes towards teaching?
- ☐ Can students see the connection between their behaviour and teaching attitudes?

At present the answers to these questions are inadequate. It will be necessary to find out more about the *learning processes* of student-teachers. As far as is known nobody in the Netherlands is doing research on these questions, and it would be interesting to hear if similar research is being done in England or elsewhere.

References

Borg, W R, Kelly, M L, Langer, P and Gall, M (1970) *The Mini-Course: A Micro-Teaching Approach to Teacher Education.* Macmillan Educational Service, Beverley Hills, California, USA.

Flanders, N A (1970) *Analyzing Teaching Behaviour.* Addison-Wesley Publishing Company, Reading, Massachusetts, USA.

McNamara, D R (1981) Teaching skill: the question of questioning. *Educational Research,* 23, 2, pp 104-109.

NTL Institute: Reading Book (1967) *Feedback and the Helping Relationship,* pp 44-47. NTL Institute for Applied Behavioral Sciences, Washington, DC, USA.

6.4 Microteaching for Adult Literacy Skills with the PET Microprocessor

M Vinegrad
University of London, Goldsmiths' College

Abstract: This paper describes: (i) the type of learning problem being tackled, (ii) the nature of the programmes that have been developed, and (iii) the results achieved to date.

The author develops the theme (with supporting data) that microteaching can simultaneously function as a tool for research into the nature of learning problems and for the diagnosis of learning difficulties.

Programmes were originally developed for use in an adult literacy centre for individuals with acute problems in learning to spell and read. The project is now receiving financial support from the Basic Skills Unit (Manpower Services Commission) in connection with the Youth Opportunities Programme (YOP). Programmes are about to undergo trials at a number of centres throughout the UK.

The programmes provide structural training on verbal material entered for the student by another person (eg a tutor). A 'self-writing' sub-routine has been incorporated that 'pokes' the verbal material into the program listing, thus enabling a permanent copy of the program plus verbal material to be made by the simple operation of re-saving the entire program. Through this technique a library of unique programmes can be built up for each student.

For the benefit of individuals with severe reading difficulties, a small inexpensive interface has been developed that allows an audio-cassette to be synchronized with the video display under the control of the PET. As many of the students fall into the 16-plus age group, some of the programmes have been cast in the form of competitive video-games.

The programmes incorporate sub-routines for recording various aspects of performance, thus facilitating quantitative analysis of learning processes. Particular attention is paid to types and effects of feedback that are available in the system.

Introduction

In September 1980, it was decided to introduce CAL into an adult literacy scheme on an experimental basis. A number of programs have been written by the author for the PET microprocessor. At the time, there was little to indicate what kind of programs might prove useful or what the reaction of the students might be. The literacy scheme, which is run under the auspices of the Adult Studies department of Goldsmiths' College at the Lee Centre in south-east London, caters for a wide range of individuals whose literacy skills vary from rudimentary to near O level standard. It was decided to concentrate on a group of hard-core individuals who were functionally illiterate. For the most part, the students concerned had been attending the centre for a considerable time but despite this continued to have problems of a fundamental kind with both spelling and reading. The students fell into two main groups: (i) school leavers enrolled in the Youth Opportunities Programme, and (ii) adults, aged 20 upwards. For many of the adults, attendance at the centre was a brave venture that had required considerable determination and courage.

Since the time of its inception, the project has received backing from the Basic Skills Unit (Manpower Services Commission) and programs are now being developed and piloted in a wide setting, mainly in connection with the Youth Opportunities Programme.

The Basic Plan

At the outset of the project it was decided to concentrate on 'functional literacy' and so to aim at programmes that would be directly relevant to the students' lives and needs. All the students had immediate literacy problems, for example filling up job application forms or writing out customers' orders or bills. This decision meant that the primary objective was to devise programmes that would provide 'first aid' training on specific words and phrases rather than to attempt remedial action of a more general nature. The programmes were therefore designed as 'empty structures' into which verbal material could be inserted according to the needs of individual students.

The basic plan of the programmes is one that enables the student to move with rapidity to the point of being able to type the target word or phrase without error. The video screen is used to prompt each successive keyboard stroke to the point where the student cannot fail to be able to make the correct response. Once successful performance has been obtained and sustained for a sufficient number of repetitions, the prompts are gradually withdrawn so that the student is left performing from memory alone. One essential feature of the procedure is that the machine does not respond to incorrect key presses; it merely waits for the right response. This is important, because many of the students concerned experience such difficulty with spelling that ordinarily they are reluctant to try out even simple sentences for fear of making too many mistakes. The experience of being able to type out a set of words without visible error has proved a powerful source of motivation. During the development of the programs, various kinds of feedback were tried in response to student errors but it was the technique of doing nothing that proved to be the best. When this procedure was adopted there was a marked change of attitude on the part of the students, resulting in quite a dramatic increase in demands to work on the programs. However, it would be a waste of the potential of the microprocessor if error responses were totally ignored. In the present project quite a lot of importance has been attached to the use of this information as a source of data for the diagnosis of learning difficulties, and as a basis for providing feedback for both the student and the tutor at the end of the learning sequence.

Strategy of Program Development

Programs were developed in two stages:

1. Programs designed to be 'operated' by the tutor working alongside the student.
2. Programs designed to be independent CAL devices.

For stage 1, a few short simple programs were written, and these were stored in the computer with a 'menu' displayed on the screen. One of these programs, for example, allowed the student freely to explore the keyboard without error messages appearing on the screen. In another, an array of letters or graphics was presented on the screen and the student was required to find the right keys to copy the display into another space on the screen. The experimenter sat alongside the student throughout, and freely discussed the various events as they occurred. It is important to remember that the students involved had a lengthy history of failure, and required a careful introduction to a new learning technique. Some had come from ESN(M) schools.

In addition, it was hoped that this procedure would be a useful step in the production of the final CAL (stage 2) programmes. The plan was to develop the initial programs into relatively independent modules that later could be combined to produce more complex program structures. During the first stage, the modules were presented and manipulated by the experimenter according to the needs of the individual student. Not only the sequence of modules, but variables within modules, such as time intervals and numbers of repetitions, were under experimenter control. By proceeding in this way, it became possible as experience grew to progressively transfer control of the various factors to the computer. By this method, fully-fledged CAL programs were created in which the modules were treated as sub-routines of a larger program.

Audio Interface

It was apparent that the presence of the tutor during stage 1 had played an essential role in providing an auditory accompaniment to the proceedings. For this reason, an interface has been developed in the psychology department at Goldsmiths' College that enables an audio-tape recorder to be run in synchrony with the video display. The interface measures 10cm x 5cm x 2.5cm and is relatively inexpensive to produce. It can be used either externally to the microprocessor and tape recorder, or it can be mounted in the microprocessor, or sometimes in the battery compartment of the tape recorder. The recording is made by the tutor in advance in the form of a sequence of spoken segments, and these are subsequently presented by the computer according to the design of the program. The addition of the audio track has been found to greatly enhance the usefulness of the microprocessor in a field of this kind. Although the sequence of segments on the audio-tape is fixed, considerable flexibility can be achieved as a sub-routine has been written that enables new recordings to be made with ease, and in a manner that ensures automatic synchronization with the video display. There is no restriction on the length of spoken segments; one may last a second or two and the next may be several minutes in length.

Computer-Assisted Teaching and Computer-Assisted Learning

The technique of presenting relatively short programme modules under experimenter control was conceived as a means of developing CAL structures. However, during the course of the project it became clear that the procedure had merit in itself as a teaching device. The experimenter was able to use the capabilities of the computer to present material in ways that otherwise would not have been possible, whilst, at the same time, the student was able to actively participate in the learning process. The procedure was conducted in an informal, conversational atmosphere. Between such an arrangement and the fully developed CAL program, intermediate stages are possible. For example, the requirement of individually based learning led to the development of the 'empty structure' programme into which the tutor inserted appropriate material. In one arrangement, the action of the program is shaped by the tutor according to the manner in which the material is entered. For example, if hyphens were used to insert the word 'Sunday', as 'S-U-N-D-A-Y', the program would operate in terms of a sequence of six units corresponding to the six letters. However, if the word were inserted as 'SUN-DAY', operation would be in terms of two units corresponding to the two syllables. A longer item such as 'Wednesday is the day after tomorrow' could be entered in various ways, for example 'WED-NES-DAY IS THE DAY AF-TER TO-MORR-OW'. Here the operational units would correspond to syllables and the whole words 'is', 'the' and 'day'. By entering a sequence of suitable items, the tutor is able to build up a lesson plan for the program to act upon. By means of such methods, it is apparent that programs can be developed in ways that make them more or less amenable to tutor control. From this point of view, it may be useful to make a relative distinction between programmes that are designed more for computer-assisted teaching than for independent learning.

Self-Writing Program and Computer Files

In order to eliminate the necessity of entering verbal material each time a programme is used, two kinds of sub-routine have been developed to store verbal material for repeated use. One of these is a 'self-writing' program which 'pokes' the verbal material item by item into the program listing as it is entered by the tutor. This means that a permanent copy of the program with verbal material *in situ* can be made by simply re-saving the entire program on a blank cassette or disc. Through this technique a library of unique programs can be built up for each student. One advantage of using cassettes rather than discs is that the computer program can be placed on one side of the cassette and the voice recording on the other.

The second sub-routine uses the more conventional 'file-writing' procedure. This is presented in a format designed for the average literacy tutor, with little or no experience of computer file procedures.

The two sub-routines form independent modules, and sometimes one is more convenient than the other. Throughout the development of the project, an effort has been made to produce this kind of independent, interchangeable module. Such a procedure means that programmes can be altered with relative ease according to invididual needs, and new programmes can be created using existing software.

Competitive Video Games

It was found useful to develop some programmes in the form of competitive video games. For example, one of these was designed to help in teaching the position of the letters on the keyboard. It consists of a simple reaction time game in which the players are able to accumulate points according to the speed with which the correct keys are located. A program of this kind is usually popular and can play a useful role as a component in a learning session.

Transfer

A basic question that is often asked concerns the degree to which skills acquired on the microprocessor transfer to other situations. For example, does learning to spell a word on the keyboard mean that the student will be able to spell the word when he or she tries to write it? It is, of course, easy enough to compare performance immediately before and after training on the computer, but it is harder to tie down any change in the longer term to the microprocessor alone. In the present project, work on the computer has almost always been integrated with other, more conventional forms of tuition, making the question of transfer even harder to answer. Because of this, it has seemed more profitable to concentrate on other questions. For example, do the students feel it helps them? In a field such as adult literacy this is very important as students often experience frustration at their slow speed of progress, and in consequence may give up. Programs of the type described, simply because they do not let the student fail, can play a significant role in bolstering confidence and morale. In addition, the simple experience of being able to work at a problem without the necessity of having someone else there to observe mistakes can be of considerable importance.

Apart from considerations of this kind, there is also the contribution the microprocessor can make to the student's insight into his or her own performance through the presentation of feedback at suitable points in the training sessions. In the present project, one of the major questions for future investigation concerns the kind and quantities of such feedback that may be beneficial to individuals of various kinds. A program module that has been tentatively tried with selected individuals provides a re-run of a programme segment, with all the student's responses recorded and played back just as they occurred. A persistent feature of many of these students' behaviour is the repetitive nature of certain kinds of error and it often comes as a surprise to the individuals concerned when confronted with this on the screen. However, more research is needed into the effects of this program module and the kind of students with whom it may be employed.

A second major emphasis for the future concerns the development of modules for detailed analysis of performance and diagnosis of learning difficulties. Modules of this type would provide a basis both for better forms of feedback and research into the learning process.

Finally, it has been decided to explore more fully the technique of developing CAL programmes through the intermediate strategy of the computer-assisted teaching design.

6.5 Training RAF Instructors in the Skills of Briefing, Monitoring and Debriefing, Using Microteaching Methodologies

J McCarthy and M Easby
RAF School of Education and Training Support

Abstract: During the past decade the RAF SOETS has identified an increasingly important need amongst Service instructors to master the skills of briefing, monitoring and debriefing practical exercises.

A most effective training method, which has found particular relevance in part-task simulation, has been developed based on microteaching principles using gaming, CCTV and microcomputers.

The paper will describe the investigation of the training need, the analysis of the skills and attitudes required in effective briefing, monitoring and debriefing, and describe in detail the training method. The paper will be illustrated by video-tapes of model and student performances.

Introduction

Much of the training in the Royal Air Force is based upon practical exercises. Over the past decade the RAF School of Education and Training Support has been involved in the analysis of the necessary skills, knowledge and attitudes which constitute effective instructor performance in the one-to-one or small-group environment. The instructor skills required in the effective management of student learning in a practical exercise include those of briefing, monitoring and debriefing.

Training in these skills was first given to tutors before their employment on the newest of our command and staff training courses: the Basic Staff Course, which is a pre-employment training course for squadron leaders about to take up staff appointments. The Basic Staff Course lays great emphasis on student-centred learning and relies heavily on the tutorial function of the instructors. The training in such tutor skills as briefing, monitoring, intervention techniques and debriefing has since been adapted to provide job-related instructor training in other areas. A special adaptation was required to train flight simulator instructors, and this has been developed further to provide special-to-type training for air traffic control simulator instructors. We will outline our concept of the principles of briefing, monitoring and debriefing, in which we have used microteaching principles, and describe how we train ground instructors and flight simulator instructors in these skills.

Model of Approach

An analysis of the principles of briefing, monitoring and debriefing, based on the observation and experience of effective instructors, confirmed that the model shown in Figure 1 was an effective training sequence.

The overall aim of briefing, monitoring and debriefing is seen to be to develop and improve student performance of individual or group skills by means of practical exercises. The elements are not discrete but are interdependent, in that the quality of the briefing will affect the degree of intervention during the monitoring phase and the scale and nature of the debriefing required to establish a satisfactory standard of student performance. Nor are the boundaries between the elements distinct; varying degrees of overlap should and will always occur, as is shown in Figure 2.

So interrelated are these instructional skills that a situation will exist where the student does not achieve the standard of performance required during the practical exercise, but may satisfy his instructor that he has achieved the exercise objectives as a result of the debriefing. The microteaching model used in instructor training is based on the well-established model used at Stanford University (see Figure 3).

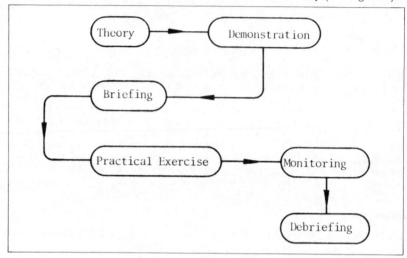

Figure 1. *Training sequence*

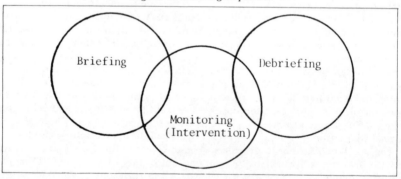

Figure 2. *The overlap of elements*

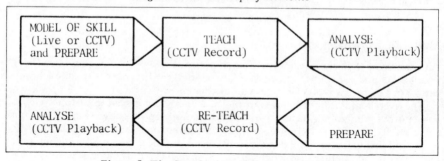

Figure 3. *The Stanford teach/re-teach sequence*

Briefing

Briefing is seen as an intense period of instruction. It does not aim to teach anything new. Rather, it is used to focus attention on the subsequent exercise as well as on those areas of theory which will be used in the practical exercise or to provide data so that an exercise can be carried out. So, briefings usually contain testing questions which are used by the instructor to check previous learning applicable to the exercise and understanding of the relevant data given in the briefing. Briefings are of short duration (generally not more than 20 minutes); they need to be logically structured and, to achieve the desired objectives, maximum use should be made of training aids.

New instructors are encouraged to plan and prepare their briefings with the aim of achieving the elements of instructor performance which are shown in Figure 4.

Introduction	Development	Conclusion
In which the instructor:	*In which the instructor:*	*In which the instructor:*
puts the student at ease	states facts	reviews main points of of the briefing
states the aim of the exercise	outlines exercise procedure	checks understanding of key points
arouses interest in the exercise	checks relevant knowledge	confirms preparation and readiness for the practical exercise
reviews the relevant background	encourages student questions	

Figure 4. *Structure of a typical brief*

Monitoring

The purpose of monitoring is to aid student learning in three ways. First, it allows the instructor to control the exercise; second, the instructor notes how a student performs in order to appraise that performance; and third, he measures achievement so as to develop and improve a student's abilities. The many skills required of the instructor for effective monitoring, including skilled intervention, are shown here:

(a) The instructor should:
   give the student all the help and information required to achieve the objectives;
   guide the student as to what to think about and look for;
   make the practice as realistic as possible whilst indicating the differences between training performance and operational performance;
   focus a student's attention on the intrinsic cues and actions and add supplementary feedback as necessary to develop the student's performance;
   appraise a student's performance by identifying the significant performances required and by recognizing the standard of performance achieved by the student;
   keep a record of the significant points in the student's performance for the subsequent debriefing.

(b) Skilled intervention is an essential part of effective monitoring and can be be verbal, non-verbal or mechanical; it requires the instructor to answer the following questions:

Why am I intervening?
How should I intervene?
When and how often should I intervene?
What will be the effect on my student?
What will the effect be on myself?
Should I give remedial instruction?
Should I suspend the exercise or take positive control?

(c) An enabling skill of effective monitoring is that of performance assessment. It is very important that the new instructor realizes that assessment should be aimed not only at measuring a student's current achievement but also at aiding the learning process. If required it can also be a predictor of a student's potential. It is often difficult to separate these functions. The first two involve 'process' and 'product' assessment. 'Process' describes the manner in which a student performs, and 'product' describes the result of his actions. For example, a student pilot may arrive at the correct location (product) in a navigation exercise, but the navigation procedures he has followed (process) may have included errors and omissions. Whereas the tester is interested in both 'process' and 'product' assessment, the trainer is primarily interested in 'process' assessment. The observation and measurement of the standard of the 'product' of a student's performance can be made by objective methods. However, the assessment of the 'process' element of a student's performance is often, of necessity, the subjective opinion of the instructor. Nevertheless, all assessment should be valid and reliable: valid in that the right performance is measured, and reliable in that the measuring device is accurate and consistent. In performance assessment, the new instructor must know the type and standard of performance he is looking for and, as the measuring device is often his own judgement, he must have the experience and training to give accurate and consistent results. Training in performance assessment is given to new instructors on the RAF Flight Simulator Instructors' Course prior to experience being gained during on-the-job training.

Debriefing

The purpose of a debrief is to provide a learning situation for the student. As such, the debrief is student-orientated. There are times when the debrief is the first time when student learning really begins. The most common uses of debriefs are: to provide students with opportunities to consolidate what they have learned; to identify strengths and weaknesses; to develop the student's ability to analyse his own performance; and to identify with the real situation (if simulation is used). The effectiveness of a debrief is enhanced by the instructor carefully eliciting from the student the lessons learned and his proposed corrective action. The instructor must also guide and motivate the student to further development.

Poorly structured debriefs can lead to loss of student confidence or general deterioration of student morale. When debriefs fail to be positive learning situations, performance on subsequent practices is affected. Hence, the instructor needs to balance the debrief with a measure of supportiveness to offset the negative attitudes which highly critical debriefs tend to produce. Just how supportive an instructor can be will depend on a number of factors, eg the amount of time available for the debrief will dictate what the instructor can concentrate on and the teaching strategy employed. Moreover, student and instructor personality and attitudes will have considerable bearing on the degree of supportiveness, as will the significance the exercise has in the training programme. To conduct an effective debrief, an instructor may often require more information than he can carry in his head. To aid effective debriefing, instructors should use information which has been noted or recorded during the monitoring phase. To this end, debriefing aids which can record a student's performance are available in modern flight simulators.

It is felt that debriefs should be structured and well-prepared, based upon the information collected during the practical exercise. There is no 'right' way to debrief because of the variations present in the training situation. However, guidelines can be helpful and these are set out here (see Figure 5).

Introduction	Development	Conclusion
In which the instructor:	*In which the instructor:*	*In which the instructor:*
puts the student at ease reviews the exercise	encourages student participation, ideas, clear thinking	reviews main points covered in the debrief
summarizes student performance in general terms	asks questions to guide the student to analyse his own performance	establishes lessons learned and what will be done to correct errors
establishes the starting points for the debrief	keeps things moving	ensures student's future co-operation

Figure 5. *Rebuilt guidelines*

The attitude displayed by a good debriefer can also be represented graphically. The instructor opens the debriefing session on a positive, supportive note, highlighting those aspects where student performance was acceptable. As the session progresses, constructive criticism is introduced and performance analysed in terms of exercise parameters. The debrief is wound up with a review of lessons learned. The round-off is supportive, yet balanced so as not to give the student wrong impressions of his performance (see Figure 6).

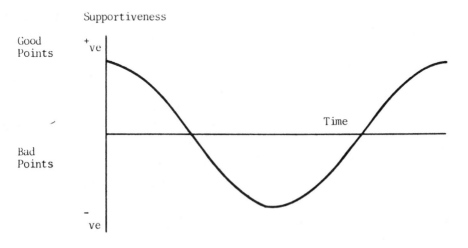

Figure 6. *The relationship between time and support*

Training using Microteaching

The RAF SOETS is responsible for the instructional techniques training of most ground training, rearcrew, air traffic control and flight simulator instructors. Special-to-type training, based on 'microteaching', is now available for RAF instructors. This scaled-down version of instruction is used to emphasize and to develop the skills of briefing, monitoring and debriefing. The student is given theory instruction in the skills and a demonstration of a model performance. He then practises the skills and analyses his performance using video-recordings, discussion with his peers, and directing staff guidance. From the lessons learned from this analysis of the first practice, he prepares and repeats the performance. This second practice is also analysed using video-recordings, peer group discussion and directing staff guidance. The lessons learned can then be consolidated by further practice if required. The aim of the microteaching training is to enable a new instructor to teach a 'student' a new skill by giving him a clear briefing, effectively monitoring the practice of the skill, and debriefing the 'student' on his performance. The effectiveness of the new instructor can be judged by the results of the 'student's' performance of the new skill (product) and by the directing staff's assessment of the instructor's performance (process). Finding a skill which would be new to the trainees, simple enough to learn in a very short period of time, consisting of distinct procedures based upon certain rules, and which could be observed and measured, was not easy!

However, two very satisfactory solutions have been found. The first is the skill of playing a card game of PATIENCE, called 'Exercise Solitaire', and the second is the skill of playing microcomputer-generated television games, called 'Exercise Dynamic Micro'. The training principle is common to both media.

Exercise Solitaire

After the theory instruction and demonstration of a model briefing, monitoring and debriefing performance, the trainee instructor is given the rules of a particular game of PATIENCE. He has 45 minutes to learn the game and to prepare a briefing. His aim is to get the student to play the game according to the rules. Each play, lasting for an hour, involves three students (the trainee instructor, the student and an observer), as shown in Figure 7.

Activity	Time	Instructor	Student	Observer
Briefing	8 minutes	Briefs student on game	Is briefed on game	Watches briefing
Monitoring	6 minutes (maximum)	Monitors and controls	Plays the game under the control of the instructor	Observes instructor-student interaction
Debriefing	10 minutes	Debriefs student on his performance	Is debriefed by instructor	Watches debriefing
Analysing	36 minutes	Analyses his own performance with Observer and DS	Watches analysis and participates when asked	Analyses instructor performance with instructor and DS

Figure 7. *Participant activities*

The briefing, monitoring and debriefing are recorded on video-tape for subsequent playback during the analysis of the instructor's performance. Should the new instructor need to be trained for an 'off-board' instructor station, an innovation can be introduced whereby the instructor monitors the student's performance at a distance via CCTV. After the trainee instructor has been allowed sufficient time to consolidate the lessons he has learned from his first performance, he then briefs a new student on the same card game in the manner just described. During this second phase, the directing staff may reduce the time allowed for the briefing, or restrict the number of interventions allowed if this will improve the new instructor's briefing, monitoring and debriefing skills.

Exercise Dynamic Micro

Whilst card games are an excellent training vehicle for microteaching, it was recognized that by using a microcomputer it was possible to increase the training value of our microteaching. 'Exercise Dynamic Micro' was developed to improve the training of instructors employed in flight and air traffic control simulators. The medium is a microcomputer-generated game in which an image moves on a television screen controlled by keyboard inputs. Several games, some commercially available, are used. All contain movement and involve hand and eye co-ordination, requiring anticipation and judgement by the player. A 'freeze' facility is available to the instructor, and the speed of the game can be altered to aid a player's learning. Microcomputer-generated games offer the following advantages:

(a) They are readily accepted because they are perceived by simulator instructors to be job-related.
(b) They are intrinsically interesting.
(c) They contain more dimensions than the card games of PATIENCE.
(d) They involve movement, the speed of which can be controlled.
(e) They contain a 'freeze/replay' facility.
(f) A hard-copy printout can be incorporated as a debriefing aid.
(g) The instructor can be stationed 'on-board' or 'off-board' as required.

'Exercise Dynamic Micro' is conducted along the same microteaching principles as 'Exercise Solitaire'.

Training in Assessment of Performance

During the Flight Simulator Instructors' Course, students discuss the principles and problems of valid and reliable assessment (a very interesting piece of training but outside the scope of this presentation). However, during 'Exercise Solitaire' and 'Exercise Dynamic Micro' the trainee instructors are encouraged to assess students' performances during the monitoring phase so that their interventions can provide supplementary feedback to aid students' learning. For example, a student may fail to recognize an intrinsic cue provided by the computer; in some instances cues are missed entirely, or misinterpreted. It is the function of the instructor to draw a student's attention to the cues by providing supplementary feedback, either in the form of further intrinsic cues or by verbal intervention. Not until a student can respond in the correct manner to the feedback provided during the practical exercise can an instructor consider the exercise to be satisfactory. During the debriefing, the instructor is expected to inform his student of the assessment he has received for the exercise.

Conclusion

The skills of briefing, monitoring and debriefing have been identified and now form part of the instructional techniques training given to new ground, rearcrew and simulator instructors at the RAF SOETS. The training method is based on microteaching and two media are used as training vehicles. Card games of PATIENCE satisfy the training requirements of all ground and rearcrew instructors, whereas microcomputer-generated TV games provide a more effective training vehicle for simulator instructors. Training in assessment of performance, as an enabling skill to effective monitoring and debriefing, is also given to simulator instructors.

6.6 The Application of Microteaching Techniques to the Testing and Training of Teachers in Oral Examination Procedures

A J Trott
Bulmershe College of Higher Education

Abstract: Many uses have been found for microteaching methodologies because many professional tasks can be broken down into skills and sub-skills.

Oral examinations based on project or experiential work are well known in the humanities, integrated studies or social studies areas. This paper describes an attempt to bring current microteaching practice to bear upon the assessment and training of oral examiners. The identification of areas of need are described; discrepancies found in a series of simulated incidents are detailed; and suggestions are offered concerning the enlargement of the pilot study and ways in which training packages can be developed.

Introduction

Oral examinations, in subjects other than languages, were significant innovations brought about by the introduction of the Certificate of Secondary Education in the 1960s. Oral assessment of one kind or another now appears as part of many CSE Mode III schemes, and it usually carries a small allocation of marks. The assessment of oral communication is acknowledged by some teachers to be a vague, grey area. This is in spite of the fact that the majority of dyadic communications in our modern world are oral.

At the present time it seems that oral assessment is used primarily on children of below average ability. Yet we see some of our most prestigious universities using a similar technique under the name of 'Viva' to examine doctoral candidates. It is possible that oral assessment could be used to good effect with the vast majority of children. Perhaps its use will uncover particular skills, knowledge or attitudes which are not identifiable by written means.

The Identification of Candidate Abilities

The Southern Regional Examination Board Working Party on Oral Assessment (Trott, 1981) suggested three areas which might be examined in this way, perhaps using a flexibility which is not available in written tests.

The Candidate's Understanding of the Nature of Evidence

(a) Can the pupil relate argument to evidence?
(b) Does the pupil appreciate the significance of evidence?
(c) Is the pupil aware of the strengths and weaknesses of the evidence, eg that evidence may be ambiguous?
(d) Can the pupil distinguish between fact and opinion?

The Candidate's Ability to Discuss

(a) Is the pupil able to explore an issue?
(b) Can the pupil incorporate new ideas arising during the discussion?
(c) Can the pupil develop an argument?

(d) Is the pupil logical and rational?
(e) Can the pupil detect bias in his own argument and correct it?
(f) Can the pupil detect bias in another person's argument and refute it?
(g) Does the pupil question hearsay evidence?

The Candidate's Understanding of Value Judgement

(a) Can the pupil identify the main issue and reject irrelevances?
(b) Is the pupil willing to concede that another point of view may be valid?
(c) Can the pupil enlarge a discussion and add depth to it without necessarily breaking new ground?
(d) Can the pupil justify a particular line of argument without being easily diverted from it?
(e) Does the pupil understand that there is a relationship between opinion, behaviour and social context?

Undoubtedly we are likely to discover mammoth pitfalls in trying to measure some of these candidate abilities. Nevertheless, there seems a need to progress quickly.

The 16-plus Examination

Recently, there has again been discussion about the proposed 16-plus implementation date. More than two years ago, Mr Mark Carlisle, the Education Secretary, suggested 1986 as a convenient time when the 16-plus would replace GCE O levels and CSE examinations. It seems likely that the 16-plus examinations in languages, social studies, integrated studies and similar areas will contain oral assessments in some form.

If pupils are assessed at 16-plus, we are examining written and oral skills which have been acquired at an earlier age. Are we right in thinking that some children are more able to express themselves orally, whereas other children might favour written assessment? Perhaps current examination procedures tend to favour children who are good at writing.

One of the questions which must be considered by those planning the implementation of the 16-plus is that of examination procedure. Relating the question to a particular subject it becomes: 'When we teach history do we examine historical skills or is that examination filtered through a procedure which is not entirely equitable or accurate?'

The Pilot Studies

Having identified these rather high-sounding aims, we felt that we should examine current procedures and build up our knowledge of 'best practice'. In order to do this, we encouraged several small-scale research studies at Bulmershe during the years 1979 and 1980 (Clarke, 1980). Simulated oral assessment interviews were recorded on video-tape and analysed with the help of four serving teachers. The tapes were viewed by the Secretary to the Examinations Board, and assessed as 'fairly typical'. Basic measurements were then made concerning four aspects of the interviews.

The Interview Structure

The mode III Social Studies oral examination seems to be very open in structure, unlike the orals in French and English, perhaps, where marking is more detailed and specific grammatical constructions are expected. In Social Studies interviews a 'traditional' structure seems to have grown up, which gives the interviews an overt similarity. After a short introduction, the interviewer asks the pupil to begin his set talk. When the pupil comes to a natural conclusion, or 'dries up', the questioning starts. After a while, the interviewer draws the assessment to a close.

From the 19 video-tapes recorded by local teachers with their pupils, it was seen that the length of the introduction varied from seven to 20 seconds; most lasted about 12 seconds. The total interview length varied between five minutes and nine seconds to 11 minutes and 30 seconds; most lasted about eight or nine minutes.

Using the same video-tapes, the length of the pupils' prepared talk was measured, compared with the overall length of the interview, and a percentage calculated. A staggering variation of between 1.4 per cent and 89.2 per cent was found.

Other, more obvious, happenings concerning the conduct of the assessment interview were noticed . . . Usually one teacher conducted the interview, although sometimes there were two. Some teachers continued to teach during the assessment interview. Some teachers allowed notes to be used; others did not. Some teachers seemed concerned about teaching their classes efficiently, creating the impression that teaching rather than learning was being examined.

Interruption of Candidates

This factor seemed to be important in the early work, but since that time has been found to occur less frequently. Nevertheless, teacher interruptions of the following types have been observed.

(a) Prompts candidate to the right answer.
(b) Repeats his own question.
(c) Repeats the candidate's answer.
(d) Answers his own question.
(e) Makes a summary of the candidate's answer.
(f) Asks further questions.
(g) Verbally rejects the candidate's answer.

Reinforcement

There is an obvious problem about the use of reinforcement in a test situation. If it is used it should be used for all candidates. If pupils are used to reinforcement when they answer in class, will they be silenced by an unfamiliar lack of reinforcement? From our observations there seem to be four main types of reinforcement present: (i) verbal, (ii) non-verbal, (iii) extra-verbal, (iv) the use of the answer by the interviewer. The most significant finding from the tapes was the low incidence of positive reinforcement. It seemed as if the teachers were not used to using this skill, and praised very few pupil contributions.

Other observed effects were those of the use of pupil names and the establishment of eye contact which seemed to encourage the pupils; and the effect of the long-standing relationship between teacher and pupil which seemed to influence pupil performance.

Questioning

'. . . frequency of questions bears no relationship to the level of pupil achievement in tests and examinations and higher level questioning is positively related to higher level performance in tests and examinations'. (Brown, 1975)

The problems of accurately measuring this skill quickly became apparent. It was noticeable that few higher order questions were asked, and few responses required analysis, synthesis or evaluation. Many questions could be answered by a quick 'yes' or 'no'.

The Focus of Previous Research

Armed with this information we began to assemble details of previous related studies to try to build up areas of concern. We found five basic areas.

(a) Establishing rapport and the relaxation of the candidate.
(b) Attending behaviour and the open invitation to talk by the examiner.
(c) Effective questioning to include: (i) the increase of pupil talk; (ii) the use of open and closed questions; (iii) the use of probing questions; (iv) prompting replies from candidates; (v) obtaining a balance of higher order, middle order and lower order questions; (vi) the refocusing of questions.
(d) The use of reinforcement (verbal, non-verbal and extra-verbal) together with the implied or open acceptance of answers.
(e) The elimination of habits which inhibit answering or disrupt the flow of discussion: (i) avoiding the temptation to teach; (ii) avoiding repeating one's own question; (iii) avoiding repeating pupil answers; (iv) avoiding answering one's own question.

It is our intention to mount trials which will test pilot materials used in conventional microteaching methods against sensitization only treatments and against control groups. Thus we are in the process of devising guidelines covering the preparation for an interview and the establishment of rapport, the beginning of an interview, questioning and reinforcement, and finally an assessment of interviews. The questioning module is complete and we expect to complete the others during this year. We would suggest that any programme attempting to train interviewers should contain elements which cover the same areas as ours. In due course, we hope to be able to make this work available for use in other contexts and that other panels and other area bodies will collaborate with us.

References

Brown, G A (1975) *Microteaching: A Programme of Teaching Skills*. Methuen, London.
Clarke, G (1980) An investigation into selected skills used during oral assessment of Certificate of Secondary Education Mode III Social Studies Projects. Unpublished BEd dissertation. Bulmershe College, Reading.
Trott, A J (1981) Interim Report of the Working Party on Oral Assessment. Mimeo. Bulmershe College, Reading.

6.7 Perception and Behaviour Progression: The Optimalization of Peer Group Microteaching when Used in a Training Laboratory

E M Buter
University of Amsterdam

Abstract: It is shown in this paper that the behaviour progression of student-teachers during classroom lessons depends mainly upon a continuous feedback loop. The loop, in turn, depends upon the input of 'weak signals' and upon cognitive schemata for control. Both of these elements have a somewhat *ad hoc* character. A model for this (PIP) cycle is presented. The use of the model prescriptively to enhance laboratory peer group microteaching is discussed.

However, to students who often expect clear cut recipes for keeping order and preventing misdemeanour, the instrumental use of 'weak signals' seems to be 'out of tune'.

In this report, experienced-based suggestions are made concerning the motivation of students towards work with the PIP cycle.

Behaviour Progression and Decisions in the Actual Teaching Situation

Since 1970 I have been analysing the way in which teachers decide on their behaviour. Some of the results support Brophy's studies on teacher behaviour. Many teachers are *proactive*, planning their lessons in a flexible way, and anticipating class behaviour well enough to cope with unexpected alternatives. As Brophy (1976) states, such teachers initiate behaviour, they do not *react* to pupil initiatives, they *proact*. It is accepted that many beginner teachers are proactive, that is, they learn to anticipate and use models to design adequate teaching-learning situations. But do they react in the same way in a real-life situation? Many subjects who took part in our experiments seemed to be able to look into the immediate future, and act accordingly. This future could be seconds or minutes away, as long as it was within the boundary of one lesson. Other subjects seemed oblivious of such futures.

The continuous behaviour progression in actual teaching will be examined in this article. Results of observations will be used as a basis for a model leading to suggestions for the use of peer group microteaching (PMT) in the training laboratory.

A Simple Research Methodology: Reflections on Video-Recordings of Teaching Behaviour

The following rather simple procedure of observation and analysis is used.

(a) A lesson is prepared to last for a maximum of 30 minutes.
(b) This lesson is presented to a peer group or sometimes a 'real' class in accordance with the perceived level of the group, thus eliminating role play.
(c) The lesson is recorded on video-tape and so is able to be reproduced immediately.
(d) After presentation, peers comment on it. Sometimes the student-teacher gives an indication of the criteria he used for his behaviour before other comments are given. Comments are sometimes written and discussed in

groups; sometimes they are stated orally during the next plenary session. It is possible to use other ways of presenting comments.

(e) Next, the student-teacher comments on his performance.

(f) A plenary discussion follows in which the reasons for behaviour at different points in the lesson are drawn out.

(g) The video-taped material is consulted and some previously identified parts of the lesson are discussed and analysed minutely. However, it would appear that this minute analysis is not always necessary.

(h) Sometimes the student-teacher and the supervisor together analyse the whole recording. An open interview method is used in which the teacher comments on what he sees and is encouraged to recall especially what his *thoughts* were when he did specific things.

(i) After each presentation, the members of the peer group fill in a simple evaluation sheet which describes what they had learned from this presentation'.

(j) In many cases *all* sessions are recorded on video-tape and transcribed for reference. Thus the process of combining video presentations with the commentary of peers and the reflections of the teaching subject is accomplished. It is hoped that some relationships are readily observable.

If recordings of a reasonable quality are available the method can be copied easily. However, time for detailed monitoring and editing must be allowed. Different methodological problems will not be mentioned here, but it does seem that patterns of reflections on recorded lessons are repeated by student-teachers, even if different settings are used.

Some Results: Weak Signals, Cognitive Structuring and Levels of Inference

Some of the trainee teachers seem to decide on behavioural change without any clear observable indication that it is necessary. Even the behavioural change itself may be unnoticed by an outside observer.

Let us look at some examples.

Example 1

The student-teacher glances at a hand-out he prepared before the lesson, and, at the very moment he is handing it out to the pupils, realizes that one specific part of the text needs elaboration. So, whilst distributing the hand-outs, in order to prevent the premature interference by some of his pupils, he imparts additional information. To an observer this might seem normal procedure because it is impossible to infer 'change of (planned) behaviour' without additional information. What is happening in this instance is that the teacher receives some clue or signal and therefore changes his plans slightly. These factors only become apparent when the video-recording is viewed and analysed.

Example 2

The student-teacher is conducting an activity with the pupils in turn. When viewing the recording, it appears that the teacher changed his planned sequence. This he did 'because he felt that one of the pupils was under pressure from other group members'; in other words, that they wanted this particular pupil to have his turn. The teacher thought that it would be wise to leave out this pupil, and to redirect the sequence to those who, in his opinion, were exerting the pressure. In this way he hoped to prevent conflict. Again, without additional information, behaviour change was not observable. It was not noticeable from the video-recording that the pupil was under any kind of stress.

Example 3

The student-teacher sees A glancing at B, and knows that this is often followed by a chat. As part of the lesson, the teacher engages B good-humouredly in discussion, asking him questions which he knows B will be able to answer easily. Thus he prevents possible chatting, which might have been annoying, and at the same time interests B in his work.

It is easy to produce many examples similar to the ones given here. From such examples we may conclude that some student-teachers are very attentive to unobstructive information coming from the environment or from their own behaviour. Signal strength of such information must be considered relatively low, so I call them *weak signals*. But the synchronization of teacher behaviour and class behaviour is based upon such weak signals.

Weak Signals and Cognition

It appears that this synchronization of behaviour is based on processes which are cognitive and often affective in character, as opposed to more conditioned and routine-based behaviour. This can be concluded from the fact that student-teachers are able to verbalize what they felt, saw and perceived, in response to video self-confrontation. From protocols it follows that student-teachers are relating their interpretations to cognitive schemes that are a mixture of what they already know, and of what they made up *ad hoc*. What seems to be even more important is that student-teachers switch the level of their verbal interpretations between two or three levels of abstraction, ie high level inference, low level inference, and a level somewhere in between (*cf* Dunkin and Biddle, 1974).

The high level inference contains sentences which are used to describe generalized conclusions about situations and behaviour. The lowest level consists of highly specific behaviour or specific feelings (in fact, these are the *weak signals* in verbal form). In between is a middle level which generalizes for *that* group, *that* situation, thus differentiating it from other groups or moments in time.

Let me give some more examples.

Example 4

In example 1, the student teacher explained his actions thus:

'I suddenly realized that some of my pupils had prior knowledge of the subject. This might have led to a discussion which was not wanted because it was not relevant for the class at this time. I thought that additional information would forestall such a discussion'.

In this example, perception and decision remain very close to the actual elements of the situation.

Example 5

The student-teacher looks at several pupils, and for each has a specific thought.

'Peter sits in a very relaxed way; it looks as if he is following the lesson easily'.
'Mary is doodling, but she does this when she is attending'.
'John makes notes that are legible even from here; it seems that he has time enough to write'.
'It seems that the class follows my theme at this speed easily. Maybe the subject is easier to follow than I thought; let's see if I can speed up a little'.

It should be noted that the student-teacher is explaining something which took only seconds in reality, and that he goes through three different levels of abstraction.

Example 6 (constructed for brevity)

As an alternative conclusion in example 5, the student-teacher might well 'translate' his conclusion into:

> 'I gave them a paragraph to read, with questions to answer, because I knew from experience or theory that this process is quicker and not so tiring as speeding up the pace of a lesson. But because I selected this alternative I had to make special provisions for individual pupils. Mary panics when asked to do things which seem to be difficult, so I gave her individual tuition. Peter is very slow and so I allowed him to work at his own pace during the lesson and then to finish it at home. There is no set homework for this class, but the procedure I adopted helped to establish the natural relationship between classwork and homework'.

From this example it can be seen that the student-teacher relates his levels of abstraction to his own behaviour. This leads to another observation.

Easy Switching between Levels of Inference

Some student-teachers switch easily from one level of inference to another, and, when they apply this to their own behaviour, often do it in reverse order. Example 6 makes this very clear. It seems as if the student is approaching his operational level of behaviour in steps.

Let us look at one final example.

Example 7

Student:

> 'I thought that the pupils were highly involved in this work. Some of the exercises seemed easy to do and yet were rewarding; even pupils A, B and C were concentrating. If the class is working like this it seems worthwhile to walk round and see what they are doing, as you told me to during training. I thought that I would look at what they were writing and drawing, so that I could comment on their work in the next lesson'.

No additional comment seems necessary here.

The Model of the PIP Cycle

We can interpret classroom behaviour, when it is functioning reasonably, as a kind of wavy line. The variations between the troughs and peaks are small, no matter what criteria we choose to measure. We find that a few student-teachers perceive weak signals in the wave line, and this could mean greater disturbances later on (see Figure 1).

A teacher who uses the preaction mode often can be described as preactive. The cycle can be repeated over and over again within a lesson period. The diagram illustrates the division of the situation into two parts: the actual and the imagined.

The Position of the PIP Cycle in the Overall Situation

The PIP cycle is used by some student-teachers to deal with perceived activities and problems in the immediate lesson future, but these are based on images in the mind of the student. Therefore, like the proactive teacher, the preactive teacher mostly generates his own behaviour. However, the reactive teacher has his behaviour enforced on him by the actions of the class (see Figure 1: 6 and A).

It now seems sensible to postulate a *post-active phase*. This follows the reactive phase during the actual lesson and relates to the reactive phase in a reflective way. The reactive and post-active phases are always easily observable, and often provide a focus for debate when classroom behaviour is being discussed. I postulate another period after the lesson which I call the *retroactive phase*. It deals with the whole lesson in retrospect and forms a natural link with the proactive phase of the next lesson.

The possible cyclic situations which undoubtedly exist between these phases will not be discussed in this paper.

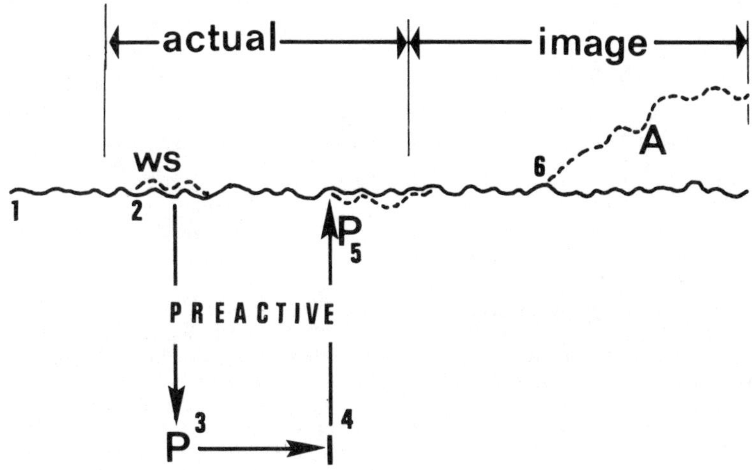

Reasonably functioning classes can be symbolized by the wave line (1). Barely perceptible cues or *weak signals* (WS) (2), can be *perceived* (P) (3) by the student-teacher, and interpreted (I) (4). These give rise to a change in behaviour which slightly interferes with the planned behaviour wave (P) (5). This interference we call *preaction*, and the cycle basic to it the PIP cycle. The cycle is actual, but it is actuated by the imagined, potential activities of the class (A) (6). A successful preaction either annihilates A or integrates it at a non-disturbance level.

Figure 1. *Preaction and the PIP cycle*

Some Critical Notes

Effects Due to the Methods of Observation

It might be suggested that the findings concerning switching between levels of inference are due in part to the ways observation is organized. It would seem logical to assume that viewing a video-recording would generate more detailed comment than just remembering without an *aid memoire*.

There are two contra-indications here. First, immediate confrontation with video-recordings brings forth many 'switching' arguments from student-teachers, and even without video-confrontation some students are able to abstract at different levels.

The second contra-indication is more argumentative. It seems quite logical to accept that high level abstractions must somehow be based on low level observations. In classrooms, these are in the *preactive phase* — that is, in the PIP cycle, and are normally suppressed. Thinking aloud is not a normal characteristic of teachers who are already in the process of communicating actively with a class. Thus, what video-confrontation seems to do is to intensify and *make explicit* the hidden wealth of reflective thinking.

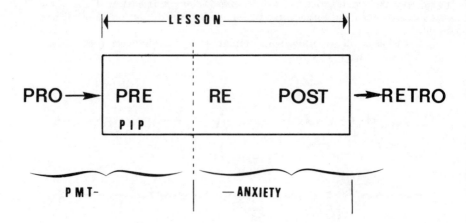

The rectangle represents the actual lesson period. Within it we can see three basic teacher behaviours: preaction (PRE) based on the PIP cycle, reaction (RE) and postaction (POST). Preparation for a lesson is done in the proactive phase (PRO), and behaviour after the lesson takes place in the retroactive phase (RETRO). PRO and PRE are dealt with especially in peer group microteaching as described earlier and are characterized by a high proportion of teacher-initiated behaviours. RE and POST are often in the forefront of the mind of beginning teachers, and cause anxiety. These create motivational problems of relevance and so need specific attention during training sessions.

Figure 2. *The phase of preactivity in context*

Observer Bias

In situations like this, observer bias can be very high. The usual methodology relies upon direct observation, the analysis of student observations and evaluations, and reflections based upon video-recordings. However, there are some contra-indications here too. First, very different students and groups of students offer the same analytical comments. Second, during discussion, very often students themselves raise the topics of switching levels and the importance of weak signals. Third, other observers come to the same analytical conclusions. It should be noted that the cyclic nature of phenomena as described here seems close to the other postulated areas of problem-solving and as used in the TOTE model.

Can This be Learned and What Place Does PIP Have in Teacher Training?

If the central importance of weak signals and the PIP cycle is real, then several questions arise. First, can students and beginner teachers who are not very preactive be trained to be so? In my opinion the answer is yes, but statistical data are not yet available in order to answer the question with any certainty. Second, the PIP cycle depends mainly on the cognitive aspects of behaviour guidance. Does this make other forms of training such as those based on a teach-analyse-reteach cycle redundant? The answer seems to be no. Skills training as a variation of the old Stanford model still seems to be necessary. But perhaps the inclusion of the new tactical item of PIP training could help students very quickly to assess their own strengths and weaknesses. The student could then be put through a more individualized series of training sessions which would focus upon his specific needs.

It would seem that between six and 10 exposures of one hour each, using peer group microteaching, are sufficient to build up a high sensitivity to weak signals and their importance for preactive teaching. Also, after the sixth or seventh round, *new* information levels off and the anticipation of a change in method should become part of the training tactics. In this way, peer group microteaching, when it is focused on preactive behaviour, can have a training as well as a diagnostic function.

Some Prescriptive Indications for the Use of Peer Group Microteaching in the Training Laboratory

Many students underestimate the significance of the more subtle aspects of teaching implied by the PIP cycle. Some students even classify these aspects as trivial. This seems to be understandable, because many students have in their minds threatening images of disorderly classes or of failures to be accepted as a person. In this respect, it seems very important that many students switch easily to high inference comments. When this is related to their own behaviour, they accept it as being 'relevant' and 'realistic'. However, if a trainer makes the same kind of high level inferences, these are assessed by the students as 'abstract' and 'non-realistic'. If the trainer confines his comments to the low inference level, the students think that he is being too specific, and that these comments are not appropriate for him to make as a trainer. So, we must deal with this problem. The students' anxiety leads them to focus their interest upon the reactive phase in the model, but peer group microteaching focuses on the proactive and preactive phases (see Figure 2).

Thus, some kind of optimization of motivation is needed for these approaches before they are started. Methods which would do this contain two elements.

(a) the creation of specific training situations which impress upon the student very quickly the importance and relevance of taking into account the minute and often subtle aspects of communication.
(b) the organization of peer microteaching sessions in such a way that specific aspects are *easily observable* and have a high degree of reality, so that the students recognize them as analogues of classroom activities.

In order to incorporate the first element, I use specific training situations in which the student experiences learning difficulties and motivation in a variety of specially contrived learner roles (Buter, 1970; Buter and Koorn, 1978). In addition, special use is made of communication exercises which focus on the importance of the trivial, and use is made of special video-tapes which make weak signals of explicit importance.

In order to incorporate the second element, I depend upon the fact that we are able to mix students so that microteaching groups contain representatives of highly divergent disciplines (eg French students are mixed with physics students). Teaching in such groups has great advantages when compared with teaching in mono-disciplinary groups, as is demonstrated in the summary tables below.

It was obvious that, for experiential work, the bi-disciplinary group was the more suitable. In practice, this type of group produced a good working atmosphere, and the group members were highly motivated. However, more effective groupings might be possible.

In MONO-DISCIPLINE groups	*In BI-DISCIPLINE groups*
1. Students have a tendency to concentrate upon the discipline itself.	1. Students have a tendency to concentrate on the difficulties of communicating.
2. Students have a tendency to remain at a high level of academic abstraction.	2. Students have a tendency to shift to a level of content and difficulty which is related to the secondary age range.
3. Students have a tendency to take each other for granted. In this area no assessment difficulties arise.	3. Students have a tendency to focus on difficulties of assessment which they seem to base upon discipline stereotypes.
4. Students, when they have communication problems, relate them to the discipline . . . 'not studied specific factors'; 'not read a specific book'.	4. Students, when they have communication problems, relate them to a wide range of criteria.
5. Students recognize *no* difficulties related to styles of learning or of presenting an argument.	5. Students recognize that many difficulties arise from the use of different styles of learning, of thinking and of presenting an argument.

Some General Conclusions

It seems that many students show proficiency in using weak signals to anticipate lesson activities. This happens in a cycle: what we have called the *preactive* phase, based on the recurring sequence of (P) the perception of weak signals, the (I) interpretation of these, and, following this, the (P) reactions (PIP cycle).

Students switch easily from high level inference to low level inference and vice versa. They are guided in their comments by different cognitive schemes.

By using peer group microteaching it seems possible to train students to become preactive teachers and to become PIP-minded. Cognitive orientated methods should be used in a number of sessions not exceeding 10, and numbers in a group should be between 15 and 20.

In order to encourage motivation, priming should be accomplished by the use of specially constructed training situations which will focus on the importance of weak signals. Situations should be as real as possible within the peer group microteaching system using bi-disciplinary groups whenever possible.

Fundamental questions which have to be answered now are:

(a) Can we find a more systematic pattern in the ways in which students structure their lesson behaviour?

(b) To what extent do students differ in their ability to use the PIP cycle as a way of guiding their behaviour?

(c) When students show a certain lack of ability in this respect, how much is it possible to teach them, and how much is it possible for them to learn? (Experience leads the writer to believe that we can be very optimistic on this point.)

It is maintained, in this article, that in any training programme for teachers, the following elements should be present and interact:

(a) A cognitive approach to weak signal observation, and instrumental use of the PIP cycle.

(b) An analysis of the student-based self-evaluation so that it can be linked
to a more individual training programme.
(c) The school-based teaching practice should be closely related to the
laboratory programme organized around the PIP cycle.

References

Brophy, J E and Evertson, C M (1976) *Learning from Teaching — A Developmental Perspective*. Allyn and Bacon, Boston, Massachusetts, USA.
Brown, G A (1975) *Microteaching, A Programme of Teaching Skills*. Methuen, London.
Buter, E M (1970) Educational technology applied to courses in educational technology. In Bajpai, A C and Leedham, J F (eds) *Aspects of Educational Technology* IV. Pitman, London.
Buter, E M and Koorn, W (1978) Media and the change of attitude of future teachers. In Clarke, J and Leedham, J F (eds) *Aspects of Educational Technology* X. Kogan Page, London.
Dunkin, M J and Biddle, B J (1974) *The Study of Teaching*. Holt, Rinehart and Winston, New York.
Wragg, E C (1974) *Teaching Teaching*. David and Charles, Newton Abbot.

Section 7:
Schools Industry Links

7.1 Industry-Education Initiatives – The Key to our Future

R H Lewin
Consultant for Technology, Berkshire LEA

Abstract: The speech by Mr James Callaghan in October 1976 at Ruskin College, Oxford centred on the necessity for changes in the education system so that it would reflect the needs of our present society. His remarks catalyzed a whole range of initiatives both large and small, from Government, industry, education and the media: within five years the growth and success of the work has become nationally recognized.

The implications of these initiatives on the curriculum and on teaching methods have been extensive. Examples from the County of Berkshire will be cited.

The aim of all these activities is to make young people aware of the role that manufacturing industry plays in the survival and future of this country; to show them at first hand through closer links with industry something of the challenge and excitement that the world can provide. The success of the industry/education movement will be measured by the attraction of more able children to join industry in a whole range of jobs from marketing, design and production to sales.

Our present success must not lead to complacency, for there is much to do, but the result could be the key to this country's prosperity.

Introduction

Recent interest in the subject of educational initiatives to meet industrial requirements was inspired by the talk given by James Callaghan at Ruskin College, Oxford in October 1976; the day he made his speech the pound was under pressure, and the interest rate had risen to the all-time high of 15 per cent. However, the (then) Prime Minister addressed his remarks to a different subject, namely the role of education in this country. He asked for improved standards of education to meet the needs of modern society, and expressed his concern that industry felt that new entrants lacked a basic knowledge required to do the job. He was worried about our ablest students not wishing to join industry. He also expressed concern that parents were questioning teaching methods. The result of this speech was the 'Great Debate', and a series of eight regional conferences on education in the following year.

Four main topics presented themselves: the concept of a basic or 'common core' curriculum to be taught at all schools; the way to assess and monitor standards of performance in education; the training of teachers; and how to improve relations between schools and industry.

The Fulmer Project

The Fulmer Research Institute is a contract research, design and engineering company concerned with aiding clients world-wide to design better products. The company, which is owned by the Institute of Physics, has a staff of over 100 graduates in a wide range of science, technology and engineering disciplines. With their background in the British education system and their work with industry, they felt that they could make some contribution to the development of industry/

education links. On the basis of a grant from the industry education unit of the Department of Industry they examined and developed ways in which schools and industry could work more closely together.

It may, at first, seem surprising that a company more closely involved with industrial research and development than with education should be actively working in this field, but this may be explained by examining the role of the engineer in an educational perspective over the last 150 years.

The British Disease

Engineers have not commanded a high status in the United Kingdom for well over 100 years because the wealth-creating role of industry, in which they play such an important part, was not recognized until comparatively recently.

Britain achieved prosperity primarily as a trading nation and not as a manufacturing nation. During the years that the British Empire was the dominant force in the world, Britain could sell to those countries products which it wished to make at the prices it decided to charge, and, in turn, purchase from them the raw materials at the prices it was prepared to pay. While this situation obtained, there was no significant role for manufacturing industry but equally there was no great compulsion for it to be efficient. In contrast, countries such as Germany and America, outside the privileged trading position afforded by the Empire, needed to become particularly efficient in order to be competitive. With this background there was no special need for this country to ensure that the educational system produced highly competitive and imaginative engineers; the main need of the educational system was to produce administrators to run an empire.

In the nineteenth century, science and engineering courses were, if anything, craft originated and aimed to produce people competent at solving purely technical problems. The courses were constructed in a highly convergent way and the education of scientists and engineers concentrated on teaching people how things behaved but gave little training as to how people behaved. This has led to the well-held belief that our top administrators should come from a liberal arts background and that scientists and engineers are best left at the bench.

The Fulmer Team believe, however, that successful designers, technologists and engineers need to have the imagination of the artist with the technical skills of the applied scientist. In their experience the British education system does little to cultivate a close link between the arts and sciences and even less to demonstrate how the major curriculum subjects relate to the real world.

Technology – The Key to our Future

It is now vital for Britain's future that it is made clear to everyone that we can no longer be indifferent or even bored with the role that industry plays in our society, because it is now the major wealth-creating activity left to us. For too long Britain has been preoccupied with the subject of wealth distribution instead of wealth creation. All parts of our society need to realize that Britain's role in the world and our corresponding fortunes have radically changed. It is a tragedy that this country, which has some of the finest universities and business schools in the world, and which is acknowledged for its creative talent, has lost motor-bicycle, car, ship, textile, and optical industries.

The solutions to our problems are complex, but we cannot continue to pay ourselves more than we earn. Manufacturing industry is the route used by prosperous nations and we must compete alongside them if we are once more to earn our living and retain the standards that we have come to enjoy. For this to happen, our products must have design-appeal, so well understood by our competitors. What a condemnation of the British car industry that, as a selling point, it announces that the body styling is Italian!

Industry/Education Activities in Berkshire

The main thrust of the Fulmer project was to see how its experience of product design, creative and scientific activities could be introduced into the school curriculum. The team's goal was to persuade more able, imaginative children otherwise bent upon a liberal arts education that they would gain more careers satisfaction from learning science and technology appropriate to a career in industry. The research programme was carried out in Buckinghamshire and Berkshire, in co-operation with the local advisory teams.

A major ingredient was to give students an opportunity to experience at first hand the work of technologists and engineers. This was initially achieved through a highly participative and interactive workshop entitled 'Technology is Fun', which lasted approximately two hours and was aimed at boys and girls aged between 13 and 15 years. Using examples taken from the child experience, the group explored the qualities and skills needed by technologists. Apart from the need to know the language of the subject, which included mathematics, physics and other natural science subjects, students considered qualities such as divergent and convergent thinking, logical and planning ability, social and communication skills, and, probably the most important qualities of all, inquisitiveness and interest in the laws of nature.

A sequel to the first workshop was a seminar entitled 'Why do Things Look Like They Do?' In this session, developed for O and A level students, the relationship between market, technology, costs, human and aesthetic factors were considered in relation to the development of a technically or commercially successful product. Further, wealth creation as the corner stone to our whole economy was considered.

In the course of the project it was interesting to move from the industrial into the educational sector in the space of a few hours, and the first thing which struck us was the complete artificiality of the education system when viewed from both the industrial and examination process points of view. The team's observations confirmed what has been said by many people before: that, on the one hand the present education system stresses the importance of analysis, criticism and acquisition of knowledge; while on the other hand it neglects the formulation of solutions to problems, planning, organization and preparing — in fact, constructive and creative activities of all kinds. Yet the future of this country is largely dependent on the education system encouraging, recognizing and producing people who have this broad range of talent. There is only one source of future industrial designers, technologists and engineers, and they are at present students in our schools. It is vital to the prosperity of this country that they are inspired to see the challenge and excitement of technology.

In parallel to Fulmer's initiative in this part of the country, Berkshire actively started to develop other work strongly linked to industry and the local Chambers of Commerce. In the Reading area a pilot scheme was started between the Reading Chamber of Commerce and Trade, the Berkshire Local Education Authority, and the Department of Industry Education Unit. An industry education officer was seconded from a local company and the project was administered by a committee comprising representatives from industry, commerce, trade unions and educationalists.

The stated aim of the project was to: 'help teachers and their pupils to become more aware of the important role of industry and commerce in the economic life of the country and to help industry and commerce to be more aware of developments in schools and colleges.' Within a year, over 30 schools and 54 companies were involved, and the picture emerged of a mutual wish on the part of both schools and employers to get closer together and to reduce the misconceptions about each other's activities and co-operate on a scale previously unknown. Some aspects of the current work are described below.

Teachers Into Industry

Teachers are attached for varying lengths of time to places of work in industry and commerce. In so doing they gain an insight into the day-to-day operations of typical firms which provide employment and contribute significantly to the local society.

Young Enterprise Companies

Young enterprise companies have now been established in Reading. These are formed by selected senior pupils from secondary schools in the area who meet for two hours each week in their own time and effectively run a business for a whole academic year.

Challenge of Industry Conferences

Challenge of industry conferences are held in local schools which are designed to give senior pupils an awareness of industry by listening to speakers from management and trade unions as well as taking part in seminars and role playing activities.

Links with Primary Schools

More recently links have been established with primary schools who are very keen to use industrial projects as a source of work in the classroom. We believe this area to be particularly fruitful since, if attitudes are to change in this country, it is necessary to start early.

There is only one source of creative talent, designers, technologists and engineers in our society, and they are the children at present in our schools. It is largely in the hands of our teachers to encourage and explain to them the challenge and excitement that industry can offer.

Conclusions

Since the beginning of the Fulmer team's work five years ago, it has produced a range of documents, audio-visual packs and, more recently, a film and radio series. The work is still in its infancy and if it is to grow, it will need effective and efficient dissemination throughout the education system in this country.

7.2 A Teacher's View of Schools-Industry Links, with Particular Reference to Berkshire

J Honeybourne
Little Heath Secondary School

Abstract: This paper comments upon schools-industry links in Berkshire, giving examples of the work done by specific firms in specific schools. The benefits to the schools will be evaluated and the benefits to the teachers will be discussed. In conclusion, trends for the medium- and long-term future are identified.

Introduction

Schools have had informal links with industry and commerce for many years. In recent times, however, a climate has developed which fosters the formal arrangement of these links.

Some of the factors which have influenced the desire for closer collaboration between schools and industry can be identified.

(a) The need to help young people to appreciate the role of industry in our economy as a means of creating wealth.

(b) In the late 1970s there was criticism of the educational system by industrialists. It stated that pupils were not being well prepared for the world of work. Dissatisfaction centred around falling standards, especially in the teaching of reading, writing and arithmetic.

(c) Teachers, it was felt, had little understanding of industrial and commercial activities.

(d) Technological change placed greater demands upon schools to equip pupils with the skills and ability to adapt to these changes, thus necessitating changes in the school curriculum.

(e) Educational cuts helped to foster liaison because schools sought help from local industry with the supply of materials.

These factors, and others, created an environment which enabled links to be developed. As a result, many new organizations came into being. These helped to establish a framework upon which initiatives were based.

Examples of these organizations are as follows.

The Department of Industry established an Education Unit which was briefed to encourage close co-operation between industry and education, to promote initiatives which would improve the attitudes of young people towards industry, and which would encourage young people to consider careers in industry.

Understanding British Industry is an organization sponsored by the CBI Education Foundation. Its aim is to provide closer links between education and industry, so that every teacher and pupil has an understanding of the role and importance of industry in our society, and that those involved in industry and commerce have an understanding of the role and function of education. It disseminates information through a network of regional liaison officers and satellite resource centres. It has also assisted examining boards in the development of new courses. An example is the O level in British Industrial Society developed by the Associated Examination Board.

Other initiatives included the appointment, in some parts of the country, of Schools-Industry Liaison Officers who promote links in their area and who set up Science and Technology Regional Organizations (SATROs).

What are the benefits derived from the creation of these new organizations and initiatives? Three interested groups can be identified: the schools (and, ultimately, the pupils); the teachers; and industry. Each of these groups has been influenced by a closer co-operation.

The Influence upon the School

The foundation upon which the work of a school is built is its curriculum. Partly as a result of the 'Great Debate' at the end of the 1970s, there has been a desire to place the activities of the school in the wider context of the community and the industrial world. The White Paper issued in December 1981, entitled 'A New Training Initiative — A Programme for Action', states:

> 'The school curriculum must develop personal skills and qualities, the knowledge needed for working life and an understanding of industrial, commercial and economic bases of our society. Links between schools and employers will help pupils and teachers to gain this understanding'.

Collaboration between schools and industry can be very successful. A Reading school has developed schemes of work in technology in co-operation with local engineering firms. One pupil, whilst following such a scheme, developed a device to help people who suffered from tinnitus. As a result he saw that his work was valuable.

Seeking to base aspects of the curriculum on industrial reality leads to a change in philosophy away from the examination-biased syllabus towards meaningful experiences related to life. The pupils in our schools are a most valuable resource for the development of our economic future. We need to provide them with learning experiences which will create healthy attitudes toward industry, and help them to develop written, oral, numerical, manipulative, social and problem-solving skills.

Examples of Link Activities

Young Enterprise

Young Enterprise is a scheme whereby pupils between the ages of 12 and 19 can establish a company for about eight months. The company is given advice and guided by managers from a local firm. The pupils are responsible for making decisions and for running the company. They are encouraged to visit local works and to interview local managers.

We have found that the project has broadened the outlook of the pupils and has developed their social skills. They have developed working relationships among themselves and with adults other than teachers. They have gained in problem-solving abilities and in self-confidence.

Visiting Speakers

Visiting speakers can relate the theoretical perspectives imparted by teachers to the real-life situation offering contextual examples which are more pertinent and up to date.

Work Experience

The placing of pupils in an industrial or commercial situation for a short time is a valuable method of gaining experience. Some educationalists consider that such work experience should be undertaken by all pupils at some time in their school career. The Schools Council Industry Project has shown, however, that such an innovation would require an additional half-time teacher per school. In the current educational climate this would seem to be an impossible objective.

Materials and Resources

When it is not possible to arrange for visits or work experience, tape-slide materials and learning packs can provide valuable substitutes. Alternatively, schools can establish informal links which enable them to obtain materials for school use, particularly in the woodwork and metalwork areas. One local school has already established a course using microcomputers, the necessary machines having been made available by a local firm.

New Courses and Developments in Examinations

There are a number of new courses and examination syllabuses which have been developed as a result of collaboration. I want to mention a few of the aims of one such course: the O level Business Studies of the Cambridge Examination Board.

The overall aim of the course is to develop young people's awareness and understanding of the industrial and commercial world. Another aim is to enable students to appreciate what work is like and how other people are motivated and rewarded. Further aims are to enable students to appreciate the interaction that takes place between one business organization and another, and between business organizations and the government.

Here we see aims which seek to develop learning experiences which are directly relevant and which also start to answer some of the criticisms previously made by industrialists. It is to be hoped that the proposed new 16-plus examination will take account of the recent work in this area, and will include measures which will allow rapid changes to be made following technological innovations.

The Employment of Pupils

If schools can build up a particular connection with local firms they can start to provide pupils for employment who have particular expertise. At best, this kind of relationship is seen when firms approach schools to recommend pupils who are suitable for a specific post.

We have considered various ways in which ordinary classroom teachers can gain from a link with industry. However, if teachers are attached to industrial or commercial concerns, different kinds of benefits emerge.

Teacher Attachment

In Berkshire we have developed a scheme whereby teachers are attached for a period of three weeks during the summer term. Naturally, the scheme is particularly helpful to members of staff who have not previously experienced such an environment. The kind of benefits are listed below.

(a) It broadens their experience and gives them insight into previously unknown areas.
(b) They become more aware of the working environment into which their pupils may go. They will see some of the tasks which young people are asked to undertake.

(c) It enables them to understand some of the problems faced by industry.
(d) They will be able to relate classroom work to industrial and commercial situations.
(e) They are able to build up contacts with local firms so that they can expand schools-industry links.
(f) They can inform people in industry about educational issues and can even clarify areas where there have been misconceptions.

The Benefits to Industry

The prime function of any business organization must be its business activities. But, increasingly, we are seeing that firms are willing to devote resources to schools. This kind of involvement has a number of advantages:

(a) It enables the pupils to be better informed about the industrial world, and the role which industry plays in the British economy.
(b) The image of dirt, noise and boredom associated with industry can be changed.
(c) When they visit schools or talk to teachers on attachment, managers can become more knowledgeable about current educational thought and practices.
(d) Industrialists are able to influence curricular change.
(e) A better community image can be developed through a good schools-industry link.

When firms have appointed staff with special responsibility for fostering such links, the links have been seen to be more effective and long lasting.

Future Developments

The aim of this paper has been to present a picture of the current activities being undertaken to develop schools-industry links. In the long term, if full benefits are to be experienced, a permanent structure must be established which will reach into schools. At present the arrangements are patchy. Some local education authorities are acting responsibly; others are not. Many of the initiatives fostered by the UBI, the Department of Industry Education Unit, and others are not permeating down into schools. Some special provision needs to be made so that in-service training for teachers can be made available.

The next few years are crucial for the development of liaison. We must build upon the first flush of enthusiasm to create a situation where those in education and those in industry see themselves as partners. When this occurs we shall see a more effective and efficient training programme nationwide.

References

Department of Employment (1981) *A New Training Initiative: A Programme for Action.* HMSO, London.
University of Cambridge Local Examinations Syndicate (1979) Business Studies for a First Examination in 1981. Circular to schools 79/1, Cambridge.

7.3 Forming Links between Education and Industry: How Educational Technologists can Help

H I Ellington, E Addinall and N H Langton
Robert Gordon's Institute of Technology, Aberdeen

Abstract: During the last eight years, the Educational Technology Unit at Robert Gordon's Institute of Technology (RGIT) has co-ordinated a large number of projects that have involved collaboration between education and industry. This paper will present a rationale for collaboration of this type, arguing that educational technology staff are, by virtue of their background and situation, ideally placed to play a key role in the formation of such mutually-beneficial two-way links.

The paper will be in two main sections. The first will identify a number of ways in which industry can make a useful contribution to our educational system — by, for example, producing educational materials of various types and running competitions, and will show how educational technologists can help them to do so. The second will discuss some of the ways in which the educational sector can help industry, such as contributing to staff development and helping to produce publicity materials, and will again examine the part that educational technologists can play in such collaboration. In both sections, the argument will be illustrated by examining specific projects in which RGIT's Educational Technology Unit has been recently involved.

The Need for More Links Between Education and Industry

One of the primary aims of an industrial society's educational system should be to prepare future citizens to play an effective role in the various industries on which that society depends. This has long been realized in countries such as Germany, but, in the UK, meeting the needs of industry has traditionally been regarded as less important than producing administrators and repelenishing the ranks of the various learned professions. Indeed, this is frequently cited as one of the main reasons for Britain's chronic industrial malaise.

All too often, education and industry operate in splendid isolation, with the result that the products of our educational system have little or no appreciation of the nature of industry and its role in modern society, and are, furthermore, poorly prepared to perform the tasks that modern industry requires of them (Snow, 1959). This was brought home to us very forcibly during a recent visit to the research laboratories of one of Britain's leading industrial combines, where it became clear that our educational system is not producing the sort of science graduates that that particular industry requires. All too often (it appears) such graduates lack the ability to tackle and solve novel problems by employing an open-minded, cross-disciplinary approach — a shortcoming that can partly be attributed to the early specialization forced on students by the entry requirements of the higher educational system, and partly to the introspective, paradigm-based nature of science education (Burgess, 1977; Kuhn, 1962).

Ideally, what Britain needs is a fundamental shift of emphasis in its educational system (Snow, 1959; Burgess, 1977) but this is (unfortunately) very unlikely to happen in the foreseeable future. In the meantime, we believe that the situation could be greatly improved by increasing the dialogue between education and industry, so that the former becomes more aware of the needs of the latter, and, as a result, takes at least some steps to try to meet these needs. Furthermore, we believe that edcuational technologists are, by virtue of their background and position, ideally placed to play a key role in the formation of such mutually-beneficial two-way links. Let us now examine some of the ways in which they can do so.

Helping Industry to Contribute to our Educational System

Until comparatively recently, contact between education and industry was limited largely to, for example, industrial visits, student placements and vacation work, staff secondment and talks given in schools and colleges by specialists from different sectors of industry. During the last decade, however, an increasing number of the more forward-looking industrial organizations have started to make a direct contribution to curriculum development, by, for example, producing resource materials and organizing competitions.

An industrial organization that wishes to make such a contribution to curriculum development invariably has the necessary financial and logistical resources to see the project through, and is also likely to have staff with specialized knowledge of the field on which the package of resource materials or competition is to be based. What such an organization often lacks, however, is people with the experience of the educational system and expertise in curriculum development and instruction design needed to translate this specialized knowledge into a worthwhile educational package. Clearly, this is an area in which educational technologists can make a significant contribution, both directly (by helping to provide the above expertise) and indirectly (by acting as an interface between education and industry).

We will now illustrate this thesis by describing two collaborative projects in which the Educational Technology Unit at Robert Gordon's Institute of Technology (RGIT) has recently been involved.

The 'Ekofisk . . . One of a Kind' Project

In the spring of 1980, we were asked by Phillips Petroleum Company to assist them in producing educational resource materials based on their Ekofisk field, which is located in the Norwegian sector of the North Sea. The Company had already produced a 30-minute film, an illustrated booklet and a set of five wall posters, dealing with various aspects of their Ekofisk operations, and wished to complement these with materials specifically designed to fit into the school and college curriculum.

Having examined the existing 'Ekofisk' materials, we recommended to the Company that what they needed was a short booklet on the North Sea oil industry that could be issued to a class as a background reader plus a comprehensive 'Teacher's Guide' incorporating detailed information about the industry, together with projects and case studies dealing with specific aspects thereof. The latter would be designed to fit into the curricula of a wide range of academic subjects, including social and general studies, geography, economics, physics, chemistry and engineering (Addinall and Ellington, 1981). We were subsequently commissioned to write these documents, plus a glossary of terms used in the oil industry and a quiz on the Ekofisk film, which was felt would enhance the value of the overall package.

The various materials described above were eventually published by Phillips as the 'Ekofisk . . . One of a kind' Multi-Media Educational Library (see Figure 1 for detailed list of contents). This is currently available free of charge to schools and colleges throughout the United Kingdom, teachers and lecturers wishing to use the materials being sent a copy of the film (which they are allowed to retain for

Teacher's Guide

An A4 booklet containing detailed background information on all aspects of the offshore oil and gas industries, plus a wide range of class studies and projects. It is divided into the following sections:

1. Historical development.
2. How oil and gas fields were formed.
3. The search for offshore oil and gas.
4. Bringing an offshore field into production.
5. Getting oil and gas ashore.
6. How oil and natural gas are used.
7. Economic, political and social aspects of offshore oil development.
8. Safety and environmental aspects of the oil industry.

Set of Class Sheets

Seventeen A4 Class Sheets designed for use in the various case studies and projects described in the Teacher's Guide. The teacher can produce as many copies as are required for a class by using the sheets as photocopy masters.

Set of Class Readers

Thirty copies of an A5 Class Reader entitled 'Oil and Gas from the North Sea'. It can be used with classes of all ages from 10 to 18, either on its own or as a back-up to the film, a taught lesson, a discussion, a case study or a project.

The film, 'Ekofisk ... One of a kind'

A 30-minute, 16mm colour film dealing with life and work in the Ekofisk field.

The quiz, 'Ekofisk ... One of a kind'

An A5 booklet, containing a bank of 95 questions based on the visual and verbal content of the film. It enables a teacher to structure a quiz to suit various levels and abilities of students.

The booklet, 'Ekofisk ... One of a kind'

A fully-illustrated, full-colour A4 booklet designed to complement the film by providing detailed information about all aspects of the Ekofisk field.

Set of Wall Posters

These five full-colour A2 posters are entitled:

1. Ekofisk ... One of a kind.
2. The Greater Ekofisk Area.
3. Ekofisk ... Communications.
4. Ekofisk ... Subsea.
5. Ekofisk ... Drilling and Production.

Glossary of Terms

A booklet entitled 'Glossary of words and phrases used in the oil, gas and petrochemical industries'. It contains over 750 entries, covering all aspects of operations, and is designed as a source of reference for both teachers and students.

Figure 1. *Contents of the 'Ekofisk ... one of a kind' multi-media educational library*

up to two weeks), plus a set of 30 of the class readers and a copy of each of the other items (none of which need be returned). The Library has proved extremely popular, and has attracted very favourable reviews in the educational press. It has also been translated into Norwegian, and is now being used in schools throughout Norway.

We believe that the development of the 'Ekofisk . . . one of a kind' Multi-Media Educational Library is an excellent example of the way in which educational technologists can help industry to produce educationally valuable resource materials. The Library could well serve as a model for other industrial organizations who want to show the citizens of tomorrow what their industry involves, and, at the same time, want to provide materials that are capable of making a real contribution to the teaching of main-line academic subjects.

The 'Project Scotia' Competition

This was a competition that was run by the Institution of Electrical Engineers (IEE), British Broadcasting Corporation (BBC) and Independent Broadcasting Authority (IBA) during 1978-79 (Ellington, Addinall and Hately, 1980). The three sponsoring bodies wanted to promote a competition that would enable pupils in the upper forms of British secondary schools to learn about the broadcasting industry by taking part in a realistic design project. It was hoped that this would not only serve as a valuable educational exercise in its own right, but would also help recruitment to the industry by stimulating pupil interest in broadcasting.

In the 'Project Scotia' Competition, the teams had to design a UHF TV network for a hypothetical highland area, write 'consultants' reports' describing their proposals, and prepare multi-media presentations of their schemes. Work on the planning of the competition and the development of the project on which it was based was co-ordinated by the Educational Technology Unit at Robert Gordon's Institute of Technology, and also involved staff of the Institute's Schools of Physics and Electronic and Electrical Engineering. The BBC and IBA provided technical advice throughout the development process, and also helped with the judging of the competition. The IEE was responsible for the actual organization of the competition, and acted as host for a 'live final' held at the Institute's London headquarters on 3 September 1979. At this final, the five leading schools in the competition had their 'consultants' reports' and multi-media presentations assessed by a panel of judges, and were also asked questions about their schemes at a plenary session held in front of an invited audience (see Figures 2 and 3).

'Project Scotia' is another excellent example of the valuable contribution that industry can make to education, and again illustrates the key role that educational technologists can play in such joint ventures. Because of the great success of the original exercise, the IEE, in collaboration with the local educational authority, subsequently organized a re-run of the competition in south-west Scotland. This also proved highly successful, and further regional competitions may well take place in future years.

Helping to Meet Industry's Own Needs

In addition to providing a useful interface between industry and education, educational technologists can sometimes make a direct contribution to meeting the needs of industry itself. As we see it, there are two main ways in which they can do so, namely by becoming involved in industrial staff development programmes and by helping industry to develop materials for publicity and other purposes. Although most work of this type is handled 'in house', there are occasions when even the largest industrial organizations feel the need to seek outside advice or help with specific projects. On such occasions, educational technologists working in the

Figure 2. *Aberdeen Grammar School's model of 'Scotia' being examined by the three judges at the live final of the 'Project Scotia' Competition (extreme right: Sir James Redmond, former Head of Engineering, BBC and current IEE President; second right: Dr Peter Clark, RGIT Principal; extreme left: Mr Tom Robson, Head of Engineering, IBA)*

Figure 3. *Lancaster Grammar School being questioned about their proposed scheme by the judges at the 'Project Scotia' final*

education sector can often provide the necessary input — or, if they cannot do so themselves, will probably be able to enlist the help of colleagues who can.

Let us again illustrate this thesis by taking a look at two specific projects in which RGIT's Educational Technology Unit has been involved in recent years.

The 'Ile de Performance' Management Training Exercise

In January 1980, Phillips Petroleum Company asked us to design a management training exercise for use at the forthcoming Annual Conference of their Petroleum Products Group, due to take place in May of that year. Specifically, Phillips wanted us to produce a mind-broadening educational exercise linked to the overall theme of the conference ('Decade of Decision') that dealt with some aspects of 'the energy problem'. They also wanted the exercise to serve as a management training tool, partly by enabling all delegates to participate in meaningful decision-making, and partly by providing a vehicle for senior staff to develop their management skills — both under competitive conditions.

During the following four months, we first designed a suitable competition based on a simulated design study that involved making plans to meet the future electricity requirements of a hypothetical offshore island (named 'Ile de Performance', after Phillips' in-house newspaper *Performance*), and then helped Phillips to build the exercise into the conference programme (Ellington *et al*, 1981). We then attended the conference in order to help run the exercise. The overall structure of the competition, in which the 100 or so delegates were divided into four teams, each under the direction of a senior Phillips manager, is shown in Figure 4. Each team had first to carry out a detailed technical and economic design study, and had then to present its recommendations at the plenary session which brought the competition to a climax.

The conference organizers and senior Phillips staff to whom we spoke after the completion of the 'Ile de Performance' competition were of the unanimous opinion that the exercise had been a great success — an impression that was subsequently confirmed by a questionnaire that was issued to the delegates. (104 of the 110 delegates who completed this questionnaire felt that similar exercises should be included in future conferences.) The main feature that distinguished 'Ile de Performance' from a conventional management training exercise was that it was designed to achieve a wide range of educational as well as purely training objectives — a mixture which Phillips acknowledged that they would not have been able to achieve without our help. The exercise is therefore a good example of the way in which educational technologists can make a very real contribution to industrial staff development.

The 'Dounreay' Tape-slide Programmes

In the summer of 1976, the Educational Techology Unit at RGIT was asked by the United Kingdom Atomic Energy Authority (UKAEA) to help revise a tape-slide programme describing their work on fast reactors at Dounreay. This had been produced by a commercial firm of media consultants, and, although satisfactory from a purely aesthetic point of view, the UKAEA were not convinced that it was capable of achieving its main objective, which was to give the general public a clear overview of the role of Dounreay in the British nuclear power programme. Having seen the programme in question, we recommended a complete re-write, using as many of the existing slides (which had been taken by the Authority's Chief Photographer, and were of excellent quality) as possible. We were subsequently commissioned to carry out this work, and the revised programme was eventually incorporated in the Visitors' Exhibition at Dounreay.

As a result of this work, we were asked to write further programmes on different aspects of Dounreay, this time for a more technical audience such as visiting

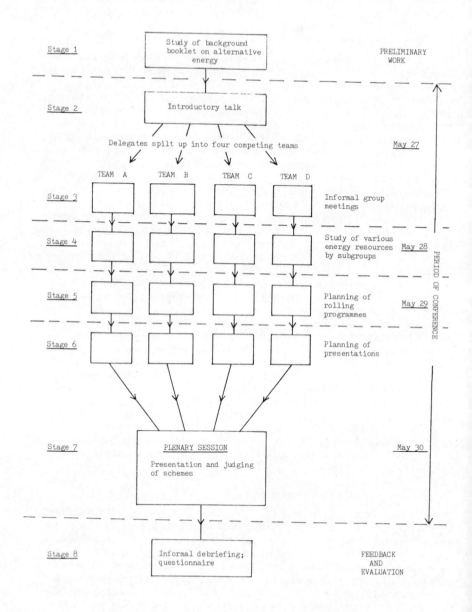

Figure 4. *The overall structure of the 'Ile de Performance' competition*

scientists and engineers etc. We have since helped to produce four such programmes, dealing respectively with 'The History of Dounreay', 'The Prototype Fast Reactor (PFR) and its Fuel Cycle', 'Fast Reactor Fuel Reprocessing' and 'Nuclear Waste Management at Dounreay'. Since much of the plant at Dounreay is inaccessible to visitors (and, indeed, to anyone else!), this series of programmes serves as a substitute 'conducted tour', and has proved extremely successful in this role.

Here, again, we have a good example of the way in which educational technologists can help an industrial organization by providing expertise that is not available 'in house'. In addition to our knowledge of the potential (and limitations) of the tape-slide medium, we had the great advantage of being able to form a detached overview of the work at Dounreay — something that scientists and engineers who actually worked there found very hard to do because of their deep involvement in their various specialist areas. This, in our opinion, is one of the great advantages of bringing in 'external consultants' to help produce programmes of this type.

Supplementary Information

It was decided, after completion of the programmes, to make available a set of supplementary information. These data were intended for use by students who wished to investigate the subject at a deeper level. The information provided here came in the form of:

(a) Booklets and papers sent from CERN, which were considered to be of relevance in this case.
(b) Reference to Nigel Calder's Book *Key to the Universe*.
(c) Paper by U Amaldi (CERN, 1979) entitled Particle Accelerators and Scientific Culture. Specific parts of this paper were drawn to the attention of the 'enthusiastic' student.
(d) There was also an audio-tape available to students of a conversation with Professor Fred Reines from the University of California. In this, he discusses his famous neutrino experiments and this was found to provide an excellent background to programmes one and three.

During the period of time that the package, 'High Energy Particles', was in use, the author was available at specific times during the week to answer any questions. Considerable feedback was obtained from the students, mostly related to the scientific content of the programmes.

Conclusion

Since it was formed in 1973, the Educational Technology Unit at RGIT has co-ordinated a large number of projects that have involved collaboration between education and industry, the four described above being typical. By demonstrating some of the ways in which educational technologists can help to form links between education and industry, we hope that this paper will stimulate further developments in this area.

References

Addinall, E and Ellington, H I (1981) 'Ekofisk . . . one of a kind' — a package of games, simulations and case studies based on the North Sea oil and gas industry. In Hollinshead, B and Yorke, M (eds) *Perspectives on Academic Gaming & Simulation 6*. Kogan Page, London.

Burgess, T (1977) *Education After School.* Penguin Books, Middlesex.
Ellington, H I, Addinall, E and Hately, M C (1980) The 'Project Scotia' Competition.
  Physics Education, 15, 4, pp 220-222.
Ellington, H I, Addinall, E, Langton, N H and Percival, F (1981) 'Ile de Performance' —
  a competitive planning exercise built into a company conference. *Simulation/Games for
  Learning,* 11, 1, pp 12-22.
Kuhn, T S (1962) *The Structure of Scientific Revolutions.* University of Chicago Press.
Snow, C P (1959) *The Two Cultures and the Scientific Revolution.* Cambridge University
  Press.

Footnote
The 'Ekofisk . . . One of a kind' Multi-Media Educational Library cam be obtained from:
Phillips Petroleum, Film Library, 15 Beaconsfield Road, London NW10 1YD.

7.4 Co-operation and Co-operatives in the Curriculum: A Pilot Project in Schools Liaison

J R W Hill
The CLEAR Unit, Co-operative College, Loughborough

Abstract: The development of links between school and university provides a stimulus to curriculum development. The following account of a joint venture between the Co-operative Union Ltd and a Rochdale secondary school, illustrates a variety of approaches to monitoring and presenting the outcome of schools-industry projects.

Dissemination of the experience gained in this pilot project is aided by educational technology, the portrayal of the outcomes being an important factor in widening the circle of involvement in future projects.

An important early step in the exploration of ideas for inclusion in the pilot project was a residential two-day course on co-operative organizations and the co-operative movement. The course was attended by a group of 15 staff from the school. Subsequently, materials were prepared in English, mathematics, drama, art, history, geography and remedial maths/English. These materials were presented to the entire first year of about 160 pupils, over a four-week period, taking up approximately 50 per cent of the timetable.

Attempts were made to monitor the progress of the project in various ways: (i) a pilot questionnaire was administered to staff to evaluate the possible relevance of key concepts; (ii) a team word association task was undertaken by all first-year pupils in a pre- and post-project design, with a second-year class as a control group; (iii) photographs were taken of pupils at work on the project and during visits to Toad Lane Co-operative Store Museum.

On completion of the project, pupils' work was presented to Co-operative Society Board members, parents, and participants at the National Co-operative Education Convention. The presentations included: visual displays, a dramatic production, a 45-minute video film, and a one-day workshop.

Three curriculum models for the organization of learning about co-operatives are described. These models are based partly on the experience gained in the pilot project in Rochdale, and partly on materials from Canada (Common and Boxer, 1976) and Scotland (Bray, 1981).

Introduction

Learning about work, unemployment, leisure, and life in communities and organizations, requires a close interweaving of conflicting ideas. But materials prepared from an employer's perspective alone are likely to leave out important strands. A major snag to be confronted, then, in attempting to increase the reality content of education by drawing on resources from industry for inspiration, is that the unattractive aspects of industrial society are likely to be minimized. Educational publications for use in schools prepared by employers ultimately serve the functions of employee recruitment, public relations or customer attraction. Consumer dissatisfaction, redundancy, under-employment and pollution rarely find a place in the picture.

In order to counter the inevitable bias and narrowness of educational materials drawn directly from industrial sources, school teachers may choose to introduce wider frames of reference. Jamieson and Lightfoot (1981) have suggested that the role of employers, especially from smaller, locally-based concerns, is to *particularize* about job content and management expectations, whereas the teacher's role is to *generalize*, that is to convey ideas about industry and work which are transferable, and which apply to a variety of organizations. General principles proposed to school teachers *about* employment, which acknowledge the irksome and enigmatic aspects, may help to increase the reality content of the curriculum. But school children bring to the classroom their own visions of reality, based on previous experience, current awareness or imagined futures. Their views about work and social organizations differ, sometimes sharply, both from those provided by industry and those provided by teachers.

The majority of secondary school courses, centred on themes such as 'Living in Modern Industrial Society' (Jamieson and Lightfoot, 1981), are not considered until the fourth or fifth form. However, a considerable amount of learning has already taken place by then and this will determine the reception given to new information and experiences concerning work and society.

As well as the perspectives on industry provided by employers, by school teachers and by school children, there are also potential contributions from trade unions, political parties and pressure groups. It is not the intention to pursue here the issue of accountability and control over the curriculum; suffice it to say that increasing the effectiveness of education by importing reality only from an employer's standpoint is most unlikely to provide a widely accepted curriculum.

There are no easy answers to the questions which have been posed in this introduction. The potential benefits of educational technology media and methods may relate to the extent to which they reveal to a larger audience the real dilemmas concerning curriculum development based on 'industrial society' themes. The generation of wider interest and participation concerning the choice of key concepts and skills, and the appropriateness of learning processes, is certainly a challenge to educational technologists. In the case study which follows, some preliminary exploration of the paths towards these goals is undertaken.

Pilot Project

Under the auspices of a partnership between the Rochdale Education Authority and the Co-operative Union Ltd, a pilot project was mounted to investigate the potential of co-operation and co-operatives as themes for an integrated curriculum development exercise. From the school's point of view the exercise provided an opportunity to consider the integration of the entire first-year curriculum. The main work was undertaken between September 1980 and June 1981. A four-stage cycle evolved creating the means to increase as rapidly as possible the involvement of school staff, Co-operative Union staff, pupils, and elected board members of co-operative societies with special commitments to education. The four stages of the cycle are summarized in Table 1.

Stage One

An important aspect of the first stage was a two-day workshop at the Co-operative College, Loughborough. A group of 15 teachers took part in an exploration of materials relating to co-operation and co-operatives. Films, documents from the archives, and current statistical reports concerning the co-operative movement were among the range of resources available.

To a large extent, the teachers planned their own use of time during the workshop and were free to work singly or in groups on ideas for curriculum development. There were also three lectures and discussion sessions based on broad views of the co-operative movement — its history, its role in third world development, and the present-day features of co-operative business in Britain. Although the lectures were delivered by Co-operative Union Ltd staff, care was taken to present contrasting viewpoints concerning the viability of co-operatives. They were portrayed as organizations which aim at a more diverse array of

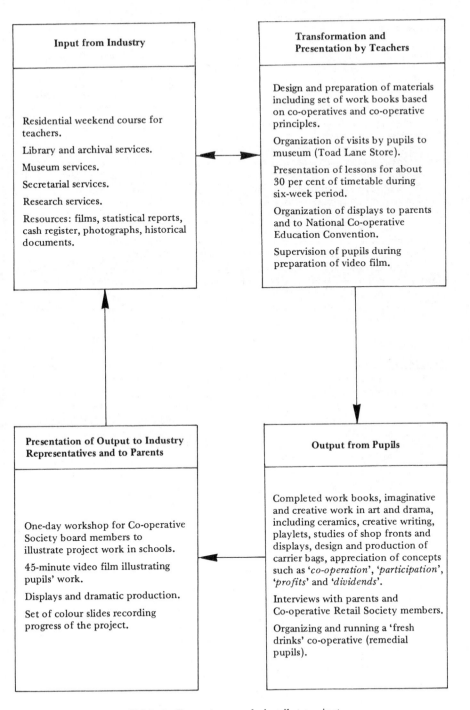

Input from Industry	Transformation and Presentation by Teachers
Residential weekend course for teachers. Library and archival services. Museum services. Secretarial services. Research services. Resources: films, statistical reports, cash register, photographs, historical documents.	Design and preparation of materials including set of work books based on co-operatives and co-operative principles. Organization of visits by pupils to museum (Toad Lane Store). Presentation of lessons for about 30 per cent of timetable during six-week period. Organization of displays to parents and to National Co-operative Education Convention. Supervision of pupils during preparation of video film.
Presentation of Output to Industry Representatives and to Parents	Output from Pupils
One-day workshop for Co-operative Society board members to illustrate project work in schools. 45-minute video film illustrating pupils' work. Displays and dramatic production. Set of colour slides recording progress of the project.	Completed work books, imaginative and creative work in art and drama, including ceramics, creative writing, playlets, studies of shop fronts and displays, design and production of carrier bags, appreciation of concepts such as 'co-operation', 'participation', 'profits' and 'dividends'. Interviews with parents and Co-operative Retail Society members. Organizing and running a 'fresh drinks' co-operative (remedial pupils).

Table 1. *Four-stage cycle in pilot project*

targets than most capitalist enterprises. The 'Rochdale principles' reflected to this day in the guiding values of the co-operative movement provide a multiple set of performance criteria which are Gothic in their scale and scope. Ideally, co-operatives are democratic, open, efficient, egalitarian and equitable in their operations, and take special care to provide educational services. The reconciliation of these ideals in practice has produced a variety or organizational types. Abundant evidence for this diversity was provided during the workshop. Any temptation to prescribe co-operation as a ready-made solution to problems of work organization and control was resisted.

A small-scale questionnaire evaluation was introduced to round off the first stage in the project cycle. This attempted a brief, single-take view of the process of concept selection by staff engaged on the project. The questionnaire invited staff to rate the relevance of potential key words to teaching about co-operation and co-operatives on an integrated basis. An open-ended section allowed staff to make their own suggestions for key words. An example of the results from the questionnaire evaluation is shown in Table 2.

A comprehensive report was circulated to the staff early during the next stage of the project, when the development of materials was under way.

This first stage of the project may be regarded as an exercise in cultural analysis, admittedly, and unavoidably, brief. Cultural analysis has been described as a compromise between the objectives model of curriculum development and the process model. Such a compromise may prove particularly appropriate for industry-schools liaison projects.

Stage Two

The design of materials and preparation of several work books was undertaken by the teachers, using ideas and resources from the workshop. A certain amount of 'writing down' was required to reach the 11- to 12-year-old age group. Efforts were made towards the integration of the curriculum. However, as may be seen from Table 2, certain concepts were more likely to be emphasized by different subject teachers.

Although these data merely hint at the difficulties in creating integrated materials, the practical problems were real enough. Nevertheless, the work by the teachers in designing the project from scratch allowed them to exercise their own judgement in balancing local, specific and concrete issues with wider ideas and generalizations about co-operation and co-operatives.

The project aims, subject by subject, and a sample of the tasks undertaken are shown in Table 3.

Stage Three

The project was presented to the entire first year during the spring term, 1981, and occupied one-third of the timetable during a six-week period.

A small-scale partial evaluation of the project was undertaken using a word association measure. Twenty words which had earlier been identified as possible key words in the project by a group of eight staff were presented to teams of three pupils. They were asked to produce four words in direct association with these key words. This exercise was administered immediately before the project and again three months after the main work had been completed, towards the end of the summer term. The aim was to obtain a quick, impressionistic measure of the ideas present among the first-year students concerning such key words as 'co-operation', 'sharing', 'profits', 'dividend' and 'participation'.

It was also hoped that word association would be a sufficiently sensitive technique to portray some of the changes in the meaning of key words resulting from the pupils' experience of the project. Some measures of learning produce

Teacher and subject / Overall relevance rating of key words	Project co-ordinator	English and drama	History	Geography 1.	Geography 2.	Mathematics	Remedial maths and English	Art
High:								
Sharing	⊛	⊛	⊛	○	⊛	⊛	*	*
Profits	⊛		⊛	*		⊛	⊛	
Ownership	*	⊛	*		*		⊛	
Participation	*	*	*	*	*		*	
Moderately high:								
Wholesale	*		*	*	*	*	*	*
Supply			*	*	*			
Customer	*		*					
Low:								
Advertising			*			*		
Balance sheet								
Board member								

Key:
Words rated as essential or very relevant = *
Words independently suggested as relevant by teachers = ○

Table 2. *Teachers' ratings of, and suggestions for, key words in terms of relevance to the integrated curriculum project on co-operation (sample only)*

Department	General aims	Sample tasks
Art and design	Awareness of the importance of architecture, advertising and display of co-operative societies' stores as commercial enterprises.	Study of Co-operative Society shop-fronts 1944 to 1980. Study of graphic art in advertising and packaging; logos and symbols. Design and construction of carrier bags. Creation of clay models symbolizing co-operation.
Drama	To 'make real' concepts and situations involving co-operation and co-operatives through movement and role play exercises.	Interviewing older local residents concerning reminiscences of co-operatives to obtain materials. co-operative games from co-operative sports and games book (Orlick, 1979).
Remedial maths and English	To establish the concept of co-operation, and to support work in the project done in other areas.	Calculation of profit and profit sharing.
Geography	Appreciation of spread of co-operatives from local beginnings to other countries.	Case study of co-operatives in the dairy industry in Denmark.
Mathematics	Acquisition of skills to aid understanding of materials on co-operation in other subject areas.	Calculation of profit on sales, dividend, interest. Study of statistical trends in inflation and in retail sales.
English	Re-creation of different experiences of schooling. Appreciation of Lancashire dialect.	Study of school rules: the factory system in education, and Owenite alternatives. Analysis of poem entitled 'Divi-day' (in dialect).
History	Imaginative re-creation of life in Rochdale in the 1840s.	Study of social and economic conditions in the mid 19th century: diet, dialect, dress, buildings, poverty, unemployment. Visit to Toad Lane Museum (first successful co-operative store). Study of prices of commodities sold at Toad Lane co-operative store.

Table 3. *Summary of pilot project on co-operation and co-operatives*

results which look drab when set against the scenery of a child's imagination. Word association is, however, an exception and the results capture some of the preoccupations, the variety, and the humour present in concepts held by children. Moreover, experience from the field of science education (eg Schaefer, 1979; Sutton, 1980), indicated that word association was a workable method for exploring concept formation, and presenting the results to teachers. A detailed analysis of the findings from this project will be the subject of a longer paper, but two samples are illustrated below:

> The principal associations to this word were *stamps, money,* and *tea.* The associations with *dividing* and *sharing* came out, though not frequently. Associations of a financial kind were *bank, loan* and *profit. Horses, gambling, betting, pools* and *coupon* were suggested by a small minority. *Co-op* was an infrequent association. *Inherit, bonus* and *luck* came into the picture once each.
>
> Total number of different associations = 94.

Table 4. *Pre-project report to teachers on word associations to key word: 'dividend'*

Associations	Frequency before project	Frequency three months after end of project
Help	16	11
Helping	9	11
Shop	8	13
Together	9	7
Co-op	9	11
Sharing	1	15
Pioneers	2	10
'Divi'	0	8
Maximum frequency possible = 44		

Table 5. *Pre- and post-project comparisons for most frequent associations to key word 'co-operation'*

The above results are merely suggestive, but indicative perhaps, that some of the historical perspectives, and the concept of sharing, were more closely associated with the concept of co-operation than they had been before the project.

Stage Four

Investigations using the key word selection questionnaires, and the team word association exercises were carefully designed to provide an appropriate technology of evaluation, bearing in mind the need to present the findings to, and involve, a wider audience. A key word selection survey was repeated at the National Co-operative Education Convention, after a display of the project by some of the pupils. Subsequently, a 45-minute video-film was made both of the pupils' work and the drama production. These were shown at a parents' evening, together with items such as the art work on shop fronts and tape-recorded recollections of the co-op from elderly local residents. There have also been two education workshops for co-operative society board members which have employed materials from the project to illustrate trends in secondary school education and industry-schools liaison.

The fourth stage had the following important functions.

1. It offered an opportunity for discussion, and criticism of the project in the wider community.
2. It provided an extra incentive to both teachers and pupils to produce good quality work.
3. It contributed to the pool of educational resources within the industry on co-operatives and co-operation, which are suitable for use with school children.

Models for Learning About Co-operatives

In contrast to the pilot project materials which were designed for 11- to 12-year-olds, there are also published materials for use with older age groups. Two sets are of particular interest. One has been produced in Scotland (Bray, 1981) and is intended to support the creation and running of a 'miniature co-operative company'. The other is from a Canadian source and consists of a collection of structured exercises and case studies (Common and Boxer, 1976). These are almost entirely original but include the well-known 'squares' exercise drawn from work by Bavelas (1960). These materials are constructed on a set of key words. Historical sources are integrated with present-day ideas and information about Co-operation in Canada.

In Table 6, a summary of three alternative approaches to learning about co-operatives and co-operation is shown. These models are an attempt to portray as succinctly as possible the options for curriculum design in this area. Any one of the three models, which drew their inspiration both from the work in the pilot project and the two published sources, may prove to be applicable, depending upon the school and community contexts in which they were to be introduced. Alternatively, it may prove useful to employ all three models in a cyclical or developmental scheme.

Conclusion

Public access to projects of this kind is an antidote to some of the problems of bias and narrowness in industry-schools liaison activities which were mentioned in the introduction. Although publications such as the recent DES booklet on 'Schools and Working Life' (HMSO, 1981) help to publicize specific projects, it is unlikely that they are read outside professional circles. In this pilot project, efforts were made to present the outcomes to 'non-professional' groups who, nevertheless, had an interest in educational trends. Video, and evaluation technology of an appropriate kind aided this process.

The research on key word selection and word association will be more fully documented and reported to establish a clearing in the conceptual thicket of ideas about co-operation which exists both in the formal literature and in informal, everyday language. Having established a tentative position on conceptual issues and made a judicious selection of key words, it may then be possible to tackle the more critical task of identifying key skills.

It is hoped that the four-stage cycle will again be applied in future projects on co-operation and co-operatives in schools, and that the outcomes should be presented to, and discussed by, as wide a public as is technologically possible.

References

Bavelas, A (1960) Communication patterns in task-oriented groups. In Cartwright, D and Zander, A (eds) *Group Dynamics: Research and Theory.* Row, Peterson and Co, Evanston, Illinois.
Bray, E (1981) *The Mini Co Kit.* Prepared by the Curriculum Development Centre for the Clydebank EEC Project, Clydebank Technical College, Strathclyde.

Model	Brief description	Key words (example)	Dominant processes	Consequence of success	Consequence of failure
Model 1 Academic study	The history, present day features and geographical spread of co-operatives and the co-operative movement. Modes of learning may include reception of information, thinking about ideas, writing about other people and places. *Context*: classroom, libraries.	OWENISM PIONEERS ROCHDALE PRINCIPLES CONSUMER CO-OPERATIVES PRODUCER CO-OPERATIVES POVERTY SOCIAL CHANGE UJAMAA OWNERSHIP DIVIDEND	Reading, writing, listening to talks by teachers, watching films, discussions concerning other places, people and times.	Mastery of facts, figures and basic principles of co-operation. Appreciation of the differences between various types of co-op. Ability to explain and define relevant concepts.	The direct costs of failure will normally be low and limited in their effects. At worst, perhaps failure to complete an essay, 'pass' a test, or comprehend a concept.
Model 2 Experiential learning	Application of the social and life skills involved in co-operation through role playing, drama, behaviour games, simulations, design of promotional materials, market research exercises, consumer surveys and feasibility projects. *Context*: Class in groups; on stage; at home; visits to co-operatives.	COMMUNICATION INVOLVEMENT PERSUASION NEGOTIATION IDENTITY DISTRIBUTION SHARING GROUP PARTICIPATION CONFLICT ADVERTISEMENT	Interview grandparents, or parents about their knowledge of co-operation. Structured exercises and activities. Role-playing, drama, creative work in art and English. Discussion mainly centred on the 'here and now'. Business games. Socially much emphasis on 'groups'.	Conviviality and laughter. Mastery of some of the component social and life skills of working with others in groups, including communication skills both verbal and visual. Acquisition of self-confidence and social status in the group. Originality and creativity.	Some social embarrassment among peers when things go wrong. Reluctance in future to take a full part in drama, discussions or learning by creative and discovery processes.
Model 3 Reality management	Operation of a real (school-based) co-operative organization such as a co-op bookshop, a gardeners' co-op, a service or manufacturing (drinks?) co-op. Creation of a new co-op or conversion of an existing organization. *Contexts*: Storeroom, playground, others' homes, parks, gardens, a stall or barrow.	EFFICIENCY SECURITY CUSTOMER COMPLAINTS MANAGER RULES ELECTION MEMBER BALANCE SHEET STOCKS RESPONSIBILITY SURPLUS DEFICIT	Business meetings, elections, buying and selling, problem-solving discussions, record keeping, manufacture and quality control work. Socially much emphasis on intergroup relations.	The establishment of a viable mini co-op organization with secure stocks, efficient management of money, well-attended meetings, group cohesion, social recognition and social responsibility in the school community. Ability to accommodate and to influence economic and social systems.	The costs of failure could be high and wide ranging. They might involve loss of cash, of stocks, of 'face' and of friends! Reduction of likelihood that co-ops will be set up again in same school in future.

Table 6. *Three models for learning about co-operation and co-operatives in secondary schools*

Common, D L and Boxer, S (1976) *Co-operative Outlooks: Social Studies, Teachers' Ideas Book.* Department of Co-operative Development, Department of Education, Province of Manitoba.

Department of Education and Science (1981) *Schools and Working Life: Some Initiatives.* HMSO, London.

Jamieson, I and Lightfoot, M (1981) Learning about work. *Educational Analysis, 3,* 2, pp 47-51.

Orlick, T (1979) *The Co-operative Sports and Games Book: Challenge Without Competition.* Writers and Readers Publishing Co-operative, London.

Schaefer, G (1979) Concept formation in biology: the concept 'growth'. *European Journal of Science Education,* 1, 1, pp 87-101

Sutton, C R (1980) The learner's prior knowledge: a critical review of techniques for probing its organisation. *European Journal of Science Education,* 2, 2 pp 107-120

7.5 Education-Industry Links: A Case Study

R S Eskdale, J Norton and J Loader
Portsmouth Polytechnic, UBI and Hampshire Education Project

Abstract: Following a short introduction, delegates will embark upon a workshop. This combined session will conclude with the presentation of a paper.
The authors describe and evaluate a scheme designed for PGCE students which attempts to help them gain an understanding of the place of industry in society and the educational consequences arising. This is a joint venture undertaken by the School of Educational Studies, Portsmouth Polytechnic, Careers Advisory Service, Understanding British Industry, and the Hampshire Education Employment Project. The scheme forms part of an Education Studies programme and the paper will be based on experiences gained since 1980.

Introduction

Since 1976, when James Gallaghan at Ruskin College initiated the Great Debate on education, there has been an outpouring of books, surveys, reports and articles which probably leaves many educationalists and others confused and bewildered. The then Prime Minister's speech needs to be seen in the context of a strong belief, held by many people, that the education system was out of touch with the fundamental need for Britain to survive economically in a competitive world through the efficiency of its industry and commerce (DES, 1977a). This theme has been examined and frequently challenged by writers in different fields and representing radically different sociological perspectives (Horricks, 1981; Lawton, 1979; Smith, 1980; Sharp, 1980).

However, it is not the purpose of this paper to examine or develop these issues — interesting and important though we find them. Rather, we wish to concentrate on the school curriculum and working life in general, and then specifically on an attempt by three agencies in South-east Hampshire, to help graduate students on an initial teacher training course gain a better understanding of industry in society and its potential as a teaching resource.

Schools and Industry

Attention has focused particularly on schools and the ways in which young people are prepared for working life. We suspect that the activities of schools are more visible, and now more legally accountable (DES, 1981) to the public than many other institutions and agencies which are part of the education system. In addition, inquiries into primary and secondary schools have been carried out recently by the Department of Education and Science (DES, 1978; DES, 1979a).

The secondary survey suggested that, in particular, careers education programmes should:

'set out to prepare young people for the transition from school to work or some form of continuing education, to encourage them to use the resources of the various helping agencies and to enable them to search for jobs whilst recognizing they will not all be successful'. (DES, 1979a)

The Mansell Report recommended, among other things, that the schools curriculum should bring an informed perspective as to the role of the young person in society (DES, 1979b).

Finally, the Schools Council and the Department of Education and Science have argued for a skills and core curriculum respectively, in which preparation for life after school plays an important part (Schools Council, 1981; DES, 1981).

In 1977, the Department of Education and Science encouraged local education authorities to set up school-industry liaison groups at local level (DES, 1977), and in 1980 the Committee of Enquiry into the Engineering Profession recommended that: 'Every secondary school should be involved in one or more liaison schemes and every company should link with at least one school'. (Committee of Enquiry, 1980). Since then, through the activities of a number of agencies acting frequently at a local level, liaison committees and working parties of different sizes and composition have been set up in many parts of the country.

It is probably too early to make any evaluation of how successful these initiatives have been. However, the Department of Education and Science recently published a guide to good practice in secondary schools, where links with local industry have been developed (DES, 1981b). The journal *View*, published by the Department of Industry, is a very useful source of information about local and national initiatives, with contributions from industry and education. The national scene appears to be confused (Morris, 1982) but the Cooper Report (1982) clearly recommended no major changes nationally at present.

It seems to us that further progress is likely to lie with local or regionally based initatives, with local education authorities playing an important role.

South-east Hampshire has a number of locally based committees, and in recent years useful links betwen industry and schools have been developed through such agencies as the Employment Education Project, the Portsmouth Careers Advisory Service, and Understanding British Industry. Further links are now being developed which include teacher training institutions in the area and the main purpose of this paper is to examine one of these initiatives based at Portsmouth Polytechnic.

Postgraduate Certificate in Education Teacher Training

In 1980, the Board of Studies for the Postgraduate Certificate in Education course in the Polytechnic supported the desirability of including an 'industrial element' in the Education Studies section of the course. This, it was argued, should be for all students, irrespective of their degree studies and the age range for which they were being trained. These are Secondary Mathematics, Secondary Science and Middle/ Secondary Children with Learning Difficulties. Part of the course's rationale is to bring students from different disciplines and age range interests together to study education, and it was within this element of the course that the Study of Industry was introduced. The only time available for placing students in local industry was in the spring term during Reading Week, when students have no timetabled commitments. Seven volunteers were placed in a variety of different organizations, including a department of Portsmouth City Council, a bank, a Royal Naval establishment, and a multinational electronics organization. Prior to these placements, all students had an introduction to industry as a teaching resource, saw a film which was intended to show how a modern industrial society works, and then played a game which examined problems of industry and pollution. However, it was not until we brought together employers and students after the industrial placements, that the level of interest increased dramatically.

The results obtained from questionnaires and discussions indicated that this section and the industrial visits were regarded by students as the most valuable.

Interestingly, some students with degrees in mathematics and physical sciences thought that many of the questions asked by students were provocative or impertinent. During the discussion, one student in particular, with a good degree in social science, widened the debate by questioning the whole basis of a capitalist society from a Marxist perspective. She later produced a paper on schooling in capitalist America, as an extension of this debate (Bowles and Gintis, 1976). One of the employers reported later that he thought a considerable amount of time was spent on challenging the methods used by employers when selecting apprentices. He went on to say that some students: 'appeared to be more interested in the morality of recruitment rather than what had been proved necessary to achieve the best results at the least risk'. A bank representative dismally suggested that this group of students will be no more able to adapt to the working environment than the present intake! However, all the employers felt it had been worth while, albeit with varying degrees of enthusiasm. The most supportive comment came from the representative of the multinational organization. He clearly had enjoyed the cut and thrust of the argument as much as the students had, and felt that this kind of session should be in the whole teacher assignment programme.

1981-82 Course

This year we decided to attempt a more detailed evaluation of this part of the Education Studies programme, particularly in respect of student attitudes to industry. The theme remained Schools and Society, but we also modified the programme to include a lecture on a systems approach to studying an industrial organization and a case study about how a local secondary school had used industry as a resource. Seventeen students were placed in local industries, with polytechnic-based activities occurring before and after the visits.

About this time, Jenny Norton was appointed Liaison Officer for Understanding British Industry, and John Loader, on secondment from Marconi, was Project Director of the Employment Education Project based at Havant. We subsequently met and devised a programme with the help of David Aryton of the Portsmouth Careers Advisory Service. For the academic year 1980-81, seven students were placed with local organizations for a three-day industrial attachment in a way similar to that used for local secondary teachers.

However, before describing our first venture into this new field, it is probably necessary to place the Postgraduate Certificate in Education course in context. Initial teacher training for graduates lasts for one academic year, and it is normal for courses to consist of teaching practice and a range of education and professional courses. There is now general agreement that such courses are too short (UCET, 1979; UCET, 1982), particularly as more demands appear to be made on the time available by inclusion of such items as Special Education (DES, 1978) and Multicultural Education (Committee of Enquiry, 1981). A recent report published by a working party of the European Commission is now suggesting the inclusion of consumer education in teacher education courses (*Times Educational Supplement*, 1982).

1980-81 Course

Portsmouth Polytechnic's Postgraduate Certificate in Education course currently recruits about 40 graduates on three programmes of studies.

On the evidence from the 1980-81 course, we assumed that we would need to convince students that all children leaving compulsory education should have an understanding of the role of industry in society. We also felt that graduates in social science were more likely to be opposed to bringing industry into the classroom than would graduates from other disciplines. Our third assumption was that students working with younger children would be unlikely to see the relevance of an 'industrial element' as being of value to them as future teachers.

Using questionnaires (see Appendix A) and discussions, the results indicated that, contrary to our expectations, almost all students supported the notion that all children leaving compulsory education should have an understanding of the role of industry in society. Most felt that it was the school's responsibility to help them gain this understanding. However, there was less certainty about the role of the individual teacher in this. Some did not see the responsibility lying with them as individual teachers, but probably it was seen as part of the work of the careers teacher rather than as a general responsibility. Again, contrary to our expectations, there were no differences of opinion among graduates from different disciplines, though students training for the age range 8 to 13 years were less willing to accept the relevance of the industrial element in the education studies course than those training for secondary schools.

Discussion

As expected, students found the industrial placements in the scheme of particular value. However, there was one case where the receiving organization had not prepared for the visit of the students, who subsequently found the visit unsatisfactory. The success of the visits depended almost entirely on the welcome the students received from the organization and the care with which the visit had been planned.

Students on PGCE courses come from a variety of backgrounds, and many now have some industrial experiences, albeit of a limited kind, to draw upon. The Portsmouth scheme uses a variety of industries for student placements to develop a better understanding of the complexity of industry in modern society.

We were surprised that most students were not opposed to industry, as we had originally thought. However, there will always be some who will wish to challenge the concept of the modern capitalist industrial society, using a different perspective from that probably held by most industrialists. This seems to us to be quite legitimate, but what is important is that argument should be heard, accepted or rejected in an atmosphere of tolerance and understanding.

It is important that a study of education and industry should not be seen in isolation from other parts of a student's course. It should also be seen in an educational context which is relevant to all students on initial teacher training courses.

Our analysis of the polytechnic-based activities showed they were most highly esteemed when students were convinced of the relevance to this work as future teachers, and convinced of the authority of the speakers.

Understandably, students who are training to teach young children are less likely to be as receptive to ideas about industry and schools as we would like. Perhaps, however, we ought to be considering such schemes as the one described as part of a general preparation for teaching in a society which, for better or for worse, still relies for its survival on being effective as a trading nation in a competitive world.

Appendix A
Industry in the Curriculum: Children and the Role of Industry

Please respond to these statements — please tick

1. All children leaving compulsory education should have an understanding of the role of industry in Britain:

   Strongly agree

   Agree

   No opinion

   Disagree

2. It is the school's responsibility to help children to gain an understanding of the role of industry in Britain:

   Strongly agree

   Agree

   No opinion

   Disagree

3. I, as a teacher, think that it is my responsibility to develop an understanding of the role of industry in Britain:

   Strongly agree

   Agree

   No opinion

   Disagree

4. As a result of the input to this course, my views on industry in the curriculum have:

   Changed towards the above three statements

   Changed against the above three statements

   Remained unchanged

Additional comments:

SCHOOLS INDUSTRY LINKS

Appendix B
Industry in the Curriculum: The Influence of Industrial Needs on the School Curriculum

Degree studies

Programme of study

Code No:

A compilation of comments made by people from education and industry on what aspects of industry should be included in the school curriculum.

(Adapted from a Schools Council Industry Project, SCIP, list)

	Own	Group
1. Understand the interdependence of working community, public industry, private industry, banks, social services (how each needs the other and society needs them all)		
2. Learn how to assess their own abilities (apart from academic exam results) by having opportunities to test and discuss them		
3. Understand the basic structure of industry . . . Buying . . . Making . . . Marketing		
4. Appreciate the basic requirements for working together as a team		
5. Know how problems are solved by teamwork		
6. Know how unions are organized and the place of the individual in them		
7. Understand the formal system of relationships between managers and trade union representatives		
8. Learn commonly used financial and economic terms used by the media		
9. Understand the needs of other people, particularly those they will have to work with		
10. Understand the need for self-motivation and acting responsibly oneself		

Appendix C
PGCE Evaluation: Industry

Degree:

Programme:

Previous industrial experience:

Key:	A	Particularly valuable	1	Particularly interesting
	B	Valuable	2	Interesting
	C	Limited value	3	Limited interest
	D	No value	4	No interest

	Value	*Interest*
1. Lecture systems approach	☐	☐
2. Lecture industry as resource	☐	☐
3. Game (industry)	☐	☐
4. Display UBI EEP	☐	☐
5. Industrial placement (where applicable)	☐	☐

Comments

6. Have any of your attitudes to industry changed as a result of this part of the Education Studies course?

   YES/NO

Comments (on 1. to 6. or other matters)

References

Bowles, S and Gintis, H (1976) *Schooling in Capitalist America.* Routledge and Kegan Paul.

Committee of Enquiry into the Education of Children from Ethnic Minority Groups (1981) *West Indian Children in our Schools.* HMSO, London.

Committee of Enquiry into the Education of Handicapped Children and Young People (1978) *Special Educational Needs.* HMSO, London.

Committee of Enquiry into the Engineering Profession (1980) *Engineering our Future.* HMSO, London.

Department of Education and Science (1979a) *Aspects of Secondary Education.* HMSO, London.

Department of Education and Science (1979b) *A Basis for Choice* (Hansell Report). Further Education Unit, HMSO, London.

Department of Education and Science (1981) *Circular to LEAs 1/81.* HMSO, London.

Department of Education and Science (1978) *Primary Education in England.* (A survey by HM Inspectors of Schools). HMSO, London.

Department of Education and Science (1977a) *Education in Schools.* A Consultative Document. HMSO, London.

Department of Education and Science (1981a) *The School Curriculum.* HMSO, London.

Department of Education and Science (1977) *Local Authority Arrangements for the Curriculum.* 14/77. HMSO, London.

Department of Education and Science (1981) *School Industry Link Schemes. A Study and Recommendations.* N Cooper, HMSO, London.

Department of Education and Science (1981b) *Schools and Working Life: Some Initiatives.* HMSO, London.

Horricks, R (1981) *Industry Understands Us.* School Technology, **14,** 58.

Lawton, D (1979) *Curriculum Planning and Technological Change.* (Stanley Lecture, Royal Society of Arts, London. Sheffield Stanley Tools Ltd, Sheffield).

Sharp, R (1980) *Knowledge, Ideology and the Politics of Schooling. Towards a Marxist Analysis of Education.* Routledge and Kegan Paul, London.

Smith, A (1980) *Education and its Part in Earning the Country's Living. Industrial and Commercial Training.* November.

Schools Council (1981) *The Practical Curriculum Working Paper 70.* Methuen, London.

Schools Council (1981-83) *Schools in Industry Project.*

Universities Council for the Education of Teachers (1979) *The PGCE Course and the Training of Specialist Teachers for Secondary Schools.* UCET.

Universities Council for the Education of Teachers (1982) *Primary Education.* UCET.

Closing Address
Quo Vadis?

K Austwick
University of Bath

Conference operators seem to work on a reverse technique to that adopted by opera composers. The latter provide an overture, before the main work gets under way, which allows late arrivals to get to their seats *cum dignitate*. Conference organizers, on the other hand, seem to settle for an epilogue to bring the proceedings to a decent close, after the completion of the main work, which enables the early leavers to slip away, also *cum dignitate*. And this allows the speaker to rationalize to his own satisfaction why so many of his audience left before he finished speaking!

There are at least two strategies one can choose from on an occasion like this: either a lecture drawn up beforehand related (or unrelated) to the conference themes, or an impromptu 'tour de force' based on one's impressions of the conference, both academic and social. Last year, Ian Morris adopted the latter strategy and, like the Lord Mayor's Show, he would be difficult to follow. I shall play it a little straighter by offering some reflections on educational technology, bearing in mind this year's conference and also that of 10 years ago, when I last performed this 'epilogue' function.

Ten years on, I suspect I could read several sections of my 1972 paper which would not seem out of place now. For instance:

'Education is not easy to quantify and so it is difficult to decide whether or not we are getting "value for money". The system contains a complex of human and material resources, a lot of interrelated social considerations, no known quality control system, a lot of decision-making made on emotional grounds, and a product (the pupil) which has a mind of its own and an ability to interact with the system through which it is passing.

However, let us try to bring a little order and systematic thinking into at least one part of this industry. At the heart of the whole enterprise is the relationship between teacher and taught — or perhaps these days we should say the learner and the manipulator of the educational environment! Either way there is a communication process. In earlier days this was perhaps a little one-sided and autocratic, whereas nowadays it is a little less formal!

There are also opportunities for this communication to be much richer and more sophisticated than it was, in the light of present day technologies'. (Austwick and Harris, 1972)

It seems we were talking about efficiency and effectiveness, amongst other things, on that occasion. But still the millenium has not arrived. *The Times Educational Supplement*, referring to our, and other, gatherings in March 1972, spoke of 'trendy new-style conferences'. I think the 'new style' referred to the much increased audience participation. The style remains; how far has the content changed? Are the questions different?

We seem to have been beset by paradoxes in educational technology. In the early days of programmed learning I can recall criticism, particularly from primary school teachers, that we were developing a formal authoritarian style of teaching (although

in fact it was a primitive form of individualized self-instruction) whereas the
prevailing fashion was for 'progressive' education, with its emphasis on discovery
learning. More recently, one explanation for the limited take-up of broadcasting
by radio, and particularly by television, has been that prevailing styles of
curriculum development — and teaching/learning in general — lean *towards*
'individualized self-instruction' as opposed to large group teaching (Hurst, 1979).
In the expansionist days of the 1960s and early 1970s it was argued that there was
no call for gadgetry that might reduce the personal role of the teacher; now, in
these days of contraction — of falling demand for teachers, of concern to protect
jobs — there again appears to be no call for systems which could in any sense take
on the work of teachers! Indeed, since the recent UGC cuts in higher education
some institutions seem to have looked on their AVA units or academic services
units as expendable. Educational technology always seems to be out of step!
Finally, and again paradoxically, demand for educational technology seems limited
in the third world where there *is* a shortage of teachers. On looking through the
conference programme there appears to have been no contribution from the third
world nor any discussion of possible applications there.

So whereabouts are educational technologists in the educational firmament?
What style or fashions of research and developments are there, and where do they
fit in?

Education as a study has come a long way from the days when a few lectures on
educational psychology and some pearls of wisdom from a master of method
formed the basis for teacher training courses.

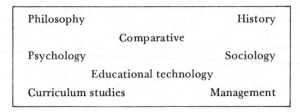

Figure 1. *Areas of educational study*

There are certain contributory disciplines from which we draw: History, Philosophy,
Psychology and, more recently, Sociology. There is also an extensive area of
comparative education. These and other (external) sources enable us to deal with
the more applied aspects of education: curriculum development, management and
educational technology for instance.

How do these interact? The main axis is perhaps the psychology/sociology line,
and this, as we shall see, is reflected in the styles of educational research which
have emerged.

Education, before and immediately after the war, was dominated by psychology,
particularly measurement psychology, in terms of intelligence, arithmetic and
English quotients, control and experimental group research designs, etc. As time
went on, cognitive, developmental and other schools of psychology had their
influence on education, and the emphasis shifted away from measurement.
Sociology in its early days was preoccupied with counting and measurement. There
were scales and questionnaires, correlations between social class, school-leaving age,
attainment, and so on. But counting and measurement gave way to more
phenomenological and other less quantitative approaches. The trend in the 1960s
and 1970s moved away from measurement, from pure science models to social
science ones. (Demands for accountability and 'value for money' are now to some
extent reviving the measurement syndrome.)

But educational technology, especially in its formative years, seemed to identify much more naturally with physical science models. Its roots were in behaviourist psychology, in electronics, and, to some extent, in systems thinking. It overflowed into curriculum development and into educational management, and stating aims and objectives were the order of the day. What are the boundaries of its domain now?

Experimental design	Surveys	Action research	Open-ended inquiry
Improve efficiency by controlled experiment		Join in and see what is happening	

Figure 2. *Research styles*

The shift in emphasis from psychology to sociology and the move away from quantitative methods in both cases have been reflected in a shift in emphasis in research styles, from numerical to non-numerical methods, as illustrated in Figure 2 which is adapted from Nisbet's inaugural address to the British Educational Research Association (Nisbet, 1974).

Measurement psychology relied on the statistical methods of the agricultural-botany model. The early work on programmed learning adopted these numerical approaches. Does anyone recall the 90/90 criterion, or those formulae for assessing gain scores? Early sociology used questionnaires and surveys — still counting, still treating individuals as 'subjects' or items in an 'observational' design. The 1960s saw the arrival of Plowden, of education priority areas, of 'action research' where 'hunches' were tried out, modified *en passant*, and consequently never evaluated in a formal or statistical sense. Much of the early work in curriculum development was of this kind. This participative movement has progressed into more subjective styles such as illuminative evaluation where the researcher immerses himself in the problem or situation before deciding what questions ought to be asked. Often, this implies a concern with process rather than product. In fact, this shift in research style is well illustrated by the 'development' of evaluation methods and techniques over the past 10 years. If evaluation is a significant part of educational technology then we are now operating in a somewhat 'non-numerical' area, since evaluation is often more subjective and qualitative than heretofore. We seem to be in step at last! So, is educational technology changing its nature — or just widening its boundaries? When is an educational technologist not an educational technologist?

Educational technology therefore began, based on an uneasy mix of behaviourist psychology and the products of the entertainment industry. It then adopted a systems-type approach which many of us probably regard as its natural form; now it may in some areas be abandoning its 'hard technology' image. Is this what we might call 'phase three' — a more qualitative stage — and does this imply an increased concern for the *context* in which educational technology is applied?

A slightly different view of a third phase in educational technology was expressed in a report (CCC, 1980) to the Council of Europe. This also saw educational technology moving into a third phase — from tools to systems to a 'reflective' phase, where the technologist had to concentrate his mind on the 'why' as much as the 'how' of his work — the implication being that educational technology has, up to now, had no value system or 'philosophical consciousness'. In other words, before developing new resources or new approaches, the educational technologist should consider and make explicit the implications of what is to be developed, and should make value judgements on its rightness or suitability. In other words, he should add a socio-political dimension to his work.

Did we hear this yesterday in relation to some projects which were criticized as 'elitist' in that they were designed to cater only for the most able children?

It was also argued in the report that the systems approach implied a certain control of the learning situation by the educational technologist with pre-determined objectives and uniform sequencing of the learning experiences for all learners. This was said to be at variance with the current trend, especially among mature learners, to seek control of their own learning programme. We are out of step again! Evaluation should not ask 'how much has been learnt of the stated objectives?' but 'what happened and why?'

But, to keep our feet on the ground, a more mundane aspect must also be taken into account! As educational technologists we like to follow a sequence of 'what is needed; for whom; what the objectives are; what the constraints are; what resources are available — hence: what is the most appropriate format or medium to use?' And how far have we succeeded? On the other hand, the consumer's approach is more likely to be: I want to teach my group about, say, probability. I would not mind a change from the usual book. Is there anything interesting on the shelf, eg a video-tape? If so, is the equipment (and a technician) available at the right time and place? This takes us back through the sequence so that our systems approach (phase 2) is reduced to a tools approach (phase 1).

Let me illustrate these points briefly by reference to a project on which we are engaged at Bath at the moment, which we call 'Mathematics at Work'. We are producing teaching resources for use by 14- to 16-year-olds based on jobs carried out by 16- to 18-year-olds at work. These materials arise from a project set up to collect information for a report called 'Mathematics in Employment' (Bailey, 1981) for the Cockcroft Committee on Mathematics Teaching. Information was collected as a result of visits to nearly 100 firms, involving interviews with employers and young employees.

Visit Report

Date
Place
Contacts
Size and nature
Recruitment and training
Employee interview

Figure 3. *Work visit report*

Using the format shown in Figure 3 for visit reports, information was collected on selection and training methods, company job descriptions, and, most importantly, employees' descriptions of their work. From these it was possible to list the mathematical skills or activities used by each employee in jobs ranging from making settees to printing books. Grouping these activities by skills produced an extensive collection of real-life work situations. An extra dimension was given by a pen portrait of each young worker in terms of his educational background and his recollections of school mathematics! These materials seemed to have the makings of some valuable teaching/learning resources.

But the essential feature was the 'real life' aspect. How could this be retained if the materials were to be used by teachers and pupils who had no direct experience of the work situations? Perhaps this is best illustrated by the 'degrees of realism' diagram shown in Figure 4.

Obviously, the teachers and pupils cannot have actual experience of all the jobs in our list. Only a few could make visits to the works concerned — if they happened to live near hand.

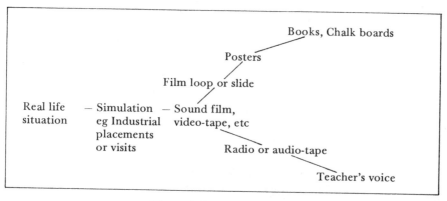

Figure 4. *Degrees of realism*

In other projects at Bath, sponsored by individual industries, we have been able to produce kits using films, tapes and slides, as well as posters, books and workcards paid for by the firm concerned, which give varying degrees of realism. In this particular project we are dealing with illustrations from a large number of firms, so provision or subsidy of illustrative material by individual firms is more difficult to arrange. We are also catering for less able pupils, whose jobs will not always lend themselves to striking forms of illustration. Again, when we talk to publishers they tend to think chiefly of books as the main format and, in this context, they are restricted by the need to keep costs down to a level which schools can afford.

So where are we? Perhaps our initial approach looks like a systems approach (phase 2). What do we want to do? What resources do we have? How best can we display them – leading to a kit or package? The reaction of publishers and the schools is to look on our function as that of producing the cheapest and simplest tools (phase 1) but this conflicts with the 'real life' nature of the initial resources.

At the same time, we are being asked whether or not we reflected upon what we are doing; what the implications are of introducing industrially oriented material into schools, as well as 'Mathematics at Work'. Are we considering maths for those 'not at work'? How do we decide whether or not to make the resources teacher-centred or pupil-centred? How will one evaluate the resources when they are produced? Phase 3 questions, if you like.

So, on the one hand some critics ask only for tools. On the other hand we are asked for reflections rather than systems. Are we technicians, technologists or philosophers? Are we efficient, or effective? Where is our technology going? Where are we going? As we leave today, the salutation is not 'farewell', but *'quo vadis?'*

References

Austwick, K and Harris, N D C (1972) *Aspects of Educational Technology* **VI**. Pitman, London.
Council for Cultural Co-operation (1980) *Educational Technology for Permanent Education.* Strasbourg.
Hurst, P (1979) *The Media in Third World Education: Performance and Prospects.* Proceedings of the 14th Annual Conference of Comparative Educational Sociology.
Nisbet, J (1974) Educational research: the state of the art; Inaugural address. British Educational Research Association.
Bailey, D E (1981) *Mathematics in Employment 16-18.* School of Mathematics, University of Bath.

Keyword Index